CW01391745

Forging Leninism in China

Forging Leninism in China is a re-examination of the events of the Chinese revolution and the transformation of the Chinese Communist Party from the years 1927 to 1934. Describing the transformation of the party as "the forging of Leninism", Joseph Fewsmith offers a clear analysis of the development of the party. Drawing on supporting statements of party leaders and a wealth of historical material, he demonstrates how the Chinese Communist Party reshaped itself to become far more violent, more hierarchical, and more militarized during this time. He highlights the role of local educated youth in organizing the Chinese revolution, arguing that it was these local organizations, rather than Mao, who introduced Marxism into the countryside. Fewsmith presents a vivid story of local social history and conflict between Mao's revolutionaries and local Communists.

JOSEPH FEWSMITH is Professor of International Relations and Political Science at Boston University. He is the author of *Rethinking Chinese Politics* (2021), *The Logic and Limits of Political Reform in China* (2012), and *China since Tiananmen* (2001).

Forging Leninism in China

Mao and the Remaking of the Chinese Communist Party, 1927–1934

JOSEPH FEWSMITH
Boston University

CAMBRIDGE
UNIVERSITY PRESS

CAMBRIDGE
UNIVERSITY PRESS

University Printing House, Cambridge CB2 8BS, United Kingdom

One Liberty Plaza, 20th Floor, New York, NY 10006, USA

477 Williamstown Road, Port Melbourne, VIC 3207, Australia

314–321, 3rd Floor, Plot 3, Splendor Forum, Jasola District Centre,
New Delhi – 110025, India

103 Penang Road, #05–06/07, Visioncrest Commercial, Singapore 238467

Cambridge University Press is part of the University of Cambridge.

It furthers the University's mission by disseminating knowledge in the pursuit of
education, learning, and research at the highest international levels of excellence.

www.cambridge.org
Information on this title: www.cambridge.org/9781316513569
DOI: 10.1017/9781009070157

© Joseph Fewsmith 2022

This publication is in copyright. Subject to statutory exception and to the provisions
of relevant collective licensing agreements, no reproduction of any part may take
place without the written permission of Cambridge University Press.

First published 2022

Printed in the United Kingdom by TJ Books Limited, Padstow Cornwall

A catalogue record for this publication is available from the British Library.

Library of Congress Cataloging-in-Publication Data
Names: Fewsmith, Joseph, 1949– author.
Title: Forging Leninism in China : Mao and the remaking of the Chinese
Communist Party, 1927–1934 / Joe Fewsmith, Boston University.
Other titles: Mao and the remaking of the Chinese Communist Party, 1927–1934
Description: New York ; Cambridge, United Kingdom : Cambridge University
Press, 2022. | Includes bibliographical references and index.
Identifiers: LCCN 2021049804 (print) | LCCN 2021049805 (ebook) | ISBN
9781316513569 (Hardback) | ISBN 9781009070157 (eBook)
Subjects: LCSH: Zhongguo gong chan dang – History. | Communism – China –
History. | China – Politics and government – 1928–1937. | BISAC: HISTORY /
Asia / General
Classification: LCC JQ1519.A5 F49 2022 (print) | LCC JQ1519.A5 (ebook) | DDC
324.251/075–dc23/eng/20211120
LC record available at https://lccn.loc.gov/2021049804
LC ebook record available at https://lccn.loc.gov/2021049805

ISBN 978-1-316-51356-9 Hardback

Cambridge University Press has no responsibility for the persistence or accuracy of
URLs for external or third-party internet websites referred to in this publication and
does not guarantee that any content on such websites is, or will remain, accurate or
appropriate.

To the memory of Gao Hua and to the Chinese scholars who have worked to deepen our understanding of modern China

Contents

Figures

Maps

Acknowledgments

I did not intend to write this book. Having gotten some understanding about how the Chinese Communist Party (CCP) worked through my work on elite and local politics in the contemporary period, I became curious about when and how this system came together. About that time, I read of Gao Hua's seminal work, *Hongtaiyang shi zenyang sheng qide?* (which has been masterfully translated by Stacy Mosher and Jian Guo as *How the Red Sun Rose: The Origins of the Yanan Rectification Movement, 1930–1945*). Gao's book opened up a party history with which I had been largely unfamiliar. It also opened up many questions, which I previously thought were unanswerable. Talking to Chinese historians and reading the many new sources that have come out in recent years, I found many clues to understanding party history. In particular, I began to probe the history of the party following the violent split with the Guomindang. I found that the ideas of Communist leaders in this period were different than I had previously thought and that local history played a much more important role than I had realized. So did violence. As I have explored this history, I have had the benefit of the guidance of many people. I greatly appreciate Elizabeth J. Perry, Joseph Esherick, and Daniel Koss for reading part or all of the manuscript. Their comments helped shape an awkward manuscript into what I hope is a readable book. I am also happy to acknowledge and thank Chris Buckley, Timothy Cheek, Chen Yung-fa, Ding Renxiang, Feng Xiaocai, Steven M. Goldstein, Han Gang, Han Shu, He Xiaocai, Huang Daoxuan, Huang Wenzhi, Jeremy Menchik, Wen Rui, Yang Kuisong, Ying Xing, and Zhang Hongqing. Needless to say, any errors in the text are solely the responsibility of the author.

It is also a pleasure to acknowledge once again the prodigious work of Nancy Hearst at the Fung Library at Harvard University, John Gaunt, whose editing has prevented many errors, and the superb staff at Cambridge University Press who have prepared the manuscript for publication.

Introduction

When one drives into the Jinggang Mountains (also known as the Jinggangshan), it is impossible to escape the celebration of revolutionary history and the role of Mao Zedong. As one is told repeatedly, you are entering the "cradle of the revolution." Maoping, once the mountain lair of Yuan Wencai, the bandit leader who would join forces with Mao, is now a thriving town of about 4,500. There are now several memorial halls recalling the heroic deeds of the Red Army. Reenactors, sent by work units for patriotic education, place wreaths before pictures of revolutionary heroes. Although some visitors seem to be having too much fun to be absorbing the lessons of the revolutionary past, perhaps most come away with an even more unquestioning acceptance of the official historiography that places Mao and his Jinggangshan redoubt at the center of a revolutionary history that has, after many twists and turns, given birth to a wealthy and powerful contemporary China, a country very different from the poor, war-torn, and exploited China a century ago.

But if you were to get into a car and drive about 100 miles to the east of the Jinggang Mountains, you would arrive at the sleepy little town of Donggu. Donggu is on the eastern edge of Ji'an county, which is anchored by Ji'an, the largest city in western Jiangxi province, along the Gan river about 150 miles southwest of the provincial capital, Nanchang. If you look hard, you can find a small memorial museum dedicated to the heroes who created the Donggu Revolutionary Base Area. The Donggu Revolutionary Base Area tells a very different story of the Chinese revolution from that portrayed in the official historiography. It is a story that has been largely suppressed and forgotten, one that is very much at odds with the historical narrative that puts Mao at the center. The Donggu Revolutionary Base Area was, in important ways, more successful than the Jinggangshan Base Area; indeed, at one point, the leaders of the Donggu Base Area literally saved Mao and his ragtag Red Fourth Army from destruction, something Mao acknowledged at the time.

1

Map 0.1 China, ca. 1920

Donggu tells the story of how the revolution moved from the cities to the countryside and how the peasants were mobilized on behalf of the revolution. It is a story about local social history and the role that local educated youth played in translating Marxism–Leninism into rural concerns. It is a story about the erosion and destruction of the traditional clan system as new, class-conscious leaders began to identify clan leaders – sometimes even leaders of their own clans – as "local bullies and evil gentry" (*tuhao lieshen*). Ultimately it is a story about the destruction of local revolutionaries and local communities as first Mao turned his forces loose on those who had developed the Donggu Revolutionary Base Area, and then the invading Guomindang (GMD) destroyed what was left of local society. This is not the story of hard struggle, sacrifice, idealism, and ultimate victory – the party narrative of the Jinggangshan – but rather a story of idealism, violence, and total defeat. This part of the revolution was destroyed by the part that ultimately won and created the myth that survives today. Out of the destruction of Donggu we find the origins of a reshaped Chinese Communist Party (CCP) that ultimately won the revolution. It was far more violent, more hierarchical, and more militarized than its earlier urban self, the version of the party that had been forced to abandon the cities by the GMD's purge of the Communists.

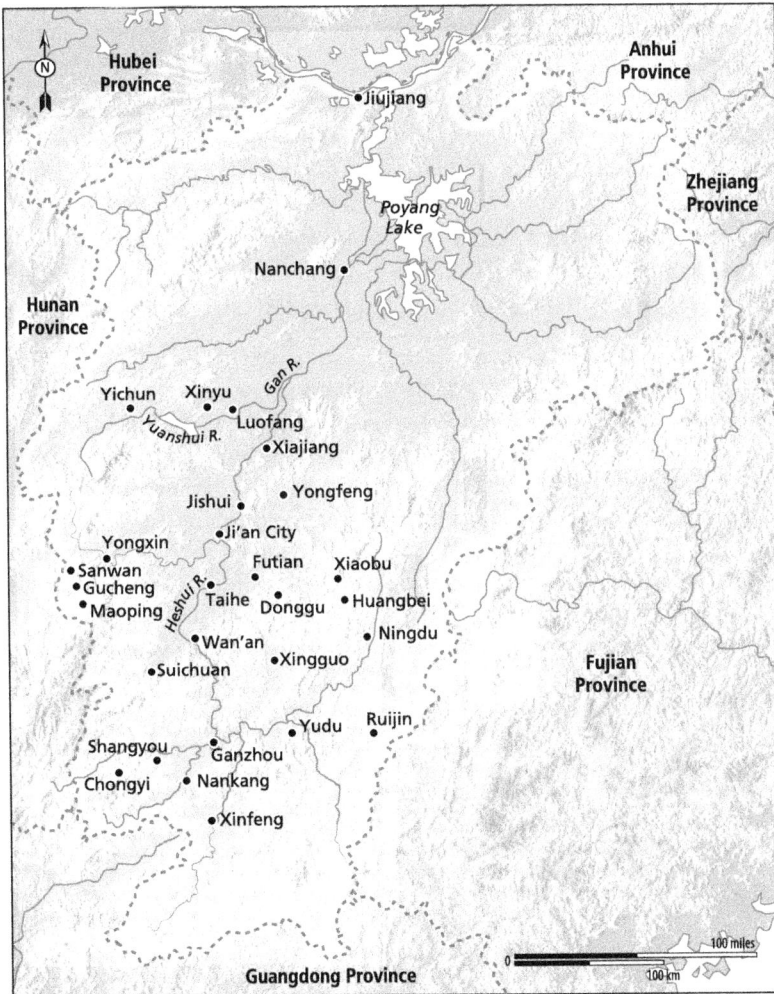

Map 0.2 Jiangxi province

The story of Donggu and, beyond that, of the Central Soviet Base Area that grew in rural Jiangxi is not easy to fit into broader narratives of revolutionary history, whether Chinese or foreign. One popular way of looking at revolution is to conceive of it as pent-up demand. For whatever reason, the dam bursts and people rise up demanding a new order.[1] This is indeed the popular image in the telling of the Chinese revolution. When R.H. Tawney wrote his 1932 classic study, *Land and Labor in China*, he detailed the harsh realities of life in rural China. "[I]t is difficult to resist the conclusion," he wrote, "that a large proportion of Chinese peasants are constantly on the brink of actual destitution."[2] Well aware of the nascent Communist movement in Jiangxi and elsewhere, Tawney declares with seeming prescience, "The revolution of 1911 was a bourgeois affair. The revolution of the peasants has still to come. If their rulers continue to exploit them, or to permit them to be exploited, as remorselessly as hitherto, it is likely to be unpleasant. It will not, perhaps, be undeserved."[3]

For a later generation, Maurice Meisner more or less took that narrative for granted. As he put it in his widely used textbook, *Mao's China and After*,[4]

While imperialism undermined the foundations of the imperial bureau-cratic state with which the gentry was so closely intertwined, gentry–land-lord proprietors found it more profitable to continue to exploit peasants in the traditional parasitic fashion – and the fashion became increasingly parasitic as traditional opportunities for bureaucratically obtained wealth ... declined along with the disintegration of the old political order ... The peasants who were the victims of that exploitation eventually were to have the opportunity to repay gentry–landlord ruthlessness in kind, although in a different way – in the ruthlessness of an agrarian social revo-lution that, in the end, was to eliminate the gentry as a social class in the mid-twentieth century.

---

[1] Jeremy M. Weinstein, *Inside Rebellion: The Politics of Insurgent Violence* (Cambridge: Cambridge University Press, 2007), pp. 34–36. Of course the building up of tensions can be a very complex process, and the "bursting" of the dam can likewise take place over time. See Charles Tilly's classic study, *The Vendée* (Cambridge, MA: Harvard University Press, 1964).

[2] R.H. Tawney, *Land and Labor in China* (London: George Allen & Unwin Ltd, 1932), p. 72.

[3] Ibid., p. 74.

[4] Maurice Meisner, *Mao's China and After: A History of the People's Republic*, 3rd ed. (New York: The Free Press, 1999), pp. 6, 7.

This narrative is enormously satisfying. In it the revolution becomes a morality play, one in which the poor and exploited rise up, however violently, and overthrow their oppressors. But the reality is much more complicated. Indeed, it is difficult to fit the history of the Chinese revolution into the literature on social movements simply because most of that literature takes for granted that political organizers work to expand a movement from the ground up. Usually such movements fail. Sometimes they lead to major social violence before being put down, and sometimes they lead to revolution. But the social-movement literature assumes that uprisings, regardless of the leadership that guides them, are essentially from the bottom up.[5]

The story of Donggu and later of the Central Soviet also fits uneasily into our general understandings of revolutions, in part because Communist leaders in Shanghai were forced to retreat to rural Jiangxi, displacing Mao and his colleagues. Even though Mao crushed the leaders of the Donggu Revolutionary Base Area, he was then pushed aside by the higher-ranking leaders from Shanghai. That contest between Mao and the Shanghai leadership is widely known, but its telling covers up the earlier history of Mao defeating local revolutionaries. It also covers up the Shanghai leadership's inheritance of the brutal suppression of rural society pioneered by Mao. That revolutionary movements have divisions and leadership disputes is not news, but the violence that stemmed from these disputes was often used against not only the civilian population, but also members of the CCP itself. To a large extent, the Communist failure in Jiangxi was the result of such self-destruction. There were other reasons as well, as will be discussed below, but this intra-party violence was a major reason for the Communist failure.

The Argument

The basic argument of this book is threefold. First, following the split with the GMD in April 1927, the CCP lost much of the organizational coherence that it had developed in the years since its founding in 1921.[6]

[5] Doug McAdam, Sidney Tarrow, and Charles Tilly, *Dynamics of Contention* (Cambridge: Cambridge University Press, 2001); Sidney G. Tarrow, *Power in Movement: Social Movements and Contentious Politics*), revised and updated 3rd ed. (Cambridge: Cambridge University Press, 2011).

[6] Hans J. van de Ven, *From Friend to Comrade: The Founding of the Chinese Communist Party, 1920–1927* (Berkeley, CA: University of California Press, 1991).

Figure 0.1 Re-enactors at the Jinggangshan

With Chiang Kai-shek's violent purge of the Communists, the CCP splintered in several directions. First, there was the Center in Shanghai, which, as a branch of the Comintern, was working closely with the Soviet Union. Even during the few short years covered in this volume, the Shanghai organization had three main leaders – Qu Qiubi, Li Lisan, and Bo Gu – each of whom followed a very different policy. Second, there were various provincial party committees vying for support from the Center while also trying to develop – and control – county-level party organizations and "special" committees, so named because they were intended to be short-term. Finally, there were party organizations scattered in many townships and villages. Such organizations were often weak, had little sense of doctrine, and often had no idea about how to organize peasants. They were also weakly controlled, if controlled at all, by higher-level organizations. Nearly all these truly grass-roots party organizations were developed by local educated youth – people who had left their villages for education either in county seats or farther afield in cities and then returned home to organize the peasants. Donggu was one such place.

It was such local organizations built by educated youth, not by Mao, that introduced Marxism to the countryside. The task of these grassroots organizations was to carry out insurrections (*baodong*) in an effort to ignite a nationwide conflagration that would allow the Communist Party to come to power quickly. This model was imported from the Russian experience. The revolution there had started in February 1917 with the overthrow of the tsar and it had continued in November 1917 with the Bolshevik victory. So local insurrections were supposed to culminate quickly in national victory. Some local party organizations carried out insurrections willingly, but many more did so reluctantly, under the prodding of higher-level party organizations. In the year following the split with the GMD, such local party organizations carried out some 100 insurrections in Jiangxi alone. Nearly all failed. One of the only local movements that survived and developed was that in Donggu. That is one reason it is of interest. But all these local organizations to some extent eroded the social institutions, what Presenjit Duara calls the "local nexus of power,"[7] particularly the clan system, that had long maintained order in rural China. In Donggu, the nascent Communist organization was able to erode the local sociopolitical order from which it had emerged to become the dominant force.

It should be noted that in order to be an educated youth during this period, one had to have come from a family of above average wealth. One of the truths of the Communist revolution that has been obscured over time is that revolutionary movements did not break out in the really poor, desperate parts of the country or among the poorest of the poor. Rather, violence erupted in somewhat wealthier places and was led by people of some social standing. At least some landlords were sympathetic toward revolution and sometimes they actually led uprisings. The story of Zeng Tianyu, told in Chapter 1 below, is a striking example. Moreover, peasants distinguished between landlords and "evil" landlords and directed their violence at the latter. The "evil" landlords were not necessarily the largest landlords, for the largest could afford to treat their tenants at least reasonably well. Frequently it was the smaller landlords who created greater tensions with the peasants because their positions in society were more precarious. Thus the image of an overwhelming local peasant demand for social justice, as suggested by Tawney, Meisner, and many others, is

---

[7] Presenjit Duara, *Culture, Power, and the State: Rural North China, 1900–1942* (Stanford, CA: Stanford University Press, 1988).

exaggerated. The reality is that local issues and political ideology were the decisive factors in the rise of the revolutionary movement.

This Communist movement was indigenous. It was created by locals, albeit locals who had acquired knowledge and ideology while outside their communities, and it attacked local institutions – clans, nearby communities, religious organizations – in an effort to build a broader social and political movement. In most places, these indigenous movements did not last long. Uprisings were poorly planned and quickly put down. However, the social conditions and physical isolation of Donggu allowed this movement to develop more successfully and over a longer period than any other such movement in Jiangxi, with the possible exception of Fang Zhimin's movement in northeast Jiangxi.[8]

The second argument in this book is that the penetration of local society by Mao and his Red Army was only possible because of what locals had already accomplished. Without this indigenous movement, it is doubtful that Mao's movement, built primarily around Hunanese, would have been able to penetrate Jiangxi society. But with the Donggu rebels providing an entrée, Mao's organization was able to penetrate deep into local society, albeit at an extremely high cost in lives.

In Donggu, Mao and his army turned on the local Communists, killed them, and took over the movement the locals had created and led. In doing so, Mao and his followers promoted a land revolution in an effort to destroy the local elite – the people who had originally built the Donggu Revolutionary Base Area. The irony is that not long after Mao had decimated the Donggu revolutionaries, he was pushed aside by the Shanghai revolutionaries who had fled Shanghai as the GMD cracked down in 1931. Because these Shanghai leaders, led by Bo Gu, ranked higher in the party hierarchy than Mao, they were able to take control of the movement. They did not have to attack Mao or his group violently (though violence did occur); Leninist discipline was sufficient. However, we will see below several instances in which Mao evaded higher-level party control. Party structure mattered, and when confronted by party authority directly, Mao had no choice but to yield. Tremendous violence then ensued, prompted in part by the Comintern,

---

[8] Kamal Sheel, *Peasant Society and Marxist Intellectuals in China: Fang Zhimin and the Origin of a Revolutionary Movement in the Xinjiang Region* (Princeton, NJ: Princeton University Press, 1988).

in part by Mao's own precedent, and in part by the tenuous existence that the party held in rural Jiangxi. Violence, it turned out, was a useful way to seize control over a movement and to extract funds from society.

Donggu and the Central Soviet were not the only areas wracked by such intra-party violence. As we will see in the final chapter, the Hubei–Henan–Anhui (Eyuwan) Base Area north of the Yangtze was similarly beset by violence, as Zhang Guotao, sent by the Party Center, moved against the local party organizations, much in the same way as outsiders had taken over the indigenous movements in Donggu. Later on, there were similar efforts in Shaanxi as Communist armies from the Eyuwan Base Area fled the GMD extermination campaigns and pushed aside indigenous Communist leaders in the northwestern Shaanxi outpost.[9]

The third argument is built on the first two, namely that Mao's development of a party army, the relative openness of local society to Mao's external forces because of local Communist leaders' development of the Donggu Revolutionary Base Area, and the subsequent crushing of that local Communist movement produced a party very different from that which had existed following Chiang Kai-shek's violent purge of the Communist Party. After the split with the GMD in April 1927, the CCP was in dire straits, not only in terms of a loss of membership but more importantly in terms of party structure. Local party cadres often operated on their own, sometimes with the support of higher-level organizations, sometimes against higher-level instructions, and often simply ignoring higher-level organs. After all, higher-level organizations were often ignorant of local conditions and had few, if any, resources to support lower-level organizations; and higher- and lower-level organizations were often in contention with one another. Moreover, party organizations at the provincial and county levels were often broken up by the GMD, leaving the lower levels to contend on their own. So shattered was the party organization by the GMD's suppression and the dispersion of party activists to the countryside that it is difficult to call the CCP after April 1927 a Leninist party. It retained the idea of hierarchy and party discipline, without which Bo Gu and others could not have sidelined Mao. But the CCP

---

[9] Joseph Esherick, *Accidental Holyland: The Origins of China's Shaan–Gan–Ning Border Region* (Berkeley, CA: University of California Press, forthcoming).

often found it difficult to realize anything resembling unified action; there were simply too many contending interests.

It was only slowly that the CCP was reconstituted, and in this process it emerged as a very different party than it had been in 1927 and before. Even after Chiang's purge in April, the CCP was extremely skeptical of military force, not only because it had been victimized by military force but primarily because it saw military force as something different from and antagonistic to mass insurrection. Military force could be used to supplement "the masses," but the masses had to be primary. Mao, however, was developing his movement around precisely such a military force, frequently drawing rebukes from the Party Center, and beginning to build a very different party, one that was far more militarized than anything party leaders had conceived of in 1927. Being a military organization had two effects. First, it invited attacks from outside forces, which took a tremendous toll on the civilian population, and second, it meant that the party army was strong enough to suppress local Communist movements, which it did with a vengeance.

There are many social movements in which factional infighting leads to the purge of one group or another, but movements in which outside elements come in and destroy the original movement are extremely rare.[10] It seems, however, that Donggu paved the way for Mao's penetration of the countryside and, in doing so, prepared the way for its own demise. What Donggu did was make Marxism and the idea of revolution legible for its own rural community, doing so in part by developing a peasant association and a military force and thus providing a new center of power in the community.[11] The fact that a local Communist force had weakened if not destroyed local institutions made it possible for an outside Communist movement to take over. In the end, Mao's revolution did not win over peasants and build itself from the bottom up; instead, it was imposed both from the outside and from the top down.

---

[10] An exception is Al-Shabaab. See Harun Maruf and Dan Joseph, *Inside Al-Shabaab: The Secret History of Al-Queda's Most Powerful Ally* (Bloomington, IN: Indiana University Press, 2018).

[11] James Scott argues that modernizing states adopt measures to make society more "legible." Here I am suggesting that educated youth in rural China made Marxism–Leninism, which had no intrinsic relationship to local society, more comprehensible to the locals, thus paving the way for Mao's movement to take over. See James Scott, *Seeing like a State: How Certain Schemes to Improve the Human Condition Have Failed* (New Haven, CT: Yale University Press, 1998).

This outsider-versus-insider struggle, no doubt inevitable, came at a particularly interesting time. As we will see below, there were many differences between Mao and local leaders, but the time in which these conflicts erupted in violence came precisely when the GMD-led First Extermination Campaign was bearing down on Donggu. One might think that in the face of such an existential threat, Mao's outsiders and the Donggu revolutionaries would bond closely together for the sake of mutual survival. But they did not; the mutual distrust was too high.

One reason for this mistrust was Mao's vaunted strategy of "luring the enemy in deep." That strategy made sense to Mao, who could use the locals' knowledge of geography to fight against outsiders who were less familiar with the locality. It made less sense to locals whose homes and families were at risk. At the same time as Mao saw the advantages of fighting in a locality that was difficult to attack and well known by locals, he was also suspicious that locals might betray him and contact the GMD. Moreover, the belief that local leaders, particularly Li Wenlin, who will be discussed extensively in the pages below, had the support of the Party Center (then led by Li Lisan), led them to be confident in their opposition to Mao. The result was that Mao turned on his erstwhile allies, accusing them of belonging to a nonexistent counterrevolutionary group, known as the AB Corps (AB standing for "Anti-Bolshevik"), and starting to arrest and purge them. The violence of this purge by outside forces led first to a violent purge of Mao's own troops – the Huangbei "suppression of counterrevolutionaries" – and then to the widely known but little understood Futian Rebellion.

The story of the Futian Rebellion has been told many times, starting with Tso-Liang Hsiao, John Rue, and Benjamin Schwartz. More recently it has been told by Chen Yung-fa and Stephen Averill.[12] What these tellings have missed, in my opinion, is first and foremost

[12] Benjamin I. Schwartz, *Chinese Communism and the Rise of Mao* (Cambridge, MA: Harvard University Press, 1979); Tso-liang Hsiao, *Power Relations within the Chinese Communist Movement, 1930–1934* (Seattle, WA: University of Washington Press, 1961); John E. Rue, *Mao Zedong in Opposition, 1927–1935* (Stanford, CA: Stanford University Press, 1966); Chen Yung-fa "Zhonggong zaoqi sufan de jiantao: AB tuan an (A Review of the Suppression of Counterrevolutionaries in the Early Period of Chinese Communism: The Case of the AB Corps), *Jindai yanjiusuo jikan*, no. 17, Part 1 (June 1988): 193–276; and Stephen C. Averill, "The Origins of the Futian Incident," in Tony Saich and Hans van de Ven, eds., *New Perspectives on the Chinese Communist Revolution* (Armonk, NY: M.E. Sharpe, 1995), pp. 79–115.

the factors that divided local interests from those of Mao and his followers. Moreover, the existence of the AB Corps has generally been accepted, but research in China has shown that no such group existed, certainly not one that had penetrated the CCP organization. The violence that stemmed from the witch hunt for AB Corps members was based on a falsehood. Finally, the Futian Rebellion has generally been taken as the culmination of conflict, whereas it really marked the beginning of a broader and even more violent suppression (*sufan*) campaign against supposed AB Corps members and other supposed counterrevolutionaries. Much of this violence was directed at CCP members and contributed significantly to the defeat of the Communist movement in Jiangxi.

It should be noted that what Mao and his Red Army did not finish, the GMD did. During both the First and Second Extermination Campaigns, GMD troops moved right through Donggu, killing and burning. The destruction was enormous. For all of its contribution to the Communist movement in the 1927–1930 period, Donggu would suffer enormously. No pre-1932 building survives in Donggu today. Other areas in the Central Soviet would suffer in similar fashion.

The *sufan* movement sprawled in a decentralized fashion throughout the Soviet area, killing tens of thousands. The violence associated with the *sufan* movement is difficult to fathom, but a movement that had started violently plumbed new depths of brutality. The fear it induced brought about a wholly new party culture, one in which orders from above were followed more quickly, fighters fought more aggressively, and violence was more readily accepted. Local society was no longer a reference point for members, at least not higher-level members, of the party. There was a new centralization as well as a new penetration of local society. The destruction of local society, something that was repeated throughout the country over the course of the revolution, would pose issues of governance that persist to the present. The clan system was destroyed and never adequately replaced. The newly imposed Communist leadership could only vacillate between the "commandism" of outsider rule and less successful efforts to rebuild local society.[13]

[13] John Fitzgerald, "Cadre Nation: Territorial Government and the Lessons of Imperial Statecraft in Xi Jinping's China," *China Journal*, no. 85 (January 2021), pp. 26–48.

In the end, the Communist Party that retreated from Jiangxi in 1934 was very different from the fractured, radical, and weak party that survived the split with the GMD in 1927. Although it would still take the Communist Party some years to work out leadership issues and doctrine, it was no longer leery of military force. On the contrary, it emerged as almost the precise opposite of what its leaders had envisioned in 1927. Instead of a party that hoped to spark a national insurrection and that criticized overreliance on military force as "military opportunism," after 1934 it relied on the military to defeat its enemies and to organize and revolutionize the areas it occupied. In short, the few years between 1927 and 1934 represent a crucial period in which the party forged the Leninism that we associate with it to this day.

Given its importance in the development of revolution in Jiangxi, one would think that the story of Donggu would be better known. This neglect is largely due to a strained historiography in which Mao had to be put at the center of a struggle to bring China out of the "century of humiliation."[14] Mao had developed the Jinggangshan Base Area, not the Donggu Base Area. Moreover, Donggu is inevitably linked to the Futian Rebellion (discussed in Chapter 4), one of the darkest moments in revolutionary history, so party historians, even those aware of Donggu, believe it better not to discuss its history. One of Mao's most famous writings, "A Single Spark Can Start a Prairie Fire," which originally had the far less memorable title "Reply to Lin Biao," mentioned different models of organization, including the "Li Wenlin type." Li Wenlin was the leader of the Donggu Revolutionary Base Area, but he had been executed in 1931 by the CCP as a supposed member of the AB Corps, so his name was simply excised when Mao's letter was published in the *Selected Works of Mao Zedong* in 1951.[15] It

---

[14] Hu Chiao-mu [Qiaomu], *Thirty Years of the Communist Party of China: An Outline History* (Westport, CT: Hyperion Press, 1973 [1951]). First published in Chinese in 1951, this narrative of the history of the CCP remained the most authoritative history of the party before the publication of Zhongguo zhongyang dangshi yanjiushi, *Zhongguo gongchandang lishi* (The History of the Chinese Communist Party), vol. 1 (Beijing: Renmin chubanshe, 1991), which only covers the years up to 1949. A second volume was intended but never published.

[15] The reference to Li Wenlin was retained in previous editions of Mao's letter, including in Zhonggong zhongyang shujichu, *Liuda yilai dangnei mimi wenjian* (Secret Party Documents since the Sixth Party Congress), 2 vols. (Beijing: Renmin

was not restored until 1989 when the Central Party School published the sixth volume of the *Selected Central Party Documents* (*Zhonggong zhongyang wenjian xuanji*). In 1994, Dai Xiangqing and Luo Huilan published their superbly researched book *The AB Corps and a Complete History of the Futian Incident* (*AB tuan yu Futian shibian shimo*).[16] Interest in Donggu was revived, especially by a seminar held in 2007 on the eightieth anniversary of the founding of the base area. That seminar led to the publication of a number of important works that have contributed mightily to the narrative below.[17]

In recent years there has been a new wave of scholarship in China that explores many aspects of the Chinese revolution, giving us a broader understanding. In particular, it forces us to pay attention to the role of rural educated youth in fostering local rebellion. Second, it shows the Maoist movement as only one strand of the revolution, one that was more militarized and coercive than is normally thought. Finally, there is the question of violence. The history of the Chinese revolution was extremely violent not only in its pursuit of landlords but particularly in its persecution of those accused of being members of the AB Corps and other groups deemed to be counterrevolutionary. Many of these supposedly counterrevolutionary groups, such as the Reorganizationalists, who demanded the reorganization of the GMD (to push Chiang Kai-shek out) and who were originally associated with Wang Jingwei's left wing of the GMD, were relatively moderate. But these moderates, including the Third Party, a party formed in 1930 by

chubanshe, 1981). See Tang Lianying, Ye Fulin, and Ding Renxiang, *Donggu geming genjudi shilun* (Historical Discussion of the Donggu Revolutionary Base Area) (Shanghai: Huadong shifan daxue chubanshe, 2019), p. 11. See also Liu Jingfang, "'Li Wenlin shi' genjudi yu Zhongguo tese geming daolu de kaipi" (The "Li Wenlin"-Style Base Area and the Opening of a Revolutionary Path with Chinese Characteristics), in Jiangxi shengwei dangshi yanjiu shi, ed., *Donggu genjudi yu Zhongguo geming daolu de kaipi: jinian Donggu genjudi chuangjian 80 nian xueshu taoluhui huiji* (The Donggu Base Area and the Opening of China's Revolutionary Path: Compilation of Academic Discussions Commemorating the Eightieth Anniversary of the Founding of the Donggu Base Area) (Beijing: Zhonggong dangshi chubanshe, 2008), pp. 41–42.

[16] Dai Xiangqing and Luo Huilan, *AB tuan yu Futian shibian shimo* (A Complete History of the AB Corps and the Futian Incident) (Zhengzhou: Henan renmin chubanshe, 1994).

[17] See especially Zhonggong Jiangxi shengwei dangshi yanjiushi et al., eds., *Donggu: Ganxinan geming genjudi shiliao xuanbian* (Donggu: Selected Historical Materials on the Southwest Jiangxi Base Area) 2 vols. (Beijing: Zhongyang wenxian chubanshe, 2007).

former Communist Tan Pingshan and former GMD leader Deng Yanda, were a fundamental threat to those who wanted a violent social revolution.[18]

This story of local revolution and the transformation of the CCP will proceed as follows. Chapter 1 looks at the response of the CCP to its crushing defeat incurred by the violent split with the GMD. The year following the April 1927 split is perhaps the most neglected period in scholarship on the CCP. Rarely mentioned are the roles of the Comintern, the educated youth, or the insurrections fostered by local party organizations, and the reasons why most of those uprisings failed. Chapter 2 explores the development of the Donggu Revolutionary Base Area. Unlike most of the local party organizations, the Donggu Base Area had a core leadership group of educated youth, held together by educational and sub-ethnic (Hakka) ties, and was able to form an alliance with the local bandit group (the Three Dot Society, *sandianhui*). Donggu's remoteness and mountainous geography protected the area in its early years; Communist groups in more exposed areas could not last long.

Chapter 3 looks at the development of the Maoist movement. Whereas the relationship between Mao and the military leader Zhu De is normally depicted as a partnership, it was actually a fraught relationship. Building a party army was a difficult matter, and it was only after Mao had been *voted* out as secretary of the Front Committee and then restored to his position due to the intervention of the Party Center that a party army began to form. The Gutian Conference in December 1929 resolved this rift, leaving Mao largely in control. Mao would face other challenges, which he would put down with violence, but the gradual formation of a party army marked an important turning point in forging China's Leninist system.

It is in Chapter 4 that we explore the clash between local revolutionaries and Mao's band of outsiders. In retrospect, this conflict seems inevitable, though if it had not been for Li Wenlin's belief that he had the support of Li Lisan, perhaps Mao might have been able to absorb the local movement into his organizations. No doubt that belief bolstered Li Wenlin's determination to oppose Mao, but the conflict was

[18] See J. Kenneth Olenik, "Deng Yanda and the Third Party," in Roger B. Jeans, eds., *Roads Not Taken: The Struggle of Opposition Parties in Twentieth-Century China* (Ann Arbor, MI: University of Michigan Press, 1992), pp. 111–134.

clearly rooted in local interests, particularly in Li Wenlin's desire to avoid a battle centered in Donggu during which the local population would be savaged.

Finally, Chapter 5 looks at how the *sufan* campaign was extended throughout the Central Soviet area after the Party Center was forced to move to Jiangxi. The logic of this *sufan* campaign was not limited to Mao's purge of local revolutionaries or Bo Gu's efforts to extend the control of the CCP (and raise funds) in the Central Soviet, but extended as well to other revolutionary base areas. A brief look at the Eyuwan Base Area in areas north of the Yangtze shows that the same logic applied to the CCP's second most important base area as well.

1 | *Disaster and Local Rebellion*

On the afternoon of April 9, 1927, Du Yuesheng, the legendary leader of Shanghai's notorious underworld organization the Green Gang, called Wan Molin, his house manager and fixer, into the living room. Seated with Du were other leaders of the Green Gang. Du asked Wan if he could find Wang Shouhua, the Communist leader of Shanghai's General Labor Union, that afternoon. Wan replied that he could. Du handed him an invitation and told him to take it to Wang. The invitation was for dinner at 8:00 p.m. on the evening of April 11.

Wang Shouhua's General Labor Union had been instrumental in organizing the general strike in February and then the climactic strike on March 21 that allowed Chiang Kai-shek's troops to enter the Chinese part of the city peacefully the next day. Tensions between the Chinese Communist Party (CCP) and Chiang Kai-shek's wing of the Guomindang (GMD) had been growing, so Wang's associates urged him not to go to dinner, or at least to take an escort of soldiers. But Wang knew Du Yuesheng, at least in part because he was himself a member of the Green Gang. With his usual self-confidence and sense of bravado, he dismissed the notion that Du would harm him. He was wrong.

When Wang Shouhua entered Du's home to attend the dinner, he was seized by four thugs. They grabbed him and stuffed him into the back of a car, where they proceeded to strangle him. The car moved through the streets of Shanghai to Fenglin Bridge. The thugs crammed Wang into a burlap bag and were about to drop him into a pit when Wang began to groan. He was still alive. One of the thugs moved to hit Wang with a shovel when one of the others stopped him. They decided to throw Wang into the pit anyway and to fill it with dirt. So Wang was buried alive, if only barely alive.[1]

---

[1] Zhang Junyi, *Du Yuesheng zhuan* (Biography of Du Yuesheng), 4 vols. (Taipei, Zhuanji wenxue zazhishe, 1968), vol. 2, pp. 1–16. See also "Wang Shouhua," in https://baike.so.com/doc/5816499-6029312.html, accessed July 17, 2019.

The next morning, April 12, 1927, at about 3:00 a.m., Chiang Kai-shek launched a coup against the CCP. Most Communist leaders were in the foreign concessions, which the GMD troops could not enter, so the coup was carried out by Du Yuesheng's Green Gang. That night some 300 CCP members were killed, more than 500 arrested, and some 5,000 disappeared.[2] It was a violent start to a very violent period in Chinese history.

On May 21, so-called Horse Day (*mari*) because of the telegraphic code used at the time, Xu Kexiang, the GMD garrison commander in Changsha, turned on the GMD party headquarters, then still dominated by Communists, and arrested about 3,000 Communists, workers, and peasants. Some 300 were killed. As the Northern Expedition had approached the Yangtze river, the left wing of the GMD had set up government in the city of Wuhan, in the middle reaches of the Yangtze, while Chiang Kai-shek had moved eastward, setting up headquarters in Nanchang, the capital of Jiangxi province, and then marching northeast toward Shanghai. The Communists were still allied with Wang Jingwei's GMD government in Wuhan, so the Communist Party headquarters were still called the GMD party headquarters. After attacking party headquarters, Xu's troops went after the provincial labor union, the provincial peasant association and other mass organizations. By June 10, Xu's attacks on Communists and those perceived to be Communists resulted in some 10,000 deaths.[3] Gong Chu, the onetime aide to Zhu De, attributes the slaughter of Horse Day to Communist actions that burned the houses of the wealthy, including the houses of GMD officers, who then demanded revenge.[4] These violent attacks reflected the rightward shift in politics and foreshadowed Wang Jingwei's decision to break with the Communists two months later, on July 15, after which he carried out his own "party purification."

Chiang's coup should not have come as a surprise to the CCP. Tensions had been rising at least since the revolutionary government

---

[2] Zhao Shenghui, *Zhongguo gongchandang zuzhishi gangyao* (An Outline Organizational History of the Chinese Communist Party) (Hefei: Anhui renmin chubanshe, 1987), p. 50.

[3] Dai Xiangqing and Luo Huilan, *AB tuan yu futian shibian shimo* (A Complete History of the AB Corps and the Futian Incident) (Zhengzhou: Henan renmin chubanshe, 1994), p. 43.

[4] Gong Chu, *Wo yu hongjun* (The Red Army and I) (Hong Kong: Nanfeng chubanshe, 1954), p. 47.

had moved from Guangzhou in the south to Wuhan. The left wing of the GMD and the CCP were increasingly alarmed by Chiang's independence and tried to rein him in. There had been simmering tensions between the left wing of the GMD, led by Wang Jingwei, and the right wing, led by Chiang Kai-shek, at least since a gunship named the *Zhongshan* moved up the Pearl river in March 1926. Saying that he suspected a coup effort, Chiang had the ship captured and the captain arrested. Chiang used the incident to reduce the influence of the Communists in the revolutionary government. Wang Jingwei, feeling insulted at not being consulted, left for Europe.

As the Northern Expedition headed north, the left wing of the GMD and its Communist allies moved their capital from Guangzhou to Wuhan in the middle reaches to the Yangtze river. Chiang Kai-shek, however, set up his military headquarters in Nanchang. From early 1927, the government in Wuhan tried to rein in the increasingly independent Chiang Kai-shek. In March 1927 the Wuhan government re-established the military council, which had been abolished following the *Zhongshan* incident, and declared that Chiang Kai-shek was subordinate to it. It also abolished the post of chair of the Central Executive Commission (CEC), which was held by Chiang, and established a Presidium of the Political Council. Meanwhile, Wang Jingwei, responding to appeals from the Wuhan government, was heading back from Europe. When he landed in Shanghai, he met with Chen Duxiu, and on April 5 the two issued a joint statement that reiterated continued support for collaboration between the CCP and the left wing of the GMD. Wang then left for Wuhan, where he became the dominant political figure.[5]

So there was plenty of warning that pressures were building, but nevertheless, Chiang's coup caught the CCP completely off guard.

The purge was disastrous for the CCP. At the time of the April 1927 split, the CCP had some 58,000 members; by the following November membership had fallen by 80 percent, to only 10,000. In Wuhan, the center of CCP power, there were 8,000 party members at the time of the split, but by early August, following the decision of the GMD left wing to split with the Communists, party membership had fallen to

[5] Tony Saich, *The Rise to Power of the Chinese Communist Party: Documents and Analysis* (Armonk, NY: M.E. Sharpe, 1996), pp. 109–115; "Wang Ching-wei," in Howard L. Boorman, ed., *Biographical Dictionary of Republican China*, 3 vols. (New York: Columbia University Press, 1970), vol. 3, pp. 369–376.

3,000. It fell to 2,000 by mid-August and to only 1,000 by September.[6] Many had been killed, but even more had simply left the party.

Despite Chiang's coup, the CCP decided to go ahead with its Fifth Party Congress, scheduled for April 1927. The congress determined that the party should maintain its alliance with the left wing of the GMD. Although the congress affirmed that the land issue was central, it still opposed confiscation of the land of small landlords. For the time being, the party decided to stick with Chen Duxiu as general secretary. But in early July 1927, Mikhail Borodin, the Comintern representative who had helped the GMD reorganize and had worked to ease tensions between the CCP and the GMD, was given the task of telling Chen that the Comintern had decided to replace him.[7] Chen was told to go to Moscow to study, but he refused. Having delivered that message, Borodin left for Moscow alone. Before boarding the train, however, Borodin designated a provisional Politburo. It consisted of Zhang Guotao, Zhou Enlai, Li Weihan, Li Lisan, and Zhang Tailei.[8]

One might think, given the disaster that had befallen the CCP, that it would hunker down, reorganize, and try to slowly rebuild its strength, this time with a strong military component. But the party was hardly humbled by its circumstances. Contrary to all evidence, the party decided that China still faced a revolutionary "high tide." If only the party could take immediate action, it might touch off the revolutionary feelings of the masses and seize power, as the Bolsheviks had done in 1917. The Comintern's new representative, Beso Lominadze, certainly encouraged such feelings and he turned to the twenty-eight-year-old Qu Qiubai as one of those in the CCP who shared his feelings. Qu was close to the Comintern and was perhaps the only CCP leader to have openly criticized Chen Duxiu before Chiang's coup, so Lominadze picked Qu to replace Chen as effective head of the Communist Party (Qu was never given the title of secretary).[9]

Like most of the leaders of the CCP, Qu was not from a working-class background; rather, he one of the intellectual elites who

[6] Yang Kuisong, *"Zhongjian de didai" de geming: Guoji dabeijingxia kan Zhongguo chenggong zhidao* (Revolution in the "Intermediate Zone": Looking at the Success of the CCP in a Global Context) (Taiyuan: Shanxi renmin chubanshe, 2010), p. 179.

[7] Zhao Shenghui, *Zhongguo gongchandang zuzhishi gangyao*, p. 59.   [8] Ibid.

[9] Wang Tiexian and Liu Fuqin, eds., *Qu Qiubai zhuan* (Biography of Qu Qiubai) (Beijing: Renmin chubanshe, 2011), pp. 206–227.

dominated the party in its early years. Qu had been born into a literary family in Changzhou, Jiangsu, but his family fell on hard times. Not being able to afford tuition, he took up the study of Russian at the newly opened Russian Language Institute in Beijing. The new school not only did not require a tuition fee, it even offered a stipend and the promise of a job following graduation. Qu soon joined the discussions on Marxism at Peking University organized by Li Dazhao, the librarian and a leader of the May Fourth Movement, the 1919 protest that objected to the Versailles Conference's decision to grant Germany's concessions in Shandong province to Japan. Li would go on to play a critical role in introducing Marxism into China and organizing the CCP. Qu then took a job as a journalist for the *Morning News*. The paper dispatched Qu to Moscow as its correspondent. He returned to China in 1923, joining Chen Duxiu in Shanghai and undertaking propaganda work for the young Communist Party.[10]

Rather than slinking back into the shadows and organizing a party that might be able to compete with the GMD, Qu enthusiastically endorsed a policy of insurrections (*baodong*). This new mood of direct action was behind the hastily organized Nanchang Uprising, which took place on August 1, 1927. Today, it is celebrated as the founding of the Red Army, but at the time it was a poorly organized and ill-conceived move to take an important city. The uprising was timed to occur when GMD troops had moved out of the city, and troops, led by He Long (who was not yet a member of the CCP) and Ye Ting, under the overall direction of Zhou Enlai, were able to seize the city. They held the city for only three days before GMD troops returned and ousted the Communists, inflicting many casualties. The defeated Communist troops, then headed south, eventually reaching Shantou in Guangdong, where they hoped to organize a new revolutionary base and launch an insurrection. Instead, they were mauled by local armies.[11]

The defeat in Nanchang, however, did not dim the enthusiasm of the Communist Party. Just days after the defeat at Nanchang, party leaders gathered in Wuhan on August 7 to hold an "Emergency Meeting." This meeting was one of the major turning points in early party history. The

---

[10] Ibid.
[11] For a wonderful description of life within the CCP during these revolutionary years, see Zhu Qihua, *China 1927: Memoir of a Debacle*, tr. Zhu Hong (Portland, ME: Merwin Asia, 2013).

first thing the meeting did was to declare that all the errors that had led to the disasters that had befallen the Chinese Communist Party were the fault of Chen Duxiu and other "opportunists" who had compromised too much and for too long with the GMD.[12] The Hunan Provincial Party Committee disagreed, arguing (correctly) that the Comintern "lacked the courage to admit its opportunist errors." The party committee was soon reorganized and the judgment that Chen Duxiu had opportunistically diverged from the correct Comintern line was fixed as the party line.[13] Up until this point in party history, the party had not blamed errors on mistakes of "line." Blaming Chen Duxiu for "opportunism" set a new and harsher tone in the party, one that would only get darker.

Second, the August 7 Emergency Meeting confirmed that China, contrary to all evidence, was continuing to face a revolutionary high tide. Seemingly inspired by the history of the Bolshevik Party, which had seized power only in November following the failure of the February revolution, the CCP insisted that peasants and workers would rise up, bringing about a national revolution. The party had articulated this thesis in a circular sent out on July 20, 1927, declaring that the "revolutionary tide throughout the country ... is actually continuing to rise."[14]

Third, in accordance with the circular of July 20, the August 7 Emergency Meeting confirmed that the revolution had opened up a new phase, that of land revolution. As Qu Qiubai put it, "Now the peasants want to launch an uprising and we control many armed forces in various areas. With such a good opportunity and such great strength, we must light the fuse and set off a rural revolution."[15] This call for land revolution did not mean that the party was thinking in terms of organizing peasants for a long, violent revolutionary struggle; rather, the party was thinking in terms of insurrections, organized by Communist activists and supported by the peasant masses who would march on the cities and seize power. It was on the basis of this judgment that the Emergency Meeting drafted a plan for the "Autumn

---

[12] See Lominadze's report to the August 7 Emergency Meeting, in Saich, *The Rise to Power of the Chinese Communist Party*, pp. 308–313.

[13] The argument of the Hunan Provincial Committee was discussed at the Politburo meeting following the close of the August 7 Emergency Meeting. See Saich, *The Rise to Power of the Chinese Communist Party*, p. 322.

[14] Ibid., p. 292.   [15] Ibid., p. 315.

Harvest Uprisings" focused on the four provinces of Hunan, Hubei, Guangdong, and Jiangxi.[16]

Finally, despite Qu Qiubai's judgment that "either we will eliminate the Guomindang or they will destroy us," Qu and the Comintern insisted that the CCP not break with the GMD, even though the left wing of the GMD, headed by Wang Jingwei, had already broken with the CCP. This stubbornness reflected Comintern policy, which was ultimately set by Stalin. Wang Jingwei was still in power in Wuhan, and the CCP still hoped to unite with him and the left wing of the GMD and launch an "eastern expedition" to oust Chiang Kai-shek. But even as the CCP was convening its August 7 Emergency Meeting in Wuhan, Wang Jingwei was arresting Communists and executing them. Slow to admit the errors of their ways, the Comintern and the CCP did not officially split with the GMD until September. Even then, many local party organizations continued their activities under the GMD banner, because that was better known and less feared than the term "communist."

The Autumn Harvest Uprisings

The best-known result of the party's call for Autumn Harvest Uprisings was Mao Zedong's failure to take Changsha and his subsequent retreat to the Jinggangshan (discussed in Chapter 4). The Autumn Harvest Uprising was really a policy of launching rural uprisings throughout the four provinces in which the party had significant influence – Jiangxi, Hunan, Hubei, and Guangdong. These insurrections were different from Mao's Hunan venture, first and foremost because they did not place as much emphasis on the military as Mao did. Although Mao had no military experience, he was obsessed with the military. He had declared in his "Report on the Peasant Problem in Hunan" that "revolution is not a dinner party" and that "power grows out of the barrel of a gun." He repeated his views at the August 7 Emergency Meeting, saying, "We must fully understand that political power grows out of the barrel of a gun."[17] But many party people opposed his militarism.

For Qu Qiubai and other party leaders, Chiang's April coup – and Wang Jingwei's subsequent split with the Communist Party on July 15 – were only temporary setbacks. They were convinced that if

---

[16] Ibid., pp. 317–319.   [17] Ibid., p. 317.

only cadres would go to the countryside and provide leadership, the masses would rise up in revolt. The divisions among the "reactionaries," whether in the GMD or among the various warlords who still ruled much of China, encouraged the CCP in this belief.

What was needed was a general insurrection, a movement that would rely on the strength of the masses, not on military power. Of course, the uprising in Nanchang used troops, but these were hastily combined and not a party army of the sort that Mao and others would eventually create. The same is true of the December 1927 Guangzhou Uprising. But in the summer of 1927, despite what had happened to it, the CCP showed little interest in building a military. In part this was because it could not imagine a prolonged struggle – it was thinking more in terms of the Russian revolution. Moreover, the CCP's history with military organizations, whether of the warlord or GMD variety, had not been pleasant. Military organizations tended to get out of control.

Perhaps more fundamentally, the CCP believed that the masses, under party leadership, could successfully launch a revolution and seize power with only a minimal role for military organizations. As one Jiangxi Provincial Party Committee document put it, "to rely on military action would not succeed, and even if it did succeed, it would have no meaning," because power would be in the hands of the military, not the masses.[18] In addition, in the face of the "revolutionary high tide," immediate action was needed. Waiting to patiently rebuild the party, carry out propaganda, and cultivate military power would waste a precious opportunity. Of course, in calling for immediate insurrection, Qu was vastly overestimating conditions in the countryside, believing that the rural areas were on the verge of exploding (*yichu jifa*).

There is, however, no evidence that the rural areas were on the brink of revolution. Although rents were heavy – tenants usually surrendered 50 percent or more of their harvest to landlords – they had always been so. Land ownership was more scattered than many accounts suggest.

[18] "Zhonggong Jiangxi shengwei tongbao (di shisan hao) (Jiangxi Provincial CCP Committee Notice [no. 13]), Zhongyang dang'an guan and Jiangxisheng dang'an guan, *Jiangxisheng geming lishi wenjian huiji (1927–1928)* (Compilation of Historical Documents of the Jiangxi Revolution, 1927–1928) (Los Angeles: Zhongwen chubanshe fuwu zhongxin, 2013), ser. 21, vol. 15, p. 40.

A 1933 survey of Shanghang county in western Fujian found that landlords constituted 3.3 percent of the population, but owned 30.5 percent of the land. But those who cultivated some land and rented some land constituted 64.1 percent of the population.[19] Similarly, a 1935 survey of Anyuan, Xunwu, and Xinfeng counties in southern Jiangxi found that 70 percent of the families owned under five *mu* (one *mu* equals one-sixth of an acre) of land, and only 2 percent of the families owned over twenty *mu*. Those who owned less than five *mu* of land certainly lived difficult lives and probably had to rent some land, but the number of families who owned no land was only 3 percent.[20]

The number of landlords and rich peasants in Jiangxi and Fujian was approximately the same as that in the rest of the country.[21] Overall, there is no evidence of extreme polarization;[22] on the contrary, there was a surprising degree of equality in Jiangxi. One source claims that hired laborers in Jiangxi wore the same clothing as those who had hired them.[23] Large landlords – those with more than 100 *mu* of land – were quite rare, approximately 0.02–0.03 percent of the population.[24] Also, taxes in Jiangxi were not particularly high, usually in the range of 4–6 percent of income.[25] Overall, Jiangxi was known as a rich agricultural area with a penchant for small commerce.[26] Even the bandits were said to join the men of the greenwood out of a desire to strike it rich rather than out of extreme poverty.[27]

Living with modest wealth dampened interest in politics. The Communist Party found it difficult to mobilize people. One report declared, "the youth of Nanchang are numb [to politics]."[28] Another report, by the party secretary of the Ji'an special committee, stated,

---

[19] Huang Daoxuan, *Zhangli yu xianjie: Zhongyang suqu de geming (1933–1934)* (Tensions and Limits: The Revolution in the Central Soviet (1933–1934)) (Beijing: Shehui kexue wenxian chubanshe, 2011, p. 26.
[20] Ibid., p. 27.   [21] Ibid., p. 32.   [22] Ibid., p. 53.
[23] Zhang Hongqing, *Nongmin xingge yu zhonggong de xiangcun dongyuan moshi Zhongyang suqu wei zhongxin de kaocha* (Peasant Characteristics and the CCP's Style of Mobilizing in the Countryside: An Investigation Centered on the Central Soviet Area) (Beijing: Zhongguo shehui kexue chubanshe, 2012), p. 22.
[24] Ibid., p. 27.   [25] Huang Daoxuan, *Zhangli yu xianjie*, p. 60.
[26] Zhang Hongqing, *Nongmin xingge yu zhonggong de xiangcun dongyuan moshi*, pp. 24–27.
[27] Ibid., p. 21. "Men of the greenwood" is a poetic term that was used to describe the bandits who lurked in the mountains.
[28] Ibid., p. 32.

The houses of the peasants are scattered and their working hours are long. In the daytime, they do not have much time to rest, and at night they go to sleep early. Because of this they are not receptive to propaganda or training. When we go to the fields to talk [with them], there are very few listeners. Each time there are at most ten or so.[29]

The mountains are said to have imparted a quick temper to the residents. Although normally calm and hardworking, when riled peasants could be quick to resort to violence. Although the Hakka and the early settlers were in many ways codependent – the mountain-dwelling Hakka supplying wood and medicinal herbs to the early settler markets, while buying rice and foodstuffs in exchange – sub-ethnic conflicts were not uncommon and they could be quite violent.[30]

Overall, however, Jiangxi was not conducive to Communist organizing. As one party report put it, "The responsible comrades of the Center believe that there is not much one can do in Jiangxi at the moment."[31] Statistics from the period bear out this observation. In July 1926, there were 11,257 members of the Chinese Communist Party, and only 105 of them were in Jiangxi.[32] Although the party expanded rapidly thereafter, it remained a weak organization. Furthermore, the party had a difficult time developing relations with the "masses," its finances were straitened, and discipline was weak. Dropping out of the party (*tuodang*) was not uncommon.[33]

There is some evidence that bandit activity and miscellaneous assessments increased in the years following the Revolution of 1911, but He Youliang's assessment that ideology and political awareness were the most important causes of revolutionary activity seems correct.[34]

Those who provided this ideology and political awareness were a group of educated youth, a slice of rural life in Jiangxi and elsewhere that has been largely ignored in the literature. Although these youth are sometimes referred to as "revolutionary intellectuals" (*geming zhishi fenzi*), they cannot really be considered intellectuals. A few had indeed gone on to college, but the vast majority merely graduated from higher elementary or high school. Such people had neither the education nor the wealth to go on to college, so they were cut off from the higher

[29] Quoted in ibid., p. 33.   [30] Ibid., pp. 28–31.   [31] Quoted in ibid., p. 34.
[32] Cited in ibid., p. 36.   [33] Ibid., pp. 35–42.
[34] He Youliang, "Geming yuanqi: Nongcun geming zhong de zaoqi lingdao qunti" (The Origins of Revolution: The Leading Group at the Beginning of the Rural Revolution), *Jiangxi shehui kexue*, no. 3 (2007), p. 95.

ranks of China's intelligentsia. But they were educated, and they saw themselves – and were seen by others – as no longer part of the peasantry. It was common for peasants to call such people "teacher" (*laoshi*), reflecting their higher and respected position in the local social order. Most of this group of youth came from middle or lower landlord or rich peasant families, families that were wealthy enough to send promising sons to school but not wealthy enough to be pillars of the social order. With the abolition of the examination system in 1905, there was no ladder of success for such youth to follow.

Taking up jobs as teachers was a possibility, and many did so, but such jobs did not pay well and were uncertain. More important, it was precisely such schools that had bred their activism in the first place. As students, they were exposed to the influence of the May Fourth Movement of 1919, but little of the liberalism of that movement survived in their thinking. Rather, their education and perhaps their participation in the May Thirtieth Movement of 1925 had radicalized them. Many had participated in student protests of one sort or another, and some had been expelled from school, further strengthening their commitment to political action. As a group, they had left their native villages to go to school, sometimes to the county seat and sometimes farther abroad, so they were no longer confined intellectually or socially to the milieu in which they had grown up. But they were still very much a part of the families and communities in which they had matured. It was this group of educated youth – not fully of their communities, not fully external to their communities, and uncertain about their futures, but politically sensitive to the forces of imperialism, warlordism, and the inequality that underpinned the old social order – who would begin to make the message of the Communist Party legible to the peasants and would start to mobilize the peasants against the "local bullies and evil gentry."[35]

After the GMD turned on its erstwhile Communist allies in April 1927, and especially after the August 7 Emergency Meeting, many of the educated youth returned to their homes, if they had not done so earlier, to continue the struggle. Looking at local party

[35] Zhang Hongqing, *Nongmin xingge yu zhonggong de xiangcun dongyuan moshi*, pp. 72–77; Tang Xiaobing, "Dageming qianhou zhongxiao zhishi fenzi de ningju yu zhengzhihua" (The Cohesion and Politicization of Middle and Lower Intellectuals before and after the Great Revolution) (n.p.).

organizations throughout China, not only in Jiangxi, it is apparent that they were dominated by educated youth.

Sometimes such youth showed a remarkable propensity toward violence. Wang Shusheng from Hubei, later a general in the People's Liberation Army (PLA), had no problem killing his uncle, the wealthiest man in his village. Wang Xiusheng, also from Hubei, killed his father, and Zhang Shixi would lead his followers to kill six "evil gentry" in Wan'an (see below). But, in general, these local party organizers were more moderate than their superiors. Those on the provincial party committees were often transferred in from other parts of the country, knew little about circumstances in individual communities, and were under pressure from the Party Center. Hence they demanded that local organizers take immediate action. This pressure meant that there was little time to do the painstaking work of organizing, spreading propaganda, and building some semblance of military force. Of course, most had no experience with the military and were unable to build a military even if they had had the time – and the guns – that would be necessary.

The Party Center, under pressure from the Comintern, was anxious to prove that China was on the cusp of revolutionary success. Because the model was the Russian revolution, no one expected a prolonged military conflict. The Center, as we have noted, embraced violence but not military power. It placed its faith in the "masses." It also opposed local organizations' doing the careful and detailed propaganda and mobilizational work required to build a solid foundation. Incremental struggles to mobilize people and build a military force were unacceptable.[36] Such efforts were dismissed by the Party Center as "pure militarism," efforts that could only "weaken the promotion of insurrections."[37] The Party Center even believed that "even if the enemy attacks and slaughters [of the masses], not only would this not be a defeat for the revolution, it would prove that the revolutionary tide is rising."[38] One of the pressures on local cadres following the August 7

---

[36] Huang Kun, *Geming yu xiangcun: Cong baodong dao xiangcun geju* (Revolution and Villages: From Insurrections to Rural Bases, 1927–1929) (Shanghai: Shanghai shehui kexueyuan chubanshe), 2006, p. 29.

[37] Zhong Rixing, *Xiangcun shehuizhong de geming dongyuan: Yi zhongyang suqu weili* (The Revolutionary Mobilization in Rural Society: Taking the Central Soviet Area as an Example) (Beijing: Zhonggguo shehuikexue chubanshe, 2015), p. 19.

[38] "Zhongguo xianzhuang yu dang de renwu jueyi'an – Zuijin zuzhi wenti de zhongyao renwu jueyi'an" (Resolution on China's Present Circumstances and

Emergency Meeting was that if they did not take action they would be accused of "opportunism."[39]

Insurrections

Qu's Qiubai's idea was that Communist organizers would direct violence toward the local elite, the so-called local bullies and evil gentry, killing them and burning their houses. The expectation was that when one area rose up, others would respond in kind, and revolution would spread like wildfire, creating conditions for a seizure of power.[40] During this period, it was widely believed that violence directed against the local bullies and evil gentry would mobilize the masses. The plan for the Autumn Harvest Uprising called for "slaughter" (*shalu*) of landlords and gentry. Similarly, following the conclusion of the August 7 Emergency Meeting, the party issued the "Resolution on the Peasant Struggle for the Near Term," which called for "eliminating (*suqing*) the local bullies and evil gentry and all counterrevolutionaries, and confiscating their property."[41] Coming out of the Emergency Meeting, party instructions called on local organizations to exercise "revolutionary dictatorship" (*geming de ducai*), which was defined in some documents as "using the strength of the masses to kill all the bullies, gentry, and landlords."[42] When the CCP's Yangtze Bureau (*Changjiang ju*) was established in September 1927, it issued a resolution that directed the party committees of Hubei and Hunan to "develop the work of confiscating the land of landlords and slaughtering the local bullies and evil gentry."[43]

Quite apart from Qu Qiubai's serious misreading of the political situation in China's rural areas, there were enormous organizational problems that stood between the party and any sort of successful insurrection. First and foremost, the party was weak. Not only had

---

the Party's Tasks – The Most Important Tasks Regarding Organizational Issues at Present), quoted in Zhong Rixing, *Xiangcun shehuizhong de geming dongyuan*, p. 19.

[39] Huang Kun, *Geming yu xiangcun*, p. 29.   [40] Ibid., p. 62.

[41] Li Weihan, *Huiyi yu yanjiu* (Remembrance and Study), 2 vols. (Beijing: Zhonggong dangshi chubanshe, 2013), vol. 1, pp. 122–128.

[42] Ren Wei, "Geming baoli de yuanqi yu tezhi: Yi 'hongse kongbu' wei zhongxin de tantao" (The Origin of Revolutionary Violence: A Case Study of "Red Terror"), *Taiwan shida lishi xuebao*, no. 51 (June 2014), p. 55.

[43] Ibid.

the numbers of party members fallen drastically in the face of repression, but also whatever discipline had been instilled in the party in its first years had been shattered. In part this was because, in the face of disaster, the party had metastasized. Instead of being concentrated in the major urban areas of Shanghai, Guangzhou, and Wuhan, party organizations were now scattered along the route of the Northern Expedition – Guangdong, Hunan, Jiangxi, and Hubei. Of course, this explosion of party groups had begun with the organization of peasant associations as the revolutionary army moved north (mostly in the wake of the Northern Expedition rather than ahead of it). But it had been accelerated by the call for insurrection. These small groups were surprisingly autonomous, being more embedded in local society than serving as local extensions of higher party authority.

They were semi-autonomous because the Center did not have the money to fund them or the organizational strength to control them. In fact, the local party organizations were expected to fund higher-level party organizations, but frequently the lower-level organizations divided the spoils from their raids on wealthy households, neglecting to send any funds upward. Furthermore, their financial independence led to a considerable degree of political independence. Higher-level party organizations could only occasionally send observers or special envoys (*xunshiyuan* or *tepaiyuan*) to the lower levels both because they lacked the necessary cadres and because traveling through hostile territory was time-consuming and dangerous. Moreover, the cadres in provincial-level party organizations (who often had to be changed because the GMD was frequently successful in breaking up such organizations) often did not have the necessary knowledge of the local areas to understand their circumstances, especially if they had been moved in from outside the province. In terms of local politics, an "outsider" could well be from a different part of the same county or from the next county over; coming from another province usually, but not always, meant an inability to act effectively.

In the summer of 1927 the CCP could not really be described as a Leninist party. As one researcher puts it, "In this period, the basic-level organizations of the party were loose (*huansan*), party branches were without substance, party members lacked training, and there was no way for the party to exercise discipline."[44] Local party organizations

---

[44] Zhong Rixing, *Xiangcun shehuizhong de geming dongyuan*, p. 24.

would often exaggerate their size and strength. After the Southern Hubei (Enan) Uprising broke out in August 1927, the Hubei Provincial Party Committee sent someone surnamed Ren to Western Hubei (Exi) to report on circumstances and to see if that district could rise up in support. When Ren reached Shashi, he received a report that one community, Dangyang, had 30,000–40,000 people who were ready to rise up; another community, Jiangling, had 10,000, and a third, Gongan, had 20,000–30,000. So Ren met with the Western Hubei cadres and decided to launch an insurrection immediately. But when Ren returned to Wuhan, he received a report that Shashi had only twenty or so party members and they were all quite backward. The other communities were equally bereft of cadres. Another report, this one from Ji'an in Jiangxi, stated that there were supposed to be "four district party committee with over 400 party members, but when one investigates the reality, the number of comrades who are really under the direction of the party, who work hard, and are loyal and reliable is probably not even fifty."[45]

Even as the Center was adopting a new and more radical policy, local party organizations were fighting for survival. After Wang Jingwei declared on July 15, 1927, that he and his wing of the GMD would split with the Communists, they carried out a "party purification" movement, just as Chiang Kai-shek and his right wing had done. On July 31, only two weeks after the split with the Communists, the movement caught up with the Jiangxi Provincial Party Committee. Seven members of the party committee were arrested and subsequently executed; only two survived, and they went into hiding.

The Yangtze Bureau was set up in September 1927 with Luo Yinong as its head. Luo was an enthusiastic supporter of Qu Qiubai's new policy, declaring, "Only if more are killed will the broad masses rise up everywhere . . . If the Chinese revolution is too civilized, it absolutely will not succeed."[46] Such calls did not attract the highest-quality cadres. In addition to the educated youth, some local organizations were basically bandit groups. As Gong Chu, later an aide to Zhu De, put it, "Because the CCP lacked correct leadership, many [organizations] in the peasant

[45] "Jiangxi shengwei zhi Ganxibian tewei de xin" (A Letter from the Jiangxi Provincial Committee to the West Ganxi Special Committee), in Jiangxisheng dang'an guan, ed., *Jinggangshan geming genjudi shiliao xuanbian* (Selected Materials on the Jinggangshan Revolutionary Base Area) (Nanchang: Jiangxi renmin chubanshe, 1985), p. 40.

[46] Ren Wei, "Geming baoli de yuanqi yu tezhi," p. 59.

movement were controlled by vagrants and hooligans, many actions
were bandit-like or they were revengeful actions devoid of discipline
and without principles."[47]

Luo Yinong transferred cadres in from Hubei to replace the local
Jiangxi cadres on the provincial party committee, whom he did not
trust. Although these outsiders did not know the local cadres or the
conditions they faced, the new committee vowed to get rid of "opportunists" and to follow the violent new policy. In December 1927, the
Jiangxi Provincial Party Committee instructed lower-level organizations to "strictly (*lixing*) carry out extreme Red terror (*hongse
kongbu*)" throughout the province.[48] Mao was certainly one of those
who called for such Red terror. In a report written in October 1928,
Mao wrote, "In the past, while carrying out the 'land revolution,' we
entirely failed to impose a severe Red terror, and to massacre the
landlords and despotic gentry ..." He advised the party to organize
"Red execution teams" that "should carry out guerrilla attacks in the
dead of night to create Red terror in the countryside."[49]

Some party organizations tried to carry out Red terror, whether
because of pressure from above or out of their own revolutionary
zeal. For instance, in September, an uprising in Xingzi, north of
Nanchang in Jiangxi on the western shore of Poyang Lake, succeeded
in occupying the county seat, but merely for one day. Only a few
peasants were involved and the Communist forces that were driven
out of the city quickly turned to guerrilla warfare.[50]

There was a sense of urgency that made cadres rush into insurrections with little organization or planning. For instance, in Yongding
county, in western Fujian, the party had considerable influence, but it
was no match for the soldiers who were in the county seat. The party
committee tried to convince people to take up guerrilla warfare, but
people did not want to – though some did want to strike out as bandits.
Others said the leaders were cowards. In the end, the party committee

[47] Gong Chu, *Wo yu hongjun*, p. 47.
[48] Ren Wei, "Geming baoli de yuanqi yu tezhi," p. 56.
[49] See Stuart R. Schram, *Mao's Road to Power: Revolutionary Wrings, 1912–
1949, vol. 3: From the Jinggangshan to the Establishment of the Jiangxi Soviets,
July 1927–December 1930* (Armonk, NY: M.E. Sharpe, 1995), p. 74.
[50] "Zhonggong Jiangxisheng zhi zhongyang xin" (Letter to the Center from the
Jiangxi Provincial CCP Committee), in Zhongyang dang'an guan and
Jiangxisheng dang'an guan, *Jiangxisheng geming lishi wenjian huiji (1927–
1928)*, ser. 21, vol. 15, p. 73.

launched an attack on the county seat and, of course, it was defeated. As cadres later reported, this was an instance of an "insurrection striking down our own C.P. [Communist Party]."[51]

However, party leaders in other areas were more cautious. For instance, in late 1927, there was an instance in which Communist cadres were openly rallying peasants in the villages in Poyang, on the east side of the eponymous lake. So the authorities sent forces to arrest them. The peasants resisted successfully at first, but at night four leaders were arrested. The next day the peasants went into the city and demanded the release of the leaders. But the local Communist leaders were cautious, and, "fearing that their locality would by ruined," mediated between the city officials and the peasants. When the peasants returned home, they were still angry and burned several homes of local bullies and evil gentry. The provincial party committee was not happy with the local leaders, whose moderate attitude clearly lagged behind that of the local peasants.[52]

Similarly, the Jiangxi Provincial Party Committee criticized the Ji'an Party Committee because the latter, understanding that it was weak, sought to compromise with the military forces in the area. The provincial party committee members were very unhappy, declaring that even if there was no hope of victory, the Ji'an Party Committee should attack courageously. If their insurrection brought about even greater cruelty on the part of the warlord army, "it would be of benefit to the overall revolution."[53] Such uprisings, even if they involved thousands of peasants, usually failed quickly. There were both organizational and sociological reasons for these failures.

Organizational Issues

Organizationally, the Jiangxi party organization lacked the necessary size and infrastructure. In July 1927, at the time of the First Jiangxi

[51] Zhong Rixing, *Xiangcun shehuizhong de geming dongyuan*, p. 19, and "Luo Ming guanyu Minxi qingkuang gei Fujian shengwei de xin" (A letter from Luo Ming to the Fujian Party Committee on Conditions in Western Fujian), in Zhongyang dang'an guan and Fujiansheng dang'an guan, *Fujian geming lishi wenjian huiji* (Collection of Historical Documents on the Fujian Revolution). Vol. 15: *Minxi tewei wenjian (1928–1936 nian)* (Documents of the West Fujian Special Committee (1928–1936)) (Fuzhou: Fujian renmin chubanshe, 1987), p. 21, quoted in Huang Kun, *Cong baodong dao xiangcun geju, 1927–1929*, p. 28.
[52] "Zhonggong Jiangxisheng zhi zhongyang xin," p. 75.
[53] Ren Wei, "Geming baoli de yuanqi yu tezhi," p. 63.

Provincial Party Conference, the party claimed 5,100 members with organizations in fifty to sixty places. But after Ye Ting and He Long, commanders in the Nanchang Uprising, left the province, the party organization "collapsed."[54] In February 1928, the Jiangxi party had about 4,000 party members in twenty-three locations; but some 2,300 of those party members were in Wan'an in southern Jiangxi, and they would have been fleeing for their lives at the time the party committee was writing its report (see below for the rise and fall of the Wan'an Soviet). It was difficult to build and sustain a viable party organization in the face of external threat, organizational neglect, lack of funds, lack of talent, and poor organizational discipline. The provincial party committee, as noted above, had been destroyed in July 1927 and its members had been replaced with outsiders. The party committee would be destroyed again in June 1928. Moreover, it felt that the Party Center in Shanghai did not value its work and it repeatedly complained about a lack of funds. For instance, in October 1927, the party committee wrote the Yangtze Bureau saying that its monthly stipend of 550 yuan was not nearly enough. The scope of its work was expanding and it was recruiting more people – the subsidy would have to be doubled![55] In January 1928, the party committee reported that it really could not manage on 550 yuan a month, and it had no funds to support lower-level party organizations. Again, in April 1928, the party committee said that it hoped the Center would value its work in Jiangxi; without funds the party work could not be done well. The party committee claimed it needed at least 5,000 yuan! Furthermore, it hoped that the Center would send some capable cadres to help with the work.[56]

The party committee realized early on that it could not possibly carry out an uprising covering the entire province, but it argued that

[54] "Wu Zhenpeng: Jiangxi dang zuzhi de fazhan yu xianzhuang" (Wu Zhenpeng: The Development and Present Circumstances of the Jiangxi Party Organization), *Jiangxi sheng geming lishi wenjian huiji (1927–1928)*, pp. 158–160.

[55] "Zhonggong Jiangxi shengwei gei Changjiangju de baogao" (Report from the Jiangxi Provincial Party Committee to the Yangtze Bureau), in Zhongyang dang'an guan and Jiangxisheng dang'an guan, *Jiangxi sheng geming lishi wenjian huiji (1927–1928)*, p. 52–55.

[56] "Zhonggong Jiangxi shengwei gei zhongyang de zonghe baogao" (Comprehensive Report from the Jiangxi Provincial Party Committee to the Center), in Zhongyang dang'an guan and Jiangxisheng dang'an guan, *Jiangxi sheng geming lishi wenjian huiji (1927–1928)*, p. 226.

organizing local uprisings was still meaningful.[57] However, the quality of local party organizations was often low, and the provincial party committee had little control over them. For instance, in Poyang, as the peasants were moving on the county seat, the local leaders, rather than lead, simply folded their arms and told the peasants to go. Worse, the party secretary of the action committee was pursuing a new girlfriend![58] Most party members, the provincial party committee reported, were "cowardly and corrupt."[59] Another report from December 1928 stated that "the lives of party members are corrupt; members use their party affiliation to benefit themselves."[60] The party committee identified the 300–400 party members in Suichuan county as "hooligans" (*liumang*) (the report also noted that they all joined Mao's forces after he seized the county seat in December 1927).[61] The report noted that the party committee in Ji'an had some 500 members, but the organization of the party was very loose and could serve almost no purpose.[62] In a report from July 1928, the provincial party committee seemed to despair of the situation, which may have been appropriate given that it had been broken up by the GMD only a month earlier. The committee reported that throughout the province there was no party organization capable of struggle. Local leaders felt that they themselves were the party and they felt no need for discipline or to go among the masses because it was too dangerous: "It can be said that they have completely given up on the mass movement."[63]

Even when a local party committee had a sufficient number of members and was willing to "go among the masses," the peasants did

[57] "Jiangxi quansheng qiubao Shandong dagang" (Outline of Inciting Autumn Harvest Uprising throughout Jiangxi), in Zhongyang dang'an guan and Jiangxisheng dang'an guan, *Jiangxisheng geming lishi wenjian huiji (1927–1928)*, pp. 25–34.

[58] "Poyang dangtuan gongzuo baogao" (Report on the Work of the Party and Youth League in Poyang), in Zhongyang dang'an guan and Jiangxisheng dang'an guan, *Jiangxisheng geming lishi wenjian huiji (1927–1928)*, p. 98.

[59] "Chuangzao Jiangxi dangde xin shengming" (Creating a New Life in the Jiangxi Party), in Zhongyang dang'an guan and Jiangxisheng dang'an guan, *Jiangxisheng geming lishi wenjian huiji (1927–1928)*, p. 127.

[60] "Zhonggong Jiangxisheng dierci daibiao dahui guanyu Suweiai quyu jueyi an" (Resolution on the Soviet Areas [adopted at] the Jiangxi Provincial CCP Second Representative Congress), in Zhongyang dang'an guan and Jiangxisheng dang'an guan, *Jiangxisheng geming lishi wenjian huiji (1927–1928)*, p. 323.

[61] "Zhonggong Jiangxi shengwei gei zhongyang de zonghe baogao," p. 223.

[62] Ibid., p. 224.   [63] Ibid., p. 258.

not always welcome the cadres or the violence they encouraged. In Shashi in western Hubei, it turned out that the peasants in the area were quite moderate, and neither the workers nor the peasants had any interest in launching an insurrection. A report from the local party committee concluded that "insurrection seems an illusion," but that if the provincial authorities wanted to launch an uprising, they should send two regiments. The request for military support only brought a rebuke. The local party committee, the provincial committee said, had no faith in the masses but only looked to military force.[64]

The moderate views of the peasants in western Hubei were not unique. When the party was planning to attack the county seat in Xianning, in southern Hubei, it could only gather together 800 peasants, hardly enough for a successful attack. Similarly, in Yuji county, the party could find no active support, and in eastern Hubei, the party's influence was extremely limited. It is said that in Yangxin county, in southern Hubei, the peasants all hated the party.[65] Sometimes such antipathy was the result of actions by the party. One report noted that in several places the troops had not behaved well, so the masses were not willing to work with them. In some places, when uprisings were defeated, the peasants turned the Communists over to the authorities as a sort of penance.[66]

At the same time, higher levels made impossible demands. The county party committee in Yongding, in preparation for an uprising, demanded that the lower levels recruit 250 party members within two weeks. Similarly, the Zhangpu County Party Committee demanded that lower levels recruit at least 300 party members within the next month.[67] Obviously such demands were impossible to fulfill.

As Lucian Bianco and others have noted, the key to organizing peasants in their villages was the educated youth, the sons and occasionally daughters of the local elite, though usually not the wealthiest of that elite. These young leaders were the offspring of relatively well-off clans in their native villages who had attended a higher middle school in

---

[64] Huang Kun, *Geming yu xiangcun*, p. 62.   [65] Ibid., p. 71.

[66] "Jiangxi gongzuo qingkuang: zonghexing baogao" (The Present Circumstances of the Work in Jiangxi: A Comprehensive Report)," in Zhongyang dang'an guan and Jiangxisheng dang'an guan, *Jiangxisheng geming lishi wenjian huiji (1927–1928)*, pp. 254–264; and "Zhonggong Jiangxi shengwei gei zhongyang de zonghe baogao."

[67] Zhong Rixing, *Xiangcun shehuizhong de geming dongyuan*, p. 24.

the county seat or perhaps even farther away. Most had not gone on to college, although some had. In any event, they had picked up new ideas in the wake of the May Fourth Movement in 1919 and especially during the May Thirtieth Movement in 1925. Because of their exposure to places beyond their natal villages, they had a greater sensibility of the issues roiling China. Their thinking was primarily dominated by ideas of opposing landlords and imperialism – sins that, if eradicated, might bring about a new and more liberated society. Their own futures were highly uncertain, spurring them to want to bring about a new society. They were, as Bianco points out, traitors to their own class with a different generational consciousness.[68] As the education of such youth suggests, they did not come from the poorest areas of China but from the somewhat wealthier areas where there were greater resources that the activists were able to use to organize uprisings.[69] Their thinking was primarily dominated by ideas of opposing landlords and imperialism; the Russian revolution provided a model of how the yoke of the old society could be overthrown in short order, and joining the Communist Party gave them ideas, organization, and sometimes discipline to feel as if they were part of a larger cause. Some returned to their native villages following the May Thirtieth Movement and more returned under the directions of the Party Center, following the split with the GMD.

The role of such educated youth is well described by one GMD official:

When we consider China's rural society [we observe that] the spirit of rural feudalism is deeply embedded in the consciousness of the people. In the villages, therefore, there is basically not much prospect for the survival or growth of communism ... However, the Communist Party has been able to expand its influence ... This has been possible ... where children of established old families have gone off to pursue modern educations ... These

---

[68] Lucian Bianco, *Peasants without the Party: Grassroots Movements in Twentieth-Century China* (Armonk, NY: M.E. Sharpe, 2001), pp. 43–44. See also Steven C. Averill, "Party, State and Local Elite in the Jiangxi Communist Movement." *Journal of Asian Studies* 46(2), 1987, pp. 279–303, and Gregor Benton, *Mountain Fires: The Red Army's Three-Year War in South China, 1934–1938* (Berkeley: University of California Press, 1992), p. 311.

[69] Communist documents usually refer to such people as "intellectuals" (*zhishi fenzi*), but most had a higher middle-school education, so, while educated, they were not intellectuals in any meaningful sense of the word. Zhang Hongqing, *Nongmin xingge yu Zhonggong de xiangcun dongyuan moshi*, p. 27.

youths have been readily won over to the heterodox notions of the Communist Party, whose ideas they have reintroduced back into the villages. Being progeny of established families, once back home on their native terrain, they possess considerable prestige and influence thanks to their clan connections ... Ultimately, their goals are in tension with [the interests of] the traditional social forces. But at the initial stage of their recruiting for the peasant movement, they constantly take advantage of their protection offered by these traditional social forces in order to survive and expand [their own influence]. Sometimes, they do this by building a following and then laying in a stock of arms. On other occasions, they infiltrate themselves into the militia ... Then, when they have built up a party of adherents, they suddenly execute a volte face and turn against the very same traditional social forces that have sheltered them until then, wiping them out in a blow.[70]

Nevertheless, such educated youth had difficulty building party organizations and leading insurrections because rural society was organized along clan lines and because there was a social gulf between such elites and peasant society. To a certain extent this gulf was bridged during the Northern Expedition when local elites supported the GMD in the hopes of reducing the depredations from bandits and warlords (and in hopes of being on the winning side). As the proliferation of insurrections in 1927–1928 shows, these educated youth could be quite violent, but they remained the linchpin of Communist organizing in the countryside. They might support the violent overturn of the social order but they rarely implemented radical land reform. They remained both elite and local, so the distance between them and the Party Center remained great.

There were both advantages and disadvantages of such educated youth assuming leadership of the revolution in rural China. First of all, rural society was still dominated by the clan system that organized both society and economy. Many villages were single-surname villages; those that were not were generally dominated by one lineage. At least within the clan, the clan leaders made decisions for the entire clan, including sometimes punishments that extended to life and death. Those from wealthy clans or wealthy lineages within a clan dominated local society. Returning from a city with a modern education gave one a special status in rural society. Educated youth returning home could

---

[70] Quoted in James M. Polachek, "The Moral Economy of the Kiangsi Soviet (1928–1934)," *Journal of Asian Studies*, vol. 42, no. 4 (August 1983), p. 817, with insertions.

use their "social capital" to recruit party members, either from their own families or from among similar educated youth who had returned home. Furthermore, their families provided protection. If authorities from the county seat came looking for someone, they were not likely to find them.

Given the clan-dominated nature of local society, Communist cadres could hardly go from village to village trying to recruit members or organize peasants. An "outsider" was quickly noticed and usually had no entrée into local society. One exception was for teachers. Given that such youth were educated they could move to a new area, perhaps a township or even a county seat and take a job as a teacher. That is one reason why schools became hotbeds of Communist organizing.

The Wan'an Uprising

As the above discussion documents, the CCP in the summer of 1927 was very far from being a well-organized, disciplined Leninist party. Lines of authority were either unclear or simply flouted. Communication between higher- and lower-level organizations was frequently interrupted. Different party organizations contested the authority of other party organizations. The Communist International encouraged some of the worst impulses of the party leadership in Shanghai, and there really was no realistic plan about how the party should build (or rebuild) itself and garner power, either locally or nationally. The radical demands coming out of Shanghai had to be implemented – or not – by educated youth, who had little experience organizing uprisings, or by older, more experienced cadres who had different and more accurate understandings of local conditions and who promoted more incremental policies as a result, much to the consternation of the higher levels.

A prime example of the latter tendency occurred in Wan'an county in southwest Jiangxi. One tends to think of southwest Jiangxi as a backwater, and in many ways it was. But those communities with access to the Gan river, either directly or through tributaries, could be surprisingly wealthy and well connected. Clans were strong, and they protected themselves not only through armed force against impositions from other clans, but also through the support of their youth by sending them to Ji'an or farther afield to gain an education. In the wake of the May Fourth Movement, such youth picked up radical ideas and returned home supporting the GMD or the CCP – or both.

Wan'an, a county of 110,000 people, straddled the Gan river south of Ji'an and north of Ganzhou. Self-cultivators or semi-self-cultivators made up 75 percent of the population, tenant farmers 13 percent, and hired laborers 7 percent, about the same as in other counties in southern Jiangxi. Wan'an was well enough connected to the wider world to have experienced demonstrations in support of the May Fourth Movement and other causes. Educated youth had led people through the county seat shouting slogans such as "Strike down imperialism" and "Abolish the Twenty-One Demands." They also threw stones through the windows of the local Catholic church.[71]

The person who would emerge as the key figure in the local party organization and the Wan'an uprising was Zeng Tianyu. Zeng was born in 1896 in Luotang township, not far from the county seat. His father was a landlord and businessman who had served as head of the Wan'an Chamber of Commerce. Zeng's older brother, Zeng Zhenwu, had studied in Japan and become a follower of Sun Yat-sen. In 1916, Zeng Zhenwu was appointed head of the Wan'an branch of the Chinese Revolutionary Party (as Sun's party was called between 1914 and 1919), and in 1919 he was elected to Jiangxi's provincial assembly. As a youth, Zeng Tianyu attended the county higher elementary school (*gaodeng xiaoxue*). The head of the school was one Xiao Bingzhang, who had studied in Japan and was, secretly, the county head of the local branch of the Tongmenghui (Revolutionary Alliance, the forerunner of the GMD). In 1913, Zeng entered the Xinyuan Middle School in Nanchang, a well-known school with a patriotic tradition. One of his classmates was Zhang Guotao, who would go on to be one of the thirteen Chinese attending the founding party congress of the CCP in 1921 – and also the center's choice to head the Eyuwan Base Area in 1931 (see Chapter 5). When he graduated in 1917, Zeng followed the path of his older brother and went to study in Japan, at Waseda University, where he met Peng Pai, later the famous peasant organizer in Guangdong. In 1918, Zeng joined with other students to oppose the

---

[71] Dai Xiangqing, "Lun Wan'an baodong" (On the Wan'an Uprising), in Zhonggong Jiangxi shengwei dangshi ziliao zhengji weiyuanhui and Zhonggong Jiangxi shengwei dangshi yanjiushi, eds., *Jiangxi dangshi ziliao* (Materials on Jiangxi Party History), vol. 5: *Wan'an baodong zhuanji* (Special Volume on the Wan'an Uprising) (Nanchang: "Jiangxi dangshi ziliao" bianjishi, 1988), p. 211.

signing of the Sino-Japanese Military Agreement to Oppose the Enemy (*Zhong Ri gongtong fangdi junshi xieding*), an agreement signed in the wake of the Bolshevik Revolution to continue to oppose Germany and Austria (China and Japan were both part of the Allies during World War I). Zeng's short stay in Japan hardened his anti-imperialist feelings and exposed him to socialist thought. Upon his return to China, Zeng enrolled in Beiping China University, a school founded in 1911 by GMD revolutionary Song Jiaoren. Zeng was thus in Beijing when the May Fourth Movement broke out.[72]

After Zeng graduated he went to Nanchang, where he joined the GMD, started a bookstore, and founded a middle school. Both the bookstore and the school became important bases for CCP and GMD activities. In 1926 Zeng joined the CCP. At this point, he does not appear to have made a sharp distinction between the CCP and the GMD, though his connections with the GMD were deeper.

Even though Zeng spent most of his time in these years away from Wan'an, he kept in touch with friends and relatives, especially Zhang Shixi, who would go on to become the CCP county secretary when a party branch was established in Wan'an in July 1926. Like Zeng, Zhang was the son of a prominent family. His father was a teacher at a private academy and he had attended school in Nanchang. When he returned to Wan'an, he took up a teaching position at the higher middle school. In 1922, when Zeng Tianyu was back in Wan'an on vacation, Zhang, Zeng, and others established the Wan'an Youth Society, the sort of intellectual group that was springing up throughout the country in the wake of the May Fourth Movement. Through the efforts of such people, three district and ten township peasant associations were established in Wan'an in 1926, making it one of the best-organized counties in Jiangxi. As in many other parts of the country, this activity was undertaken by mobilizing elite contacts – friends, relatives, and local relations. Therefore, when Zeng returned to Wan'an in late 1926, he took up his natural position as a leader in local society.[73]

---

[72] Ying Xing and Li Xia, "Zhonggong zaoqi difang lingxiu, zuzhi xingtai yu xiangcun shehui: Yi Zeng Tianyu jiqi lingdao de Jiangxi Wan'an baodong wei zhongxin" (Local Leaders, Organizational Circumstances, and Rural Society in the Early Communist Period: Taking Zeng Tianyu's Leadership of Jiangxi's Wan'an Uprising as the Focus), *Shehui*, vol. 34, no. 5 (2014), pp. 7–8.

[73] Ibid.; Chen Liming, "Zeng Tianyu," in Zhonggong Jiangxi shengwei dangshi ziliao zhengji weiyuanhui and Zhonggong Jiangxi shengwei dangshi yanjiushi,

Clan feuds were an inevitable part of local society, and when nearby clans encroached on interests in Luotang township in early 1927, Zeng led the organization of a self-protection army. The results of the CCP's August 7 Emergency Meeting were relayed to the Jiangxi Party Committee in early September, and it drew up an "Autumn Harvest Uprising Plan," which decided that uprisings in western Jiangxi should begin in Wan'an. A representative from the provincial party committee, Wang Qun, went to Wan'an in October. He was joined by Zeng Yansheng, who was not related to Zeng Tianyu but was the older brother of Zeng Shan, who would become a close aide to Mao Zedong and play a prominent role in Donggu and the Futian Rebellion (see Chapter 4). In 1927 Zeng Yansheng was a representative of the West Jiangxi Special Committee. Meeting at Zeng Tianyu's house, the group established an "action committee" (*xingdong weiyuanhui*) with Zeng Tianyu in charge.[74]

Following instructions coming out of Shanghai, the Jiangxi Provincial Party Committee called for the "immediate arrest and killing of the evil landlords, rotten gentry, and reactionaries, confiscation of the land of large landlords, and the establishment of a peasant government." Establishing a peasant government meant taking the county seat, a formidable task. In any event, the West Jiangxi Special Committee urged the Wan'an Party Committee to take action. Zhang Shixi led his followers in Yaotou township to kill six local elites, but the less violent Zeng Tianyu held back. He opened a night school for peasants, led a movement to reduce rents, and even obstructed the movement to kill and burn that was led by Zeng Yansheng and Zhang Shixi.[75]

Zeng Tianyu had many reasons for his moderate, incremental approach. He was concerned that leading a violent movement would press against Hakka interests and set off sectarian violence. He was also concerned that attacking the county seat would hurt the interests of the leading clans there, who were actually supportive of the Communist cause. Zeng's approach was to try to reconcile local interests while bringing about a more progressive government. He even continued to

Jiangxi dangshi, vol. 5, pp. 160–185; and Chen Liming and He Longliang, "Zhang Shixi," in ibid., vol. 5, pp. 186–210.
[74] Dai Xiangqing, "Lun Wan'an baodong," p. 216.
[75] Ying Xing and Li Xia, "Zhonggong zaoqi difang lingxiu, zuzhi xingtai yu xiangcun shehui," p. 23.

conduct activities in the name of the GMD, despite the fact that Wang Jingwei and the left wing of the GMD had split with the Communists in July.

What tipped his hand was that the head of the 14th Army in Ganzhou sent troops to Luotang, where they discovered propaganda for the Communist Party and the Communist Youth League. Knowing that the commander was preparing to bring a sizable army into Wan'an to suppress Communist activity, Zeng decided to strike first. On November 19, 1927, in a poorly arranged attack, Zeng led his small force to the county seat. Meeting strong resistance, Zeng quickly withdrew. Zeng's hesitation to attack, followed by his ill-prepared effort, angered the provincial party committee. Therefore the committee sent one Wan Xiyan to Wan'an. Representing the provincial party committee and the Yangtze Bureau, Wan abolished the action committee, demoted Zhang Shixi from county party secretary to committee member, and appointed one Yu Qiu, a Sichuanese who was from the Central Bureau, as Wan'an party secretary.[76]

It made no difference. Zeng Tianyu had never held a post on either the Wan'an Party Committee or the West Jiangxi Special Committee. With the abolition of the action committee, Zeng had no position whatsoever. Nevertheless, the troops remained tightly under his control, and the very next day he led his force of roughly 100 troops to Taihe, the next county over, to co-operate with forces there to seize the county seat.[77]

Reflecting the views of Wan Xiyan, the provincial party committee wrote a blistering letter to the West Jiangxi Special Committee, which supposedly controlled the party committee in Wan'an. The letter accused the Wan'an Party Committee of not developing close relations with the provincial party committee. The work in Wan'an, it said, was undertaken by individuals who were called "teachers" and who had no consciousness of the party as an organization. Not only had the party committees of the various districts not convened meetings, but even the county party committee had not called meetings. The work for an uprising in Wan'an was carried out by an action committee, and the county party committee never asked about it, nor did it have any ability to ask about it. All actions were decided by just a few people.

[76] Ibid., p. 29. [77] Ibid., p. 30.

The planning work ignored the masses and relied too much on the military.[78] Local leaders, the letter complained, were military opportunists:

It is as if revolutionary victory can be achieved by an armed peasant army and the strength of the masses is not needed. And the armed peasant army is only the tool of a handful of people and not the armed force of the party. This truly does not recognize clearly the meaning of an uprising of the masses.

Finally, the letter called for clearing out all opportunists and all cowardly, backward elements.[79] Of course, Communist activities in Wan'an were following the contours of local society. Zeng Tianyu was sympathetic to the Communist program, as he understood it, but as one of the local elite he accepted the divisions in local society. Peasants were intended to follow, not lead.

Even as this letter was being written, Zeng Tianyu was leading a second attack on the county seat. This second attack, and a third attack on December 31, were also thrown back. Finally Zeng coordinated with Mao Zedong, still up in the Jinggangshan. When Mao was attacking and occupying the county seat in neighboring Suichuan county, Zeng was hiding his troops in ambush. When the defenders fled from the Suichuan county seat, Zeng's forces attacked them. Realizing that Mao's forces had joined with Zeng's, the defenders in the Wan'an county seat fled, and Zeng and his forces were able to occupy the city. On January 11, 1928, Zeng and his followers organized the first county-level soviet in Jiangxi.

The good news did not last long. On January 23, the GMD sent a large force to attack the county seat, and Zeng was forced to flee. On March 5, GMD troops caught up to Zeng in Luotang and killed him. Thus ended the Wan'an Uprising and Zeng's short but eventful life.[80]

The angry letter from the Jiangxi Party Committee reflected the radical views coming out of Shanghai, but it also reflected the views of outsiders. Luo Yinong, the head of the Yangtze Bureau, was unhappy with cadres in Jiangxi, so he replaced them with cadres from Hubei, including Wan

[78] Zhonggong Jiangxi shengwei gei Zhonggong Ganxi tewei de yifeng xin" (A Letter from the Jiangxi Provincial Committee to the CCP West Jiangxi Special Committee), in Jiangxisheng dang'an guan, *Jinggangshan geming genjudi shiliao xuanbian*, pp. 8–14.

[79] Ibid., p. 12.

[80] Ying Xing and Li Xia, "Zhonggong zaoqi difang lingxiu, zuzhi xingtai yu xiangcun shehui," p. 32.

Xiyan. Having just come to Jiangxi, these cadres did not know local circumstances and they were hardly sympathetic to the situation in Wan'an. Like Qu Qiubai and the leaders in Shanghai, these cadres believed that the party in Wan'an could organize a peasant uprising with little or no military force. However, the description of Zeng Tianyu's actions laid out above suggests a radically different reality. Zeng, like most local revolutionaries at the time, was an intellectual who had returned from Beijing and Nanchang to organize a revolutionary movement. But such educated youth necessarily relied on social capital, recruiting friends, relatives, and those whom they knew from their localities. They did not have deep roots among the peasantry, so, in a sense, the provincial party committee was correct in saying that those in Wan'an had ignored the masses. The organizations they built were based on local elites who were sympathetic to the Communist cause – though their understanding of that cause was not deep. They did not listen to the party because they did things the way they had always done them – based on individual connections and individual prestige. It was only natural that Zeng Tianyu and other leaders were addressed as "teacher" (many, in fact, were teachers). The reality was that the revolutionary hopes coming out of the Comintern and Shanghai, at least for now, would have to be implemented by local elites who depended more on social capital than on strong organization.

Conclusion

The 1927 split with the GMD – both Chiang's coup in April and Wang Jingwei's decision to break the alliance in July – was disastrous for the CCP. For the first six years of its organizational life, Chen Duxiu had provided the leadership that kept the fissiparous tendencies of the party in check and even instilled a degree of Leninist discipline.[81] No other leader could easily slip into the role that Chen had created. About one decade older than his protégés in the leadership, Chen had the prestige of being one of the true intellectual leaders of modern China. He no doubt had a tendency to act as the party's "patriarch," deciding many issues on his own. Perhaps he bore some blame for not preparing the party for the betrayal by the GMD, but it is difficult to see what he

---

[81] Hans J. van de Ven, *From Friend to Comrade: The Founding of the Chinese Communist Party, 1920–1927* (Berkeley: University of California Press, 1991).

could have done differently. Caught between the Comintern's unrealistic reading of the situation, the complete absence of any military apparatus, and the increasing demands for social revolution by activists in Wuhan, compromise was probably the only thing he could do to ward off disaster. But this was not enough. Tragedy ensued and Chen was blamed for it. He had not only made a mistake, the Comintern held, but he was guilty of "opportunism." However, the charge of "opportunism" was not something directed solely at Chen; instead, it became a weapon that could be directed at anyone who proposed any form of moderation. Radicalism – "Red terror" – and violence were the order of the day.

Despite this call for "Red terror," the party had no coherence. The educated youth who returned to their villages were dedicated Communists, but they were also the progeny of the rural elite. They could organize the peasants because they had the social standing to do so. Often the peasants would join the attacks on the county seats because they hoped to partake of the loot if the attack was successful. It is not surprising that the vast majority of these uprisings failed. They did not create base areas, and they did not develop a hierarchical, well-disciplined party, much less any sort of coherent ideology. Rather, they brought death and destruction, weakening an already weak party. The story of Zeng Tianyu may be exceptional in that he was truly at the top of the local social order, but it illustrates the degree to which the nascent "rural revolution" was dependent on the social capital of the rural elite – the presumed target of the revolution. This was no Leninist party, as is plainly revealed by Zeng Tianyu's leading his small force to Taihe county the day after his action committee was abolished. Forging a Leninist party would take more time, better organization, the destruction of the local leadership, and far more bloodshed.

During the year following the August 7 Emergency Meeting, over 100 uprisings, large and small, were launched in Jiangxi, most of which failed very quickly. What is surprising is that some of these revolutionary movements survived and even grew. The best known of these is Fang Zhimin's base area in northeast Jiangxi. The least well known was the most successful, the Donggu Revolutionary Base Area in Ji'an county. It is to that base area that we turn in the next chapter.

2 | The Donggu Revolutionary Base Area

Perhaps no area better illustrates the theme of the previous chapter – educated youth returning to their native villages and organizing peasants to carry out insurrections – than Donggu. Donggu was an agricultural community located in the eastern part of Ji'an county, near the intersection of Ji'an, Yongfeng, Jishui, Taihe, and Xingguo counties, roughly equally distant – about seventy miles – from the county seats of each of those counties. Although nested among mountains, it was largely a plain and thus a rich agricultural area. A small river connected it to nearby communities such as Futian, allowing for a flow of goods. The economy was based on agriculture, but it also produced commodities such as tea, rapeseed, and tung oil. Although not as wealthy as some of the surrounding areas, Donggu could not be considered poor. Like much of southern Jiangxi, the livelihood of the people was passable (see Figure 2.2).

In 1919, Donggu had some 3,200 families with a population of about 15,000.[1] The majority were Hakka, who had moved into the area from northern Guangdong and Fujian during the late Ming and early Qing period (the seventeenth century). Perhaps 10 percent of the population consisted of the She nationality, a hunting community that lived primarily in the mountains (today the area is officially known as Donggu Shezu township). It was a multi-surname area with no one clan predominating. Most of the people were tenant farmers, cultivating temple land owned by large clans such as the Wangs of Futian and the Hus of Beixia.[2] The community was certainly not wealthy, but good natural conditions and

---

[1] Tang Lianying, Ye Fulin, and Ding Renxiang, *Donggu geming genjudi shilu* (On the History of the Donggu Revolutionary Base Area) (Shanghai: Huadong shifan daxue chubanshe, 2019), p. 31. Different sources give different numbers and population figures at the time were inexact.

[2] This was where Hu Lijiao, later governor of the People's Bank of China (1964–1966) and second chairman of the People's Standing Committee secretary of Shanghai (1981–1988), was born. He was born in 1914, too late to get caught up in the anti-AB Corps movement.

Figure 2.1 The countryside around Donggu

rich soil allowed the residents to eke out a living. Rents were heavy, but life was sustainable. As Yuan Xiaoxian, head of propaganda for the Jiangxi CPC Party Committee in 1929, reported, "Semi-self-cultivators made up the majority" of farmers in this area. Similarly, a survey by the nearby Wan'an County Party Committee in 1928 states that "70–80 percent of peasants there were self-cultivators or semi-self-cultivators."[3] Looking at such data, Wang Caiyou concludes about Donggu, "just considering the land usage and degree of exploitation, it is hard to imagine that a revolution would happen here."[4]

This did not mean that there were no stresses or strains. The fact that some 80 percent of the land was owned by the Wangs of Futian certainly was a source of communal tensions.[5] Commercial forces

[3] Wang Caiyou, "Tudi geming de difang yinying: Yi Donggu genjudi fentian yundong wei zhongxin" (The Local Response to Land Reform: Taking the Division of Land in the Donggu Base Area as the Focus), *Kaifang shidai*, no. 8 (August 2011), pp. 5–6.

[4] Ibid. See also Guo Dehong, *Zhongguo jinxiandai nongmin tudi wenti yanjiu* (The Land Problem of Peasants in Modern and Contemporary China) (Qingdao: Qingdao chubanshe, 1993).

[5] Ding Renxiang, "Dongjinggang geminshi gaiyao" (Overview of the Revolutionary History of East Jinggang), in Zhonggong Jiangxi shengwei dangshi yanjiushi et al., *Donggu, Ganxinan geming genjudi shiliao xuanbian*

were also entering the area, bringing a degree of prosperity but also the uncertainties that come with changing economies and market competition. There were traditional rivalries between villages and clans, exacerbated by the differences between Hakkas, such as in Donggu, and the "early settlers,"[6] the Han populations that had settled the area before the arrival of the Hakka. The Wangs in Futian were one such early settler clan. Christianity had also entered the area, bringing about clashes with traditional ways of thought; non-Christians perceived the converts to be enjoying the advantages that came with foreign protection. Also present were the secret societies and bandits typical of poor mountainous areas. In this part of Jiangxi, the "Three Dot Society," which had its roots in Fujian, was the predominant organization for men of the greenwood. Most of all, the end of the Qing dynasty and the inability of the Yuan Shikai and later governments to exert control meant that local authority was weak and shifting. Under these circumstances, local elites jockeyed for advantage.[7]

Perhaps the biggest change, however, consisted of the new ideas swirling around China, including in hinterland areas like Ji'an. With the fall of the dynasty and the collapse of Yuan Shikai's imperial pretensions, the May Fourth Movement ushered in all sorts of new thinking – liberal, Marxist, idealist, anarchist, and so forth. With the imperial exam system having been abandoned in 1905, new schools were being set up, some emphasizing traditional learning, others focusing on modern, "Western," learning. Students were going abroad in ever-increasing numbers. Some 10,000 traveled to Japan during the first decade of the twentieth century, and increasingly students were also looking to Europe and America. Although these new currents largely affected the east coast – Guangdong, Shanghai, and nearby

(Selected Historical Materials on the Donggu and Southwest Jiangxi Revolutionary Base Area), 2 vols. (Beijing: Zhongyang wenxian chubanshe, 2007), vol. 1, p. 492. Note that sometimes Donggu was referred to as East Jinggang as a play on Mao's base area of Jinggangshan.

[6] I am following the usage Stephen Averill adopted in *Revolution in the Highlands: China's Jinggangshan Base Area* (Lanham, MD: Rowman & Littlefield, 2006) to indicate the non-Hakka locals native to the area before Hakkas migrated in.

[7] You Haihua, "Jitai pendi de shengtai huanjing yu Donggu geming de xingqi" (The Ecological Environment of the Ji–Tai Basin and the Rise of the Donggu Revolution), in Jiangxi shengwei dangshi yanjiushi et al., eds., *Donggu genjudi yu Zhongguo geming daolu de kaipi* (The Donggu Base Area and the Opening Up of the Chinese Revolutionary Path) (Beijing: Zhongyang dangshi chubanshe, 2008), pp. 523–546.

places – a surprising amount of "new learning" penetrated the interior of China as well.

A number of local youth, all from relatively wealthy families, became the early promulgators of Marxism. For instance, Yuan Yubing was born in nearby Taihe county and tested into Jiangxi Provincial No. 2 Middle School in Nanchang in 1918, just in time to be an active participant in the May Fourth Movement. In the latter part of 1919, Yuan and seven classmates organized the Poyang Lake Society, which soon changed its name to the more ambitious Transformation Society (*Gaizao she*). One of the society's guidelines was to study Marxist theories. The Transformation Society soon published a journal, *New Jiangxi* (*Xin Jiangxi*), which republished *The Communist Manifesto* and introduced other Marxist works.[8] In 1922, Yuan tested into Peking University, where he was deeply influenced by Li Dazhao.

In nearby Wan'an, Zeng Tianyu and Zhang Shixi, discussed in the previous chapter, published a magazine called *Youth* (*Qingnian*), and Zeng Tianyu managed a leftist bookstore, Bright Star (*Xingming shudian*) in Nanchang. In Xin'gan county, another activist, Zou Nu, who tested into Jiangxi Provincial No. 1 Normal School, soon joined the Communist Youth League. In the summer of 1924, Zou returned home and organized the Xin'gan county branch of the China Socialist Youth League. Also in 1924, Zeng Yansheng, whom we met when discussing the Wan'an uprising, tested into Shanghai University, where Qu Qiubai, Yun Daiying, Zhang Tailei, Cai Hesen, and other Communist Party luminaries were teaching. Zeng would soon join the Communist Party and would become one of the early leaders of the Communist movement in Ji'an.[9]

In Ji'an, Luo Shibing, born in 1896, came from a wealthy family, studying at a private academy in his youth before testing into the famous Luling Higher Elementary School and then Jiangxi Provincial No. 1 Normal School in Nanchang. Returning to Ji'an in 1919, Luo accepted a position as a teacher at Provincial No. 7 Normal School. As a provincially established normal school, it attracted poorer students hoping to find jobs as teachers. But getting jobs was difficult. The majority of those who graduated in 1923 were unable to find work.

[8] Tang Lianying, Ye Fulin, and Ding Renxiang, *Donggu geming genjudi shilu*,
    pp. 60–61.
[9] Ibid., pp. 62–63.

This uncertainty about their life chances was one of the factors that inclined them to radicalism.[10]

In 1919 Lai Jingbang, who would go on to establish the first Communist Party branch in Donggu, tested into Provincial No. 7 Normal School. Born in 1899, Lai was twenty years old when he entered normal school, about the same age as Mao Zedong was when he entered No. 1 Normal School in Changsha. In any event, when the May Fourth Movement burst out only a few months later, Luo Shibing led the students, evidently including Lai Jingbang, in protest. Luo went on to Shanghai University in 1924 and joined the Communist Party in the same year. On his return to Ji'an, he began to recruit people into the Communist Party.[11] In January 1926 he helped organize a branch of the Socialist Youth League (the predecessor to the Communist Youth League) in Ji'an, choosing the Provincial No. 7 Normal School as its locus. He would go on to organize another branch of the Socialist Youth League in Yanfu township, north of Ji'an, and then, in March 1926, a special branch of the CCP in Ji'an. At the time it was established, there were thirty-three members of the CCP in Ji'an; by April there were forty-two party members – half the number of party members then in Jiangxi.[12]

One of the people Luo recruited was Liang Mingzhe, who had been a classmate of Lai Jingbang at Provincial No. 7 Normal School. It was Liang, by then head of the Ji'an Education Bureau, who not only introduced Lai into the CCP but also appointed him as an inspector in the Education Bureau, a position that allowed him to move from school to school, making contacts, spreading radical thinking, and developing new Communist Party members. Most of the leaders of the Communist Party in Donggu followed a similar path. For instance, both Zeng Bingchun and Gao Kenian, who worked with Lai to establish the Donggu party branch, were his classmates at Provincial No. 7 Normal School.[13]

---

[10] Ibid., p. 64.
[11] You Haihua, "Jitai pendi de shengtai huanjing yu Donggu geming de xingqi," pp. 523–546; Tang Lianying, Ye Fulin, and Ding Renxiang, *Donggu geming genjudi shilu*, p. 63.
[12] Tang Lianying, Ye Fulin, and Ding Renxiang, *Donggu geming genjudi shilu*, p. 64.
[13] You Haihua, "Jitai pendi de shengtai huanjing yu Donggu geming de xingqi," pp. 523–546.

In late September 1926, the Northern Expedition reached Ji'an. The troops that entered the city were from the Second Division, led by Ye Jianying, who was soon to reject GMD overtures and instead join the Communist Party. Because Ji'an was controlled by the left wing of the GMD, which was still allied with the CCP, Zhou Tingpan, a CCP member, became county magistrate and Liang Mingzhe became head of the Education Bureau. In February, Lai and classmates Zeng Bingchun, Gao Kenian, and others secretly organized the first Communist cell (*xiaozu*) in Donggu. Shortly thereafter, Lai helped organize District 9 (Donggu) Peasant Association and a small self-defense force.[14] At the time, peasant associations were legal, but the Communist organizers maintained secrecy while using the peasant associations to mobilize support.

"Peasant association" is a widely misunderstood term. Although members of such associations were indeed peasants, often owner–cultivators, the leaders were usually those of some social standing. The original version of Mao Zedong's famous "Report on the Peasant Movement in Hunan" contains a list of peasant associations in the counties Mao went to (which is not included in Mao's *Selected Works*). One can see from this list that most of the associations were led by intellectuals, many of whom were local teachers.[15] In Donggu, the peasant association was similarly organized by educated youth. Peasants normally looked up to such people, calling them *laoshi* ("teacher"). When such educated youth asked peasants to join the peasant association, of course they complied. As we saw in the previous chapter, Zeng Tianyu organized peasants in Wan'an in this manner. At the time, the phenomenon of educated youth taking control of local politics was clearly widespread.

Peasant associations did two things. First, they were a way of displacing clan authority and uniting the village under a new leadership. Clan leaders tended to acquiesce to such centers of power in times when the new organizations were encouraged by outside political forces, such as during the Northern Expedition, or when conflict with outside

[14] Tang Lianying, Ye Fulin, and Ding Renxiang, *Donggu geming genjudi shilu*, p. 68.
[15] See Mao Zedong, "Report on the Peasant Movement in Hunan," in Stuart R. Schram, ed., *Mao's Road to Power: Revolutionary Writings, 1912–49*, vol. 2: *National Revolution and Social Revolution, December 1920–June 1927* (Armonk, NY: M.E. Sharpe, 1994), pp. 442–444.

groups required a more organized response. Moreover, the leaders of these peasant associations were often sons of local clan leaders.

Second, these peasant associations organized the villages in which they were located. One of the secrets of Communist success was its organization of local society. The Communists gave everyone jobs, and thus became the center of local life. In Donggu, the Communist Party adopted the slogan "All power to the peasant associations," and the peasant associations undertook everything from organizing elementary schools (known as "Lenin schools") to organizing a hospital and a pharmacy. The peasant association even constructed a post office and factories to repair farm implements and to produce stencil paper. Among other things, women in the villages were organized to sing "patriotic" songs supporting the revolution.[16] This got women out of the house and built public support, which made it difficult for those who would have preferred to hold back or perhaps to quietly oppose these new political trends. Everyone had to participate, making peasant associations the center of village life.

As Mao noted, if the military occupied a place for only a short period of time, the organizations established would "immediately crumble" when the army departed. But if the village had been in Communist hands for a longer period of time, it was very difficult to restore the old order – clans would have been destroyed, lands redistributed, and new organizations established. Organization and mobilization were keys to control. But in other places where there were well-established party organizations, then the army could help the areas expand and solidify control.[17] This did not mean, however, that villagers would willingly sign up for military service, especially if it meant fighting outside the county. We will see the importance of such localism in later chapters.

In any event, one of Lai Jingbang's strategies for organizing peasants was to mobilize opposition to one of the largest landlord families in the area, the Wangs of Futian. Futian was a very wealthy town about twenty miles from Donggu, and one of the things the Wangs did with the money they earned from milling rice and processing tung oil was to

[16] Ding Renxiang, "Dongjinggang geminshi gaiyao," vol. 1, pp. 500–502.
[17] Mao Zedong, "The Significance of Dividing the Troops to Win Over the Popular Masses, and Our Line," in Stuart R. Schram, ed., *Mao's Road to Power: Revolutionary Writings, 1912–49*, vol. 3: *From the Jinggangshan to the Establishment of the Jiangxi Soviets, July 1927–December 1930* (Armonk, NY: M.E. Sharpe, 1995), p. 275.

invest in land in Donggu. The vast majority of the land in Donggu was owned by the Wangs from Futian and the Hu family in Beixia. Reflecting the wealth of the clan, the Wang family temple in Futian was the largest family temple in the province. On top of the landlord–tenant relationship that existed between Futian and Donggu, there was also sub-ethnic tension – Donggu was largely populated by Hakka and Futian was populated by early settlers. Finally, Lai Jingbang, who was Hakka, had a personal grudge against a scion of the Wang clan, one Wang Chuxi. As classmates in a traditional school, the Jiandong Academy, before Lai went on to Provincial No. 7 Normal School, they had become embroiled in a fight. The principal punished Wang, who, in anger, withdrew from the school. Thereafter, Lai and Wang had maintained a personal grudge.[18] So attacking Wang Chuxi was a good way to combine township rivalries, economic resentments, and personal animosities.

Having organized a peasant association, Lai used its name to draw up a list of Wang Chuxi's "crimes" and leveled accusations against him in Ji'an. Not surprisingly, Lai's petition was supported by the county magistrate, the Communist Zhou Tingpan and Ye Jianying, so Wang was seized and thrown into prison. The fact that Wang was simply imprisoned suggests that serious community-level violence had not yet begun. Large-scale violence emerged only later in that year after the GMD's violent split with the CCP. Thus Wang was fortunate. The political situation soon changed and Ye Jianying moved his troops north to Wuhan. More conservative troops moved into Ji'an, and Wang Chuxi was released and he returned to Futian. The absence of violence was not to last.

When Wang Jingwei, the leader of the left wing of the GMD, split with the CCP in July 1927, he followed the precedent set by Chiang Kai-shek and began his own "party purification" movement. That effort to exterminate Communists reached Ji'an on August 6 when the head of the Ji'an county General Labor Union, Liang Yiqing, was arrested and executed. With conservative troops of Zhu Shigui then in charge in Ji'an, Wang Chuxi worked with Zhu and other local leaders to break up the peasant associations and hunt down the Communist leaders. Specifically, getting wind that Lai Jingbang was heading for

[18] You Haihua, "Jitai pendi de shengtai huangjing yu Donggu geming de xingqi," p. 528.

Figure 2.2 The Donggu Revolutionary Base Area Museum

Ji'an, he organized a blockade to capture him. Alerted by sympathizers in nearby towns, Lai turned back to Donggu and avoided the trap.[19] The jailing of Wang Chuxi and Wang's effort to capture Lai certainly hardened the enmity between the Communists in Donggu and the conservatives in Futian.

Even as political fortunes were changing at the national level, Communist leaders were organizing locally. In late June, Fang Zhimin, the well-known Communist leader in northeast Jiangxi, was driven out of the Nanchang area and came to Ji'an and nearby counties to organize peasant associations. Fang emphasized the need for local leaders to take matters into their own hands,[20] advice that leaders in Donggu would heed closely. As the crackdown hit Ji'an, Lai Jingbang and others were able to escape from Ji'an and return to Donggu.

As noted in the previous chapter, the August 7 Emergency Meeting called on local party organizations to carry out insurrections, known

[19] Ding Renxiang, "Dongjinggang geminshi gaiyao," vol 1, p. 493.
[20] Zhonggong Jiangxi shengwei dangshi ziliao zhengji weiyuanhui and Zhonggong Jiangxi shengwei dangshi yanjiushi, eds., *Jiangxi dangshi ziliao* (Materials on Jiangxi Party History), vol. 10: *Donggu geming genjudi zhuanji* (Special Volume on the Donggu Revolutionary Base Area) (Nanchang: "Jiangxi dangshi ziliao" bianjishi, 1986), p. 3.

collectively as the Autumn Harvest Uprisings. There has been some debate as to whether word of this meeting reached Donggu before Lai Jingbang and other leaders started organizing – there were certainly plenty of other reasons to organize – but it seems probable that it had.[21]

In any event, in September 1927, Lai gathered with eleven other party members in Aoshang, the village in Donggu where Lai was born, and convened a secret meeting. They formed a party branch (known as the Donglong party branch because it was formed jointly with nearby Nanlong township) with five party cells. This meeting is usually regarded as the start of the Donggu Revolutionary Base Area, although, as we have seen, there was quite a bit of organizing prior to this meeting.

In addition to deciding to set up a party branch, the group talked quite a bit about reaching out to the local bandit chief, Duan Qifeng. Duan was born into poverty, surviving as a youth by watching water buffalo and apprenticing as a tailor. His strength was said to be "startling," and he became adept in the martial arts. Eventually, he became head of the local Three Dot Society.

There were three views regarding whether or not to ally with Duan. The first view held that Duan, like other men of the green-wood, raised the slogan "Robbing the rich to aid the poor" (*jiefu jipin*), and that if they could win him over it would be good for the revolution. The second view was that Duan was simply a bandit, and that if they allied with him it would hurt the reputation of the CCP. It would be better to attack Duan militarily and seize his weapons. The third view was to live and let live, to adopt an attitude of mutual nonaggression. The first view prevailed for the obvious reason that it held many advantages for the fledgling revolutionary group, giving it the armed strength of the bandits. But what made the alliance possible – and made the alliance last – were the personal ties that connected them. Lai Jingbang's elder sister was married to Duan Qifeng's older brother. Moreover, one of the party members at the Aoshang meeting, Duan Weilin, was a cousin (*tangdi*) of Duan

---

[21] Ye Fulin, "Donggu Aoshang huiyi yu dang de baqi huiyi guanxi kaobian" (Investigation into the Relationship between the Aoshang Meeting in Donggu and the August 7 Meeting), *Jinggangshan daxue xuebao*, vol. 32, no. 3 (May 2011), pp. 9–13.

Qifeng.[22] Later on, these ties would be extended when Lai Jingbang's elder daughter married Duan Qifeng's son.[23]

Being a bandit was certainly low on the local social scale, so the offer of respectability by being associated with Lai Jingbang and other educated youth must have been appealing to Duan, and Duan's group gave Lai a force he could not muster on his own. This sort of reaching out to family, friends, and other social relations was very common in the development of local Communist (and other) groups.[24] In any event, it was Lai Jingbang who first wrote to Duan and then followed up by visiting him in person. Then, bringing family relations to bear, Duan Weilin went to visit Duan Qifeng.[25] Duan Qifeng would soon join the CCP, though it is said, no doubt with understatement, that his understanding of Communism was still "superficial."[26]

Family lore has it that Duan Qifeng thought of Lai as the scholarly sort, and he urged him to stay back from the action. But Lai had practiced martial arts for many years and so he challenged Duan to a match. When Lai won, Duan recognized him as the leader. While this story seems apocryphal, it was true that Duan was willing to subordinate himself to Lai, and this superordinate–subordinate relationship remained until Lai's death in the following year. When the rather grandiosely named "Donggu Workers and Peasant Army," with some thirty people and ten or so guns of various sorts, was formed in October 1927, Lai Jingbang was head (*duizhang*) and Duan Qifeng was deputy head.[27]

---

[22] Huang Huiyun, Shi Jingsong, and Liu Jun, *Donggu geming genjudi jianshi* (A Short History of the Donggu Revolutionary Base Area) (Chengdu: Bashu shushe, 2011), p. 32.
[23] Tang Lianying, Ye Fulin, and Ding Renxiang, *Donggu geming genjudi shilu*, pp. 90–92.
[24] Ying Xing, "Suqu difang ganbu, hongse wuzhuang yu zuzhi xingtai" (Local Cadres, Red Armed Forces, and the Organizational Situation in the Soviet Areas), *Kaifang shidai*, no. 6 (June 2016), p. 59.
[25] Tang Lianying, Ye Fulin, and Ding Renxiang, *Donggu geming genjudi shilu*, p. 91.
[26] Ibid., p. 92.
[27] Zhang Shouchun, "'Li Wenlinshi' Donggu geming genjudi" (The "Li Wenlin"-Style Donggu Revolutionary Base Area), at www.jsdsw.org.cn/web/detail/detail.html?id=787, accessed April 19, 2021.

The Development of Military Force

In many ways the development of the Donggu Revolutionary Base Area was much closer to what Qu Qiubai and other CCP leaders had in mind than was Mao Zedong's redoubt in the Jinggangshan. As we will see in the following chapter, Mao conceived of his base area as a military-cum-political experiment that would spread revolution forcefully. Certainly after Zhu De joined Mao there was a strong professional military component. In Donggu, however, there was no real military component before Li Wenlin (see below) became the leader. Its "military force" was entirely based on Duan Qifeng and other bandit leaders.

The Donggu group began an armed struggle in November, two months after it had been organized, when its leaders got wind that the GMD military force occupying Ji'an had been transferred away. Sensing an opportunity, the Donglong party branch started planning an insurrection. On November 12, Lai and Duan led sixty people to Futian, where they planned to seize Lai's old nemesis, Wang Chuxi. Wang, however, got wind of their approach and fled. Lai and his comrades were nevertheless able to seize Wang's younger brother, Wang Liangzhao, and search his house. They took six rifles and some cash, and distributed food and clothing to the peasants. The following day they went to nearby Yonghewei and beat eight "local bullies" while seizing over 10,000 yuan. A few days later, they seized more rifles from the self-defense force of a town in Jishui county. Collectively, these actions became known as the "Donggu insurrection."[28]

Donggu was not the only place in southwest Jiangxi that was developing armed forces. In the neighboring counties of Jishui and Yongfeng, party activists, working with local bandits, developed similar guerilla groups. Another group, known as the Red Seventh Column, was established in the Jishui–Yongfeng area, and in February 1928 these groups were merged into the Donggu Revolutionary Army. The Donggu leadership formed the core of this new Seventh Column; Lai Jingbang became the chief of staff and, after a brief hiatus, Duan Qifeng became the commander. This force, based on Donggu's Yangjun Mountain, now consisted of about 150 men with eighty rifles.[29]

---

[28] Huang Huiyun, Shi Jingsong, and Liu Jun, *Donggu geming genjudi jianshi*, p. 34.

[29] Yu Boliu and Ling Buji, *Zhongyang suqushi* (History of the Central Soviet), 2 vols. (Nanchang: Jiangxi renmin chubanshe, 2017), vol. 1, pp. 90–91.

At the same time, another group developed in Yanfu, north of Ji'an on the west side of the Gan river. Something of the composition of these groups is evident when we learn that some officers in this new developing force, which became known as the Ninth Column, plotted to seize and kill the Communist leaders and set off on a life of banditry. Their plot was discovered and it was they who were executed, but the incident does suggest that the line dividing these Communist guerilla groups and bandits was murky at best.[30]

In May 1928, Lai led the Red Seventh Column to attack the self-defense forces of a community in the northern part of Xingguo county, south of Donggu. This strong self-defense force had been threatening Donggu, so Lai thought it best to attack first. Lai and the Red Seventh Column were initially successful, but then reinforcements from Xingguo arrived and the Seventh Column was forced to retreat. Lai, however, was captured and eviscerated.[31] Zeng Bingchun, Lai's old classmate and one of the original organizers of the Donglong party branch, took over.

With the death of Lai Jingbang, the West Jiangxi Special Committee, based in Ji'an city, took more direct control of the Donggu Base Area. The chief secretary (*mishuzhang*) of the special committee was Li Wenlin, who later would emerge as one of the most effective guerrilla leaders in western Jiangxi. Li decided to merge the Seventh and Ninth Columns to form the Second Independent Regiment of the Jiangxi Workers and Peasants Revolutionary Army. Li became commander and party secretary.

This could have been a difficult transition. Local politics were very sensitive as to who was regarded as an insider and who was seen as an outsider. Lai Jingbang was from Dongggu and his personal relationships with his fellow educated youth and the bandit leader Duan Qifeng had knit together a strong and stable leadership core that few other local movements could match. Li Wenlin was from the southern part of Jishui county, not far from Donggu, and he shared the social customs and the local dialect of Donggu. Like Lai Jingbang and other leaders in

[30] Zhongyang dang'an guan and Jiangxisheng dang'an guan, *Jiangxi geming lishi wenjian huiji (1927–1928)* (Compilation of Historical Documents on the Jiangxi Revolution, 1927–1928) (Los Angeles: Zhongwen chubanshe fuwu zhongxin, 2013), ser. 21, vol. 15, pp. 333–334.
[31] Huang Huiyun, Shi Jingsong, and Liu Jun, *Donggu geming genjudi jianshi*, p. 41.

Donggu, Li Wenlin was a Hakka. An exceptional person, he quickly overcame the challenge of being an outsider and soon emerged as the acknowledged leader of the Communist movement in western Jiangxi.

Li Wenlin was born in 1900 to a wealthy agricultural household. He graduated from Provincial No. 6 Normal School, so he was able to draw on the same social networks that Lai Jingbang had drawn upon. In 1921 he tested into Jiangxi Law and Politics Academy in Nanchang, where he quickly became involved in political movements, particularly the Great Alliance for People's Rights Movement. Then in 1925 he tested into the fourth class of Whampoa Military Academy. Graduating in October 1926, he returned to Nanchang, where he joined Zhu De's Third Army as an instructor. He also joined the Communist Party that year. The following year, he took part in the Nanchang Uprising, and then he followed the CCP troops south to Guangdong. When the troops were dispersed by military defeat, Li made his way back to his hometown, where he continued to participate in revolutionary activities. In July 1928, he was appointed chief secretary of the West Jiangxi Special Committee.[32]

Therefore Li Wenlin was a native son of the area around eastern Ji'an, if not of Donggu specifically. He had all the social connections that came with being from a fairly wealthy family and having attended a local normal school. He had long participated in socialist and Communist activities and his training at the Whampoa Military Academy had provided him with the military expertise he needed. This was a resumé that no other local cadre could match, with the possible exception of Fang Zhimin in northeast Jiangxi. So, despite his being an outsider – though barely so – from the perspective of Donggu, his military experience and personal network allowed him not only to be accepted by the Seventh and Ninth Columns, but also to be able to merge the two units into the new Second Independent Regiment and take personal command.[33] At the same time, he became the political commissar of the regiment, so party and military leadership was unified in his hands, and the military force was bound together by ethnic, social, clan, and educational backgrounds. These relationships were solidified by appointing Duan Qifeng, the former bandit leader, as his second in command. This local political and military force was

[32] Ying Xing, "Suqu difang ganbu, hongse wuzhuang yu zuzhixingtai," p. 64.
[33] Ibid., p. 64.

very different from the one Mao Zedong and Zhu De would soon lead into the area.

In total, the Second Independent Regiment numbered over 300 people.[34] Li based his troops in Donggu, and from there he successfully conducted guerilla operations in the counties of Ji'an, Jishui, Xinyu, Fenyi, and Anfu. By December he had crossed the Gan river and defeated the local self-defense forces defending the Le'an county seat, capturing twenty-three men and, more important, fifty-seven rifles. In February 1929, he reorganized the Fifteenth and Sixteenth Columns of the southern Jiangxi army into the Independent Fourth Regiment, with Duan Qifeng as commander. Li was both secretary and political commissar of a newly formed "action committee," with command over both his Second Regiment and the new Fourth Regiment. Altogether he had command over a total of some 1,500 soldiers and 800 rifles. It was the strongest military force in the region.[35] By the end of 1929, the Donggu Base Area covered twenty-three townships, each with its own peasant association and a total of 4,000 members (see Map 2.1).[36] This was a far larger area than the Jinggangshan Base Area ever covered.

As mentioned above, one of the unique features about the Donggu Base Area was that, despite the guerilla warfare conducted out of it, the party organization maintained secrecy. It did not attempt to set up a soviet to exercise political power openly; rather it established peasant associations and used them to wield power. For open activities, Li and his associates used the name "Red Dawn Society" (*Hongse shuguang she*) to cover party activities. The secrecy obscured the difference between the base area and the surrounding white areas, allowing the base area to influence other areas. Unlike in the Jinggangshan, there was no clear border between "red" and "white" areas, making the Donggu Base Area less vulnerable to attack.

[34] *Donggu geming genjudi gaishu* (Introduction to the Donggu Revolutionary Base Area), in Zhonggong Jiangxi shengwei dangshi ziliao zhengji weiyuanhui and Zhonggong Jiangxi shengwei dangshi yanjiushi, *Jiangxi dangshi ziliao*, vol. 10, p. 11.
[35] Ye Fulin, "Donggu geming genjudi zhuanti yanjiu" (Specialized Research on the Donggu Revolutionary Base Area), Ph.D. dissertation, East China Normal University, 2010, p. 38.
[36] Tang Lianying, Ye Fulin, and Ding Renxiang, *Donggu geming genjudi shilu*, p. 86; *Donggu geming genjudi gaishu*, p. 6; Ye Fulin, "Donggu geming genjudi zhuanti yanjiu," p. 38.

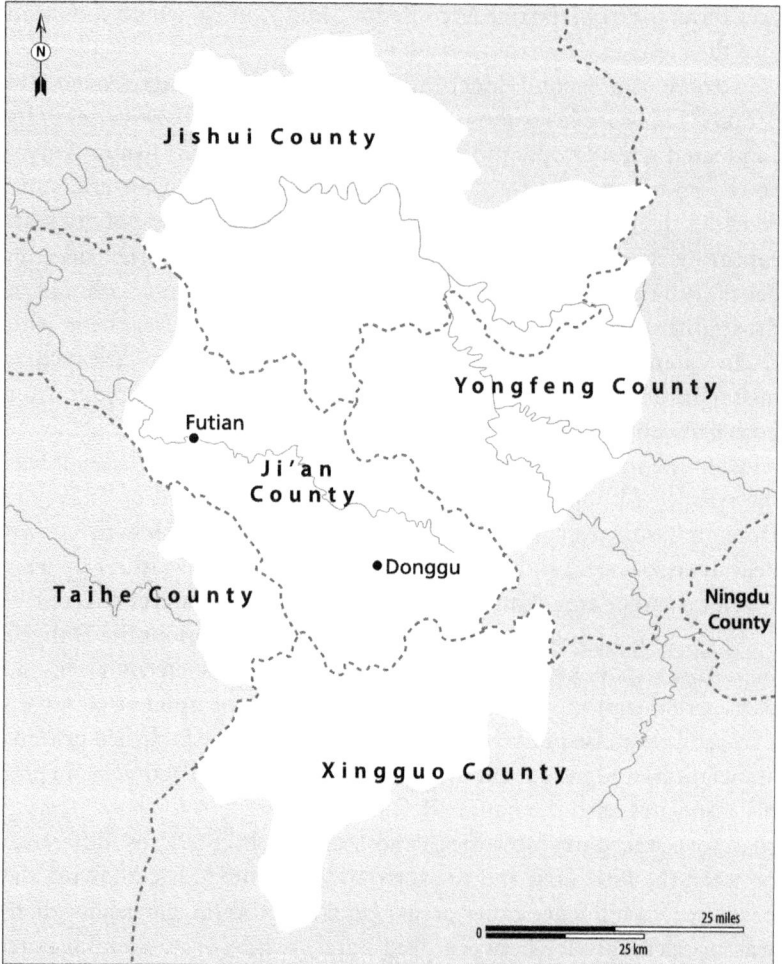

Map 2.1 Extent of Donggu Revolutionary Base Area, February 1929 to October 1929

This secrecy saved the movement in early 1928 when Lai's old nemesis, Wang Chuxi, worked with "local bullies and evil gentry" from surrounding areas to organize a band of 100 people, sending them into Donggu with the intention of exterminating the Seventh Column. They entered Donggu but could find no trace of the military forces. Similarly, militia from Xingguo and other areas also entered Donggu, staying for twenty days but without engaging the guerillas.

These encroaching forces then set a trap, offering peace talks with the Donggu guerillas. They offered the guerillas an amnesty and incorporation into their own forces, a traditional tactic that had resolved many a local disturbance. However, the guerillas responded by setting their own trap. They offered to meet the militia commanders but they pre-positioned their soldiers in the nearby mountains. When the militia and their leaders appeared, the Donggu fighters attacked. It was the last time local militia tried to attack Donggu. The militia did, however, set up a blockade, denying Donggu many supplies. In response, Donggu established its own primitive arsenal to make hand grenades, gunpowder, and bullets.[37]

Another difference with the Jinggang Base Area was that Li Wenlin and his followers paid close attention to building the economy. Li held back from carrying out thoroughgoing land reform. There were few large landlords in the immediate area, and a policy of confiscating and dividing the land would have put the Communist leaders at odds with the middle peasants who predominated in the area. Rather the Communist leaders sought to attract the middle peasants to their cause and to create a strong mass foundation for their movement by emphasizing resistance to rents, cruel and miscellaneous taxes, and high-interest loans, thus improving the lives of the peasants.[38] The base area also established the Donggu Commoners Bank (*Dongggu pingmin yinhang*), which printed the first paper money in any of the base areas. In late 1928, the base area in Donggu established the first school for the common people, and it soon established "Lenin elementary schools" throughout the area to provide free education. In contrast, in the Jinggangshan, Mao adopted a policy of confiscating all land – a policy he could pursue only because he was an outsider with a considerable military force. But as Mao later admitted, this had alienated the local peasants.[39]

Saving Mao Zedong

By February 1929 Mao and the Red Fourth Army were in desperate shape. Mao and Zhu had led their 3,600 troops down from the

---

[37] Tang Lianying, Ye Fulin, and Ding Renxiang, *Donggu geming genjudi shilu*, p. 36.
[38] Ibid., p. 33. [39] Ibid., p. 279.

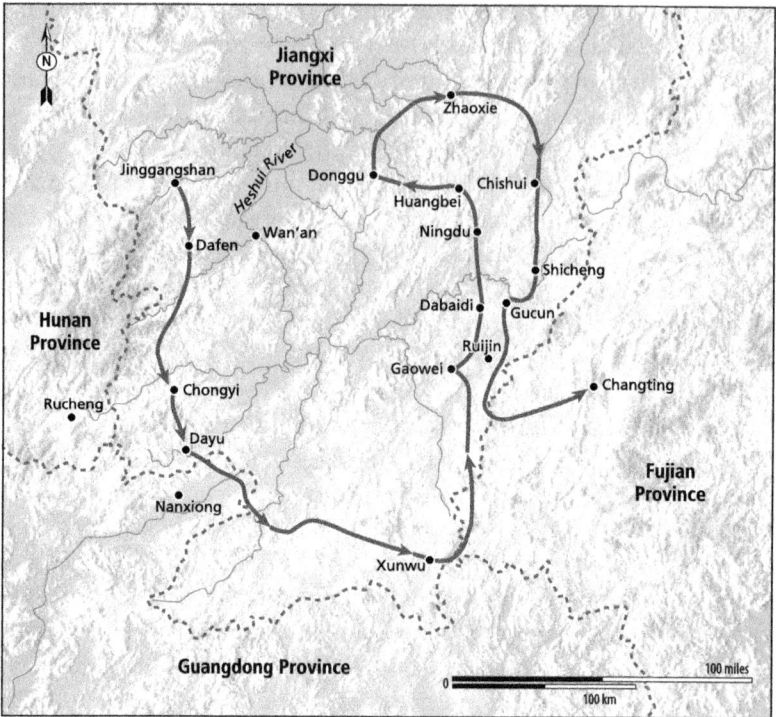

Map 2.2 Mao's route leaving the Jinggangshan

Jinggangshan on January 14 (leaving Peng Dehuai, who had just arrived, with the unenviable task of defending the now abandoned base area). The GMD quickly sent troops to block Mao's escape, and at Dayu, just east of the Jinggangshan, Mao lost some 300 troops in a battle with the pursuing GMD troops. Although Mao tried to avoid military clashes, his troops nevertheless faced battles in Xinfeng, Anyuan, and Xunwu (see Map 2.2). They reached Xunwu in southeast Jiangxi on February 1, hoping for some rest. But the very next day, GMD commander Liu Shiyi attacked. Mao, who normally did not pick up a rifle, this time had no choice but to do so. Mao and Zhu De barely escaped with their lives. Chen Yi was captured briefly before escaping. Mao and the others then headed north to Dabaidi in Ruijin county, where they used the mountainous terrain skillfully to lure GMD troops into a trap and to inflict a severe defeat, capturing some 800 men and their guns. But the Dabaidi area was not hospitable. Fearing Mao's troops as they would fear a bandit gang or a marauding army, the peasants fled into the mountains, leaving Mao's troops with difficulties in finding food and replenishing supplies. The soldiers were forced to search houses for foodstuffs, leaving behind IOUs as they went. Later, when they returned to the area, they are said to have left cash, but the facts are impossible to verify. Despite its victory at Dabaidi, the Red Fourth Army was in terrible shape, exhausted and with many sick and wounded troops. As Mao said, "Since we started out from the Jinggangshan, we have lost a total of over two hundred guns and six hundred men ... The hardship we encountered this time was the greatest in the history of the Red Army."[40]

Trying to avoid a head-on clash, Mao headed to Luofuzhang near where Jiangxi intersects with Guangdong and Fujian. The Red Army stopped not only for a conference to discuss where to go next but also to make a decision that would have major ramifications in the coming months, namely the abolition of the Military Committee. The Military Committee was an intermediate organ between the Front Committee and the various divisions. It was composed of both party and military people and would discuss the instructions of the Front Committee and decide how, and indeed whether, they should be followed. Abolishing the Military Committee gave the Front Committee, especially Mao, who dominated discussions, more direct control over the military, something that would rankle Zhu De and other military commanders.

At the time, this decision did not seem very important; the threat of GMD troops was more pressing. The Nationalist commander, Li Wenbin, had caught up to the Red Fourth Army and inflicted heavy losses. The Red Fourth Army decided to head off to Donggu where it hoped to find some relief.[41] Mao was aware of the Donggu Revolutionary Base Area because in the previous year he had exchanged letters with the leaders there.[42] When Mao reached Ningdu on February 13, he wrote to the Second Regiment. The

[40] Mao Zedong, "Letter from the Fourth Red Army Front Committee to the Central Committee," in Schram, *Mao's Rise to Power*, vol. 3, p. 150.
[41] Zhang Shouchun, "'Li Wenlinshi' Donggu geming genjudi."
[42] Liu Dai, "Donggu songxin dao Jinggang" (Donggu Sends Letters to Jinggang), in Zhonggong Jiangxi shengwei dangshi ziliao zhengji weiyuanhui and Zhonggong Jiangxi shengwei dangshi yanjiushi, *Jiangxi dangshi ziliao*, vol. 10, p. 137.

Ningdu party organization forwarded Mao's letter, and Li Wenlin sent a company (*lian*) to Yongfeng to welcome Mao.[43]

On the afternoon of February 22, the two armies had a formal meeting at Donggu's Luokeng riverbank. Many friendly and happy words were exchanged. Mao's Red Fourth Army gave Li's regiments two machine guns and a mortar, while Li's regiments contributed 4,000 silver dollars and five cases of bullets to Mao's army. Li's forces also provided food and cotton to Mao's bedraggled troops.[44] The meeting of the two armies must have presented quite a contrast. Mao's army was ragged, whereas the Donggu fighters were well fed and well dressed. Xiao Ke, recalling the meeting, writes that what he remembered most clearly was that the representatives from Donggu wore the long cotton robes, "like gentry (*shenshi*), not like soldiers," and that their speeches at the meeting were "both elegant and impassioned."[45]

After a month of difficult warfare, the meeting at Donggu provided Mao's troops with a much-needed respite. They spent a week resting and reorganizing, a time that Mao recognized as vital to the survival of the Red Fourth Army. As Mao put it, "If in that year we had not had that week of rest at Donggu, the Red Fourth Army would have collapsed, even less could it have opened up the southern Jiangxi base area."[46] Some 300 sick and wounded, including Mao's younger brother, Mao Zetan, were able to heal in an improvised hospital.

Mao was obviously deeply impressed by what he found in Donggu. He wrote to the Center, stating, "the fighting capacity of the Independent Second Regiment is very strong, almost equal to that of the Fourth Army's Thirty-First Regiment" (i.e., Mao's troops).[47] More important, Mao was impressed by the control Li Wenlin's party organization exercised over the military. As Mao said, "They cannot allocate

[43] Zhang Shouchun, "'Li Wenlinshi' Donggu geming genjudi."   [44] Ibid.
[45] Xiao Ke, *Xiao Ke huiyilu* (Xiao Ke's Memoir) (Beijing: Jiefangjun chubanshe, 1997), p. 117.
[46] Shi Zhongquan, "Cong 'zuozuodangshi' dao 'fajue dangshi'" (From "Looking at Party History" to "Developing Party History"), in Zhonggong Jiangxi shengwei dangshi yanjiushi et al., *Donggu: Ganxinan geming genjudi shiliao xuanbian*, vol. 1, p. 6.
[47] Tang Jingtao, "Zhongyang suqu de diyikuai jishi: Li Wenlin ji Li Wenlin-shi genjudi" (The Number One Cornerstone of the Central Soviet Area: Li Wenlin and the Li Wenlin-Style Base Area), *Dangshi zongheng*, no. 6 (1992), pp. 39–41.

one bullet without asking the Party. They have absolute Party leadership."[48] This was a thought that would stay with Mao.

Relations between Mao and Li Wenlin were good enough that after Mao left Donggu, there was some co-ordination between them on troop movements.[49] There was apparently even some consideration of Li Wenlin merging his troops into Mao's Red Fourth Army. But Feng Ren, secretary of the West Jiangxi Special Committee, held Li back. The Donggu Revolutionary Base Area was under the authority of the West Jiangxi Special Committee – that is how Li Wenlin took over command of the Second Independent Regiment – but the authority of the Special Committee depended on who was the secretary and on the agreement of lower units, such as the Donggu Base Area. There was very little funding for the Special Committee. Its funding was supposed to come from the Jiangxi Provincial Party Committee, but, as noted in the previous chapter, the party committee hardly had the funds to support itself, much less to dispense funds to lower-level organizations. So, in reality, the Special Committee was dependent on the Donggu Base Area for funding. Its way of raising funds was the same as the bandits had long used – raiding wealthy people and extorting funds, a practice widely known as "sheep hangings" (*diaoyang*) because people were strung up like sheep until the raiders were satisfied that they had extracted all the money and valuables that could be obtained. Even this method was uncertain; those with significant wealth moved to cities like Ji'an, and lower-level party organizations did not always pass money upwards. Thus party authority was generally weak. But it was strong enough that Li Wenlin felt obliged to heed Feng Ren's instructions not to merge with Mao's Red Fourth Army. We can conclude, however, that Mao's relations with Li were good in February 1928 and that the inevitable tensions that would develop

---

[48] Mao Zedong, "Letter to Lin Biao," in Schram, *Mao's Road to Power*, vol. 3, p. 180.

[49] Jiang Boying, "Cong Mao Zedong de lunshu kan Donggu geming genjudi de lishi gongxian" (Looking at the Historical Contributions of the Donggu Revolutionary Base Area from Mao Zedong's Remarks), *Dang de wenxian*, no. 5 (2007), pp. 53–58. The Front Committee reported to the Center that the Red Fourth and Fifth Armies, as well as the Second and Fourth Regiments (Li Wenlin's troops), were carrying out guerrilla fighting in southern Jiangxi and western Fujian. Quoted in Pang Xianzhi and Jin Chongji, eds., *Mao Zedong zhuan* (Biography of Mao Zedong), 2nd ed., 6 vols. (Beijing: Zhongyang wenxian chubanshe, 2011), vol. 1, p. 195.

between local party organizations and outsiders were not prominent at this time. Those conflicts would come soon enough.

Conclusion

The Donggu Revolutionary Base Area was truly a local movement. Its founders – Lai Jingbang, Zeng Bingchun, Gao Kenian, and others – were bound together by all coming from the area; they were all classmates at Provincial No. 7 Normal School, and they were all Hakka. As educated youth, they were prominent in their communities, and they had all had been radicalized by their time in Ji'an. They also had kinship ties with Duan Qifeng, the leader of the Three Dot Society. It was this alliance with local bandits that provided a core leadership that remained together even after Lai Jingbang was killed. Li Wenlin had a much wider social network, not only coming from a fairly wealthy family, but also having studied in Nanchang and then at Whampoa Military Academy. He was not as elite as Zeng Tianyu in Wan'an, but he had much better military training and organizational skills.

Rents in the area were heavy, as they generally were in rural China, and the natural frictions between landlords and renters were exacerbated by the fact that the Wang family members who owned the land were early settlers. But it was the radicalization of Lai Jingbang and the others that led them to accept communism and that launched them on their revolutionary careers. Communism at this point was still a protean concept, as the many debates in the party would show. As locals, the Donggu revolutionaries did not embark on a course of land confiscation and radical land redistribution; rather, they fought to reduce rents, lower interest rates, and eliminate miscellaneous fees. It was only in the fall of 1929 that they began to implement land distribution in accordance with the Xingguo Land Law. In doing so, land was redistributed by the district (*xiang*), which allowed for considerable evasion because those in charge of distribution were often landlords or rich peasants themselves.[50]

Moreover, as a local movement, the leaders were very conscious of the importance of developing the economy, especially after conservatives in other areas had blockaded the Donggu area. They opened small-scale mines and an arsenal that could fix rifles, make simple

---

[50] Ding Renxiang, "Dongjinggang geminshi gaiyao," vol. 1, p. 502.

mortars, manufacture gunpowder, and forge spears and large swords. They set up schools, established a simple bank (more like a revolving credit union than a modern bank), printed money, and established a consumer co-operative.

The Donggu Revolutionary Base Area was subordinate to the West Jiangxi Special Committee, and it was that committee that appointed Li Wenlin to replace Lai Jingbang as head of the Donggu Revolutionary Army. However, the control of the West Jiangxi Special Committee does not appear to have been especially tight. The city of Ji'an was some seventy miles away, transportation was not easy, and the Ji'an party organization was dependent on the Donggu Revolutionary Base Area and other local movements for financial support. Decisions on when and where to fight appear to have been set by Li Wenlin, and the social and economic policies were likewise decided upon by the local party committee. In short, the Donggu Revolutionary Base Area was first and foremost a local movement. Such relative independence, however, was not to last.

3 | A Different Approach to Revolution

Building a Party Army

On April 12, 1927, as Du Yuesheng's Green Gang was taking control of Shanghai, Mao Zedong was in Wuhan attending a meeting of the GMD's Central Land Committee (*Zhongyang tudi weiyuanhui*). This GMD was, of course, the wing headed by Wang Jingwei, which was still collaborating with the CCP. By this time, Mao was one of the CCP's leading policy specialists on land and peasant issues. In May 1926 he had been named director of the Peasant Movement Training Institute (*Nongmin yundong jiangxisuo*) in Guangzhou for the sixth class. In October of that year, Chen Duxiu appointed him secretary of the newly established CCP Central Peasant Movement Committee (*Zhonggong zhongyang nongmin yundong weiyuanhui*). Sending his wife and children off to Hunan, Mao set off for Shanghai, and wrote the Plan for the Current Peasant Movement (*Muqian nongmin yundong jihua*),[1] which was approved by the Central Bureau. The plan called for focusing on the four provinces of Hunan, Hubei, Jiangxi, and Henan – the areas through which the Northern Expedition was marching. Having completed this task, Mao set off on an inspection tour, traveling to Jiangxi, Hunan, and Hubei and meeting with their respective party organizations.

The timing was propitious. The Northern Expedition had been launched in July 1926. As it marched north through Hunan and Jiangxi, peasant associations were being set up in its wake. In Hunan, some thirty students whom in the previous year Mao had trained at the Peasant Training Institute in Guangzhou were helping to organize peasant associations. By January 1927, some 2 million peasants had been organized and had begun launching movements to lower rents and interest.

---

[1] "Plan for the Current Peasant Movement," in Stuart R. Schram, ed., *Mao's Road to Power: Revolutionary Writings, 1912–49*, vol. 2: *National Revolution and Social Revolution, December 1920–June 1927* (Armonk, NY: M.E. Sharpe, 1994), pp. 411–413.

Mao reached Wuhan in December 1926 and established a Central Peasant Committee Office (*Zhongyang nongmin weiyuanhui ban-gongshi*) in Hankou, one of the three cities that made up Wuhan (the other two being Wuchang and Hanyang). Then, from December 13 to 18, Mao participated in a CCP Central Special Conference. This conference declared that the peasant movement was veering left and was threatening the United Front. The conference decided to restrict the labor and peasant movements in the hopes that the alliance with Chiang Kai-shek would continue and, at the same time, the CCP would support Wang Jingwei as GMD leader in the hope that he could restrain Chiang's military power. At the conference, Chen Duxiu said that the peasant movement was "excessive" (*guohuo*), "immature" (*youzhi*), and "an obstacle to the United Front" (*fang'ai tongyi zhanxian*). Mao said nothing in response. Later, he would explain his silence, saying that he did not have sufficient evidence to confront the party secretary.[2] More likely, Mao was still deferential to the older, better-educated, and far more famous leader.

Just at this time, Mao received an invitation from the First Hunan All-Provincial Representative Congress of Peasants (*Hunan quansheng diyici daibiao dahui*) to come to Hunan. On December 17, he left Hankou for Changsha. At the congress, Mao answered questions and helped draft resolutions, including one that declared that the central task at the moment was to "thoroughly root out the feudal political power of the local bullies and evil gentry and establish the political power of the peasants."[3]

Following this, Mao used his status as an alternate member of the GMD Central Committee to inspect the peasant movement. Prior to his depature, the Hunan provincial GMD held a meeting of its standing committee and decided to send Dai Shuren of the GMD Control Commission to accompany Mao. So, on January 4, 1927, Mao and Dai set off on a thirty-two-day expedition through the counties of Xiangtan, Xiangxiang, Hengshan, Liling, and Changsha, covering some 700 kilometers.

---

[2] Pang Xianzhi and Jin Chongji, eds., *Mao Zedong zhuan* (Biography of Mao Zedong), 2nd ed., 6 vols. (Beijing: Zhongyang wenxian chubanshe, 2011), vol. 1, p. 124.

[3] Ibid., p. 125.

After the end of the trip, Mao's enthusiasm for rural revolution was unlimited. In his well-known "Investigation of the Peasant Movement in Hunan," he famously wrote,

For the present upsurge of the peasant movement is a colossal event. In a very short time, several hundred million peasants in China's central, southern, and northern provinces will rise like a fierce wind or tempest, a force so swift and violent that no power, however great, will be able to suppress it.[4]

Mao admitted that his information was based on the reports of people working in the peasant movement, but he did not allow this evident bias to curb his enthusiasm.

Mao would soon learn that the countryside was not so simple, and a great tidal wave of peasant enthusiasm would not rise up and wipe out "feudal" authority, not even in places like Donggu where there was a substantial revolutionary movement. As he wrote to the Party Center a year and a half later,

But since the feudal family system is widespread in every *xian* [county], and all the families in a village or group of villages often have the same surname, a fairly long time will be required for class polarization to take place in the villages and for the clan ideology to be overcome. In the countryside, where clan organizations prevail, the most troublesome are not the despotic gentry, but the intermediate classes. This is the biggest problem.[5]

Overcoming this structure from the outside was not easy; breaking it down from the inside was the role of the educated youth, whom Bianco described as "class traitors," in places like Donggu.[6]

But that was later. Mao's full report was published in whole in April 1927 as a pamphlet. Qu Qiubai, soon to be leader of the CCP, wrote a full-throated preface, urging his fellow revolutionaries to read Mao's work. "What China's peasants want," he wrote, "is political power and land." Mao and Peng Pai were, according to Qu, "the kings of the peasant movement." Even Bukharin endorsed Mao's work at an

---

[4] Mao Zedong, "Report on the Peasant Movement in Hunan," in Schram, *Mao's Road to Power*, vol. 2, p. 430.

[5] Mao Zedong, "Report of the Jinggangshan Front Committee to the Central Committee," in Stuart R. Schram, ed., *Mao's Road to Power: Revolutionary Writings, 1912–49*, vol. 3: *From the Jinggangshan to the Establishment of the Jiangxi Soviets, July 1927–December 1930* (Armonk, NY: M.E. Sharpe, 1995), pp. 103–104.

[6] Lucian Bianco, *Peasants without the Party: Grassroots Movements in Twentieth-Century China* (Armonk, NY: M.E. Sharpe, 2001), p. 44.

executive chair meeting of the Communist International.[7] On April 2, at the Fifth Enlarged Meeting of the GMD Standing Committee, Mao was named to the Land Committee, along with Deng Yanda and three others.[8]

Returning to Wuhan, Mao attended the Third Plenary Session of the Second GMD Central Committee as an alternate member. Just back from his investigations, he spoke out on adopting a more radical land policy. It was necessary, he said, to confiscate the land owned by family temples, otherwise it would not be possible to smash the clan system. Mao spoke out in support of regulations on punishing local bullies and evil gentry, as had been raised by the Hubei Party Committee. "It is necessary to use revolutionary methods to deal with local bullies and evil gentry," Mao said. "Peaceful methods will not overturn the local bullies and evil gentry." The plenary session agreed and adopted the regulations. The following day, March 16, the session also adopted the "Resolution on the Peasant Problem" and the "Manifesto to the Peasants" that Mao and Deng Yanda had proposed.[9] So it is no wonder that this insistent voice on rural matters was attending another meeting on the peasant issue when Chiang Kai-shek and the Green Gang struck.

Despite Chiang's coup, the Communist Party decided to go ahead with its previously scheduled Fifth Party Congress, which convened from April 27 to May 9. Giving the political report and a separate report on the organizational situation, the beleaguered Chen Duxiu admitted that the Organization Department "in fact does not exist, because whether it is me or the others, none of us worked in the Organization Department before."[10]

Prior to the Fifth Party Congress, Mao had met with Peng Pai, Fang Zhimin, and others responsible for peasant associations in other provinces and they drew up a proposal to immediately solve the peasant land question. They sent their proposal to the Center just prior to the convening of the Fifth Party Congress, but Chen Duxiu refused to even

---

[7] Pang Xianzhi and Jin Chongji, *Mao Zedong zhuan*, vol. 1, pp. 128–129.
[8] Ibid., p. 130.
[9] Zhonggong zhongyang wenxian yanjiushi, ed., *Mao Zedong nianpu, 1893–1949* (Annual Chronicle of Mao Zedong, 1893–1949), 3 vols., revised ed. (Beijing: Zhongyang wenxian chubanshe, 2013) (hereafter cited as *Mao Zedong nianpu*), vol. 1, p. 185.
[10] Zhao Shenghui, *Zhongguo gongchandang zuzhishi gangyao* (Organizational History of the Chinese Communist Party) (Hefei: Anhui Renmin chubanshe, 1987), p. 53.

discuss it. The CCP, desperate to maintain its alliance with Wang Jingwei's government, was not willing to go as far as the left wing of the GMD had been willing to go just three weeks earlier.

As Mao contemplated rural policy and stewed over the way his views had been dismissed, his thoughts turned to violence. When a delegation from Hunan arrived in Wuhan to appeal for sanctions against Xu Kexiang for his Horse Day massacre of Communists, Mao urged everyone to return to their posts, saying that if Changsha could not be held, and if the cities could not be maintained, then they should go to the countryside and arouse the peasants. Those in the mountains should go to the mountains, those near the lakes should take to their boats. They should pick up their guns and carry out the revolution. It was necessary to use armed force to protect the revolution.[11] Mao would soon have a chance to put his ideas into practice.

On July 24 the Politburo decided to reorganize the Hunan Party Committee, placing Mao in charge. Mao went to Changsha to understand the situation, and he declared that it was necessary for the armed forces in each county to concentrate their strength. It was necessary to use armed force to oppose armed force, and necessary to use guns to oppose guns. One could not merely wait around and watch.[12] As Mao would soon find out, there was little organization and there were few arms at the local level. Organizing the few armed forces to resist the conservative power in Hunan would prove difficult. Perhaps that is why Mao, upon returning to Wuhan, told a Politburo meeting that one way to survive was to "go to the mountains" (*shangshan*). "Heading up into the mountains," Mao said, "could create a foundation for military strength." "If we don't preserve our military strength, then the next time something happens, we won't be able to do anything."[13]

In early August, Mao drew up a plan for an insurrection in southern Hunan. The plan called for using military strength to seize Rucheng

---

[11] *Mao Zedong nianpu*, vol. 1, p. 201.   [12] Ibid., p. 202.

[13] Ibid., p. 203. In a conversation with Chen Duxiu, Zhou Enlai, Zhang Guotao, and others on July 4, Mao suggested that the Hunan Peasant Association could "go up to the mountains." By doing so, Mao said, "we can create a foundation for a real military force." Several days later, on July 20, the Central Committee issued a circular that had included Mao in the drafting. In particular, as Schram points out, Mao's influence was reflected in a section that again suggested that peasant associations might "go up to the mountains." Thus Mao had been clearly thinking about retreating to the mountains for some days before this Politburo meeting. See Schram, *Mao's Road to Power*, vol. 3, pp. 11, 18.

and four or five other counties. The idea was to transfer three regiments – one from Guangdong that was then in Rucheng, one from the Liuyang–Pingjiang area in northeast Hunan, and one from Jiangxi – to form a division that would have enough strength to take control of the southern Hunan area.

Mao's plan was part of the larger effort to launch the Autumn Harvest Uprisings throughout the four provinces of Guangdong, Hunan, Jiangxi, and Hubei. This plan reversed the Communist International's view that the peasant associations in Hunan had been "immature" and their actions "excessive," saying now that workers and peasants exercising "democratic dictatorship" in alliance with the petty bourgeoisie was correct. Insurrections should aim at "consolidating all power in the hands of peasant associations, slaughtering (*jianmie*) local bullies and evil gentry, and confiscating their property."[14]

At the Emergency Meeting on August 7, Mao had repeated the injunction in his "Report on the Peasant Movement in Hunan" that "all power grows out of the barrel of a gun" and stated that if the insurrections failed, they should head to the mountains. Several days later, Mao reiterated his views, telling party leaders that if his plan failed, his forces, such as they were, should not go to Guangdong as many were then advocating, but rather they should head for the mountains.[15]

Because of GMD military strength in southern Hunan, Mao focused his attention on attacking the provincial capital, Changsha. When Mao and the Hunan Party Committee discussed the attack, they considered using two regiments. But the Party Center opposed this plan, saying, "This reliance on military force seems as if you do not believe in the revolutionary strength of the masses. The result is a type of military adventurism." The Hunan Party Committee defended itself rather feebly, saying, "Our plan to seize Changsha relies primarily on the workers and peasants. Moving these two regiments to attack Changsha is only intended to supplement the insufficient strength of the workers and peasants, and it is not [intended] to be the main force."[16]

---

[14] *Mao Zedong nianpu*, vol. 1, p. 205.   [15] Ibid., p. 207.
[16] Huang Kun, *Geming yu xiangcun: Cong baodong dao xiangcun geju, 1927–1929: Zhongguo gongchandang geming genjudi zenyang jianli qilaide* (Revolution and the Villages: From Insurrections to Rural Bases, 1927–1929: How the CCP Revolutionary Bases Were Established) (Shanghai: Shanghai shehui kexueyuan chubanshe, 2006), p. 57.

The Party Center was not opposed to violence. As pointed out in Chapter 1, the Center loved violence. It certainly supported the Nanchang and Guangzhou Uprisings, but it opposed the organization of large-scale military force. Mao disagreed, regarding military force as essential to organize peasants and to preserve the party. This was an argument Mao would win, but it would take time.

Mao left for Hunan on August 12. On August 18, he called a meeting of the Hunan Party Committee and once again presented his views on military affairs. He expressed how his views on uprisings differed strongly from those espoused by Qu Qiubai and other leaders, saying, "If we want to initiate uprisings, relying solely on the strength of the masses will not do. There must be military assistance. With one or two regiments, then something can get going. Otherwise, everything will end in defeat." Mao went on,

Developing uprisings is to seize political power. If we want to seize political power, to try to do it without the support of military force is just self-deception. The mistake of our party in the past was to ignore military affairs; now we should place 60 percent of our attention on military affairs so we can carry out [the reality that] political power grows out of the barrel of a gun and we can establish political power.[17]

When the Center received the Hunan Party Committee's plan for an uprising to take Changsha, one person commented that Mao's theory of "power growing out of the barrel of a gun" was different from the Center's policy. "The Center," this unnamed party leader said, "trusts purely in the strength of the masses; military strength can only be of assistance." When the Center replied to the Hunan Party Committee, it stated that the committee's plan was overly reliant on military force and the result could only be "military opportunism."[18]

At the beginning of September, Mao went to Anyuan, where he had worked with Li Lisan and Liu Shaoqi to organize miners in 1922. He called a meeting at nearby Zhangjiawan to map out plans to advance on Changsha. It was decided that they would move in from three directions, starting from Xiushui, Tonggu, and Anyuan in Jiangxi and then converging on Changsha. They were to instigate peasant uprisings as they went. But on September 6, the garrison at Changsha intercepted orders from the Hunan Party Committee to the various

---

[17] Pang Xianzhi and Jin Chongji, *Mao Zedong zhuan*, vol. 1, pp. 144–145.
[18] Ibid., p. 146.

party branches and accordingly ordered martial law to be established starting on September 8. As Mao was traveling to Tonggu, he was seized by a local self-defense force. On his way to probable execution, he made a break and ran into some tall grass around a pond, where he managed to hide. By the time he reached Tonggu on September 10, the uprising had already started. The armed forces did not converge as planned, and one unit mutinied. Seeing the probability of disaster, Mao stopped the attack and began to retreat.[19]

On September 29, the remnants of Mao's army reached Sanwan village in Yongxin county, Jiangxi, where Mao reorganized his troops, setting up party organizations at each level and adopting a system of "soldier committees" (*shibing weiyuanhui*) to give ordinary soldiers a channel through which they could express their opinions. This reorganized group of soldiers, totaling about 1,000 men, would become Mao's 31st Regiment, the core of his personal military strength.

After carrying out this reorganization, Mao and his troops moved south to Gucheng, where they stopped for a two-day conference. A representative of Yuan Wencai, the bandit leader based in Maoping in the Jinggangshan, attended the meeting along with cadres from the party organization in Ninggang county. This conference seems to have made at least a tentative decision to co-operate with Yuan Wencai. Mao then met with Yuan and they discussed co-operation over dinner. Mao presented Yuan with 100 rifles, and Yuan presented Mao with a large amount of money. Yuan agreed to allow Mao and his troops to enter Maoping and he promised to feed them and care for the sick and wounded. Thus, on October 7, the fledgling Red Army went to Maoping.[20] Yuan would later provide Mao with an introduction to Wang Zuo, the other bandit leader in the area. The bandits led by Yuan and Wang would go on to form the 32nd Regiment, so these troops were never integrated with Mao's own troops. Personal relations between commanders and troops remained important.

Mao's decision to go into the mountains and seek co-operation with the bandits should not be a cause for surprise. He had expressed the

[19] Ibid., pp. 148–151.
[20] Stephen C. Averill, *Revolution in the Highlands: China's Jinggangshan Base Area* (Lanham, MD: Rowman & Littlefield, 2006), p. 160.

idea of heading into the mountains many times. As he had said, a mountain base would give him time to build a military force; co-operating with bandits would give him an entrée into local society and would teach him the basics of guerilla warfare. Furthermore, co-operating with local Hakkas might overcome the social gap between his non-Hakka fighters and the many Hakka communities in and around the Jinggangshan.

Mao's actions may not be cause for surprise, but they were very different from what was going on throughout the rest of south China. As discussed in Chapter 1, organizations and uprisings else-where were being developed by local people, mostly by those edu-cated youth whose passion for revolution had been ignited during their schooling, away from their villages. But Mao and his troops were very much outsiders. Moreover, whereas organizers in most parts of China were satisfied with merely setting off insurrections, Mao was aiming at building a base area with military force. That is why co-operation with Yuan Wencai and Wang Zuo was important; it would give Mao a guide to the complicated environment, both physically and socially, and it would provide desparately needed fighters.

Zhu De

Mao's situation in the Jinggangshan would be complicated in April 1928 by the arrival of Zhu De. Zhu De is one of the more intriguing figures in Communist Party history. Born in 1886, he was adopted by a wealthy uncle when he was nine years old. In 1909, when he was twenty-three, he was admitted to Yunnan Military Academy. For a number of years he was an opium addict and a minor warlord. He finally kicked his opium habit and, in 1922, went to Germany, where he studied philosophy at Göttingen University. There he became involved in political activities and he met Zhou Enlai, who was one of his sponsors for membership in the CCP. In 1925 Zhu went to Moscow, where he studied at the Communist University of Toilers of the East for a year before returning to China. When he returned to China in 1926, he was first sent to Sichuan, where he worked with the warlord Yang Sen. Then, in January 1927, he was sent to Nanchang, the capital of Jiangxi province. At the time, Zhu Peide, commander of the Third Army of the GMD National Revolution Army, was in charge of Nanchang, Jiujiang, Ji'an, and Jinxian, an area south of Poyang Lake.

Fortunately for Zhu De, Zhu Peide was an old friend. Both were from Yunnan, and they were classmates at the military academy in Yunnan. Zhu Peide would soon be trailing Mao and Zhu through the hills of Jiangxi trying to exterminate them, but at this time the alliance between the Communists and the GMD was still on, and Zhu Peide had conflicts with Chiang Kai-shek. Thus there were a number of reasons for the two Zhus to co-operate, and Zhu Peide asked Zhu De to run a newly established officer training academy (*Guomin gemingjun disanjun junguan jiaoyu tuan*) under his Third Army to replenish the officers lost in battle.[21] In April 1927 Zhu De also became head of the Nanchang Public Security Bureau. These positions allowed him to play an important role in attacking the AB Group that Chiang Kai-shek had set up in Jiangxi to wrest control from the Communists, but that is a story for later (see Chapter 4).

Thus Zhu De was in Nanchang when the CCP decided that its first uprising after the disastrous split with the GMD would be in Nanchang.[22] The decision was made on July 15, just days after Beso Lominadze, the Comintern agent who had replaced Borodin, arrived from Moscow and, coincidentally, the same day that Wang Jingwei announced his split with the Communists. The uprising took place on August 1, led by He Long and Ye Ting, who had defected from Zhang Fakui's GMD forces. The uprising succeeded in taking the city, but the Communists were forced to retreat only three days later when they were confronted by larger GMD forces. Zhu De had played only a minor role, but he followed He Long and Ye Ting's troops south toward Guangdong, where they hoped to create a new base and launch a Communist version of the Northern Expedition.

When the Communist troops reached northern Guangdong, Zhu De was left at Sanheba ("embankment on three rivers"), east of Meizhou city, to protect the main forces from the pursuing troops led by Nationalist general Qian Dajun. The forces Zhu commanded were primarily from Ye Ting's army and they were not sufficient to defeat Qian Dajun's larger and better-equipped army. After three days of

---

[21] Zhonggong zhongyang wenxian yanjiushi, ed., *Zhu De zhuan* (Biography of Zhu De), 2 vols. (Beijing: Zhongyang wenxian chubanshe, 2016), vol. 1, p. 83.

[22] On Zhu De's role in the Nanchang Uprising, see ibid., pp. 89–93.

heavy fighting, Zhu withdrew his remaining troops and headed south to join the main force. It was on the way to join Ye Ting and others that Zhu De learned that the Communist troops had been dealt a devastating defeat at Qiaoshan. The army had been defeated and all the leaders had fled. Because there was no way to establish contact with party leaders, Zhu was on his own, with the nationalist troops in pursuit.

With approximately 2,500 troops, Zhu De headed north and west along the border between Guangdong and Fujian, and then into Jiangxi. Along the way, battles and defections reduced Zhu's forces to only 800 men. Among them, however, were major leaders of China's future PLA: Lin Biao, Chen Yi, Xiao Ke, and Su Yu. Finally, as the ragtag army approached the Hunan border, Zhu learned that his old friend and classmate Fan Shisheng was based in Rucheng in southern Hunan. Zhu was extremely close to Fan; they were sworn brothers and they both had secretly entered Sun Yat-sen's Revolutionary Alliance. They had fought together under Cai E against Yuan Shikai in the Protect the Nation movement (1915–1916). Fan then went on to achieve a high position in the Yunnan military.[23] Now, Fan welcomed Zhu to Rucheng.

Therefore, some two months after leaving Sanheba, Zhu De, in December 1927, met up with Fan Shisheng. Fan supported Zhu by giving his troops new uniforms that matched the uniforms of his own troops and giving them a Nationalist Army designation (the 140th Regiment of the 47th Division of the 16th Army). Thus they were "hidden" as part of Fan's own troops. The food, rest, and military supplies that were afforded by Fan no doubt saved Zhu's troops from destruction.

However, Fan's deception was soon discovered, and in January Chiang Kai-shek ordered that Fan arrest Zhu and disband his troops. Fan, who was not on good terms with Chiang, told Zhu he had to leave, but he gave him 10,000 dollars as a parting gift.[24]

Zhu headed west toward Yizhang. Approaching the city, Zhu had a collaborator, one Hu Shaohai, who was from a prominent family in Yizhang, write a letter to the leaders of Yizhang, inviting them to dinner to welcome the 140th Regiment. Yizhang's elite, believing that the 140th regiment had been dispatched by Fan Shisheng, declared that

[23] Ibid., p. 113.   [24] Ibid., pp. 116–118.

they would host the dinner. In a scene right out of the *Romance of the Three Kingdoms*, Zhu hid his soldiers near the dining hall, and on a signal from Zhu, they burst in. In one swift coup, Zhu's troops seized 400 of the city's elite. Having seized control of the city, Zhu set about replenishing his troops and co-ordinating with local party organizations to touch off the Southern Hunan Uprising (*Xiangnan baodong*). The troops from Yizhang would form the core of what would become Zhu's 29th Regiment; they would also be the cause of one of Zhu's most severe defeats (see below).

Southern Hunan had originally been the target for Mao's Autumn Harvest Uprising, but the reinforcement of Nationalist troops in the area had forced Mao to focus on Changsha instead. However, the situation in early 1928 was different. A war between Chiang Kaishek's Nationalist troops and Tang Shengzhi, who had dominated Hunan and Hubei, broke out in northern Hunan. Therefore the military forces in southern Hunan were moved north and the remaining forces were few and far between. Moreover, despite the repression following Horse Day, the party organization in southern Hunan was still fairly strong. Although quiet, it had been able to organize several guerrilla forces that would be able to support the uprising.[25]

The party organization in southern Hunan was much the same as elsewhere at this stage of the revolution; that is to say, it had been built and was run by educated youth. In his memoirs, Huang Kecheng provides a vivid account of his youth and early days in the party. Huang himself had grown up poor, but members of his clan recognized that he was smart and fond of learning, so they supported him to attend school. As he stopped and started school, progress was slow. When Huang was eighteen years old, he was still in elementary school. He writes that at the time this was not unusual. There were students in his school even older than he. When he was twenty, he tested into Hengyang Provincial No. 3 Normal School, where he became radicalized. Being in Hengyang opened his eyes. Hengyang was bigger and more prosperous than the county seat in his native Yongxing county. Books and newspapers were plentiful. Reading them, he felt he better understood the social problems and the future of the country. He also thought about his own future.[26]

[25] Ibid., p. 120.
[26] Huang Kecheng, *Huang Kecheng zishu* (Autobiography of Huang Kecheng), (Beijing: Renmin chubanshe, 1994), pp. 8–9.

Hengyang Provincial No. 3 Normal School had a revolutionary tradition, hosting a branch of Mao Zedong's Wenhua shushe (Culture Book Society), an early publishing venture and bookstore. Two of its teachers were members of the Communist Party who used their teaching posts as cover for their organizing activities, a common practice at the time. In 1924, Huang organized a mutual-aid society of Yongxing students in Hengyang to read and discuss issues. Huang's later party contacts and associates in the Southern Hunan Uprising – Huang Ping, Liu Shen, Liu Mu, Li Bucheng, and Huang Tingfang – were all members of this society.[27]

Something of the atmosphere of the time can be gleaned from Huang's memory of a party meeting in December 1927 at which the spirit of the August 7 Emergency Meeting was conveyed. Members of Huang's party branch all agreed that the branch should organize a peasant uprising, but when discussions began about how to go about it, Huang suggested preparing the ground by first engaging in mass work. One of his comrades, Kuang Zhenxing, immediately called him a coward and a rightist opportunist, the charge that had first been used to indict Chen Duxiu but was soon used to condemn anyone deemed "conservative." Huang tried to defend his point of view, but the majority agreed with Kuang, and Huang was criticized as a rightist opportunist. For a while he was not permitted to participate in county party meetings.

The Southern Hunan Uprising turned out to be a bloody affair. At the time, the party secretary of the Southern Hunan Special Committee was Chen Youkui. In 1920, Chen had gone to Changsha for further education when he serendipitously ran into Mao Zedong and He Shuheng, who were organizing the short-lived Hunan Self-Improvement University (*Hunansheng zixiu daxue*) to recruit poor students. Chen enrolled, and in the following year Mao and He introduced him into the party. Chen held a number of positions on the Hunan Party Committee during the following years, becoming head of the provincial party Organization Department in 1926 and party secretary of the South Hunan Special Committee in 1927. As Huang says, Chen was "extremely leftist." He ordered all counties to "burn all and kill all" (*dashao dasha*). Not only were the houses of the gentry to be burnt but also all the shops along the streets in town were to be burnt

27 Ibid., p. 17.

as well. In Chenzhou, he ordered people to burn all houses on the road between Hengyang and Pingshi for fifteen *li* (about four and a half miles) on both sides. The idea was that when the enemy attacked, it would have nowhere to stay.[28] This step was one too far for the peasants. At a mass rally to mobilize people to burn the houses, the peasants rose up and killed all nine members of the party committee on the platform. Chen was not there, but he was later arrested and executed in April 1928.

The Southern Hunan Uprising was the largest uprising launched during this period. It encompassed at least six counties, and a million peasants are said to have participated, though most were no doubt onlookers. But the killing and burning were too much, and local elites mounted a counterattack. Any support for the CCP was lost, and, as Mao said when the Hunan Party Committee was pressing him to return to southern Hunan, "From the time Zhu's army arrived in Leiyang in February, Zhu could not raise a penny and he had to rely on selling opium to eat."[29] So Zhu De, Chen Yi, and their troops were driven out of southern Hunan as the uprising collapsed. Thousands of people had been killed, and the wanton violence meant that Zhu and Chen could not remain in the area. Having no choice, they turned eastward and climbed the Jinggangshan, finally meeting with Mao in Ninggang county on April 28, 1928.

The Jinggangshan

This is not the place for an extended discussion of Mao in the Jinggangshan, a task that has already been undertaken admirably by Stephen Averill.[30] However, there are some aspects of Mao's time there that underscore his evolving role as he began to emerge as a major leader and that highlight the differences between the Jinggangshan and Donggu.

---

[28] Ibid., p. 36.

[29] "Zhonggong XiangGanbian tewei he hongsijun junwei xiang Zhonggong Hunan shengwei de baogao" (Report from the Hunan–Jiangxi Border Special Committee and the Military Committee of the Red Fourth Army to the Hunan Provincial CCP Committee), in Jiangxisheng dang'anguan, ed., *Jinggangshan geming genjudi shiliao xuanbian* (Selected Historical Materials of the Jinggangshan Revolutionary Base Area) (Nanchang: Jiangxi renmin chubanshe, 1985), pp. 47–49.

[30] Averill, *Revolution in the Highlands.*

First and foremost, the Jinggangshan Base Area was developed on the basis of military control imposed from the outside. This is not to say that party organization was not important – it was – but military power was also central. The military at the time was composed of three basic groups. The first group, consisting of Mao's troops, can be subdivided into three parts: the troops that had originally been part of the unit around Lu Deming, a graduate of Whampoa Military Academy and previously head of the guard unit around Zhang Fakui (Lu himself was killed in an ambush as Mao's troops were heading toward the Jinggangshan, but the troops remained); the workers from the Anyuan mines; and the peasants Mao and others had organized in Pingxiang and Liuyang. Originally this force was composed of about 5,000 men, but by the time Mao arrived on the Jinggangshan, only about 700 remained. They were organized into the 31st Regiment. The second group was made up of the fighters with Yuan Wencai and Wang Zuo, the bandit leaders who lived on the Jinggangshan and used it as their base. Mao won them over with a gift of guns and expressions of solidarity. They formed another regiment, the 32nd Regiment, composed of about 400 men. Third, Zhu De brought two regiments of troops. The 28th Regiment was composed primarily of troops originally under Ye Ting's command, but these troops were then led by Zhu across northern Guangdong into southern Hunan, as described above. By the time they reached the Jinggangshan, they were loyal to Zhu De. Mao would complain that they still had the old habits of warlord armies, but they formed a capable military force of about 1,100 men. As veterans of the Nanchang Uprising, they were also contemptuous of the troops that Mao had led up the mountain.[31] Zhu's other regiment, the 29th Regiment, was made up of peasants recruited in Yizhang in southern Hunan.[32] These troops were hardly committed to the revolution, at least not a revolution away from their homes, and they would push Zhu into an unwise incursion into southern Hunan in the summer of 1928. In what became known as the "August defeat," these troops

---

[31] Ying Xing, "Hongsijun lingdao jigou de bianhua yu zhuli hongjun de zuzhi xingshi" (The Evolution of the Leadership Organ of the Red Fourth Army and the Organizational Forms of the Main Force of the Red Army), *Suqu yanjiu*, no. 3 (2016), p. 17.

[32] "Du Xiujing xiang Zhonggong Hunan shengwei de baogao" (Report of Du Xiujing to the CCP Hunan Provincial Committee), in Jiangxisheng dang'an guan, *Jinggangshan geming genjudi shiliao xuanbian*, pp. 42–46.

were routed; many simply fled the battlefield to return to their homes.[33] The differences between these various forces suggest some of the fissures that would create tensions between Mao and Zhu, cleavages that would become much more serious after they left the Jinggangshan.

Mao and Zhu were not only military figures. They were outsiders in a society that took very seriously the distinction between locals and outsiders. Being outsiders meant that Mao and Zhu related differently to the local population than Lai Jingbang and Li Wenlin related to the people in Donggu. Mao and Zhu could impose radical land reform; Lai and Li could not. Under Mao, the CCP confiscated all land, reassigning it mostly on a per capita basis. Land sales were forbidden. This radical land policy hurt the interests of the rich and middle peasants, and it hurt the local economy.[34] Moreover, as outsiders, the forces of Mao and Zhu were not concerned with the families and properties of the peasants in the area; they could conduct guerrilla warfare without worrying that counterattacking forces would harm the interests of the peasants. This is something that Lai Jingbang and Li Wenlin could not do in Donggu.

Being outsiders also meant that they could not recruit local peasants into the army. As Mao put it,

The Red Army was not made up of locals. It was completely different from the local armed Red Guards (*chiweidui*). The peasants in the counties in Ninggang around the Hunan–Jiangxi border were only willing to join the Red Guard in their own county and they were unwilling to join the Red Army. Because of this, the Red Army simply could not recruit peasants from the Hunan–Jiangxi border area.[35]

Another important difference was that Mao and Zhu were very clear that they were raising the flag of rebellion. They occupied a high massif that was relatively defensible and they used that redoubt to mount

[33] On the August defeat, see Averill, *Revolution in the Highlands*, pp. 274–290.
[34] Tang Lianying, Ye Fulin, and Ding Renxiang, *Donggu geming genjudi shilu* (On the History of the Donggu Revolutionary Base Area) (Shanghai: Huadong shifan daxue chubanshe, 2019), p. 279.
[35] Mao Zedong, "Jinggangshan de douzheng (1928 nian shiyiyue ershiwu ri)" (The Struggle in the Jinggang Mountains (November 25, 1928)), in Zhonggong zhongyang wenxian yanjiushi, ed., *Mao Zedong xuanji* (Selected Works of Mao Zedong), 2nd ed., 4 vols. (Beijing: Renmin chubanshe, 1991), vol. 1, p. 63. Quoted in Tang Lianying, Ye Fulin, and Ding Renxiang, *Donggu geming genjudi shilu*, p. 275.

assaults on the surrounding areas. The distinction between the red areas and the white areas was clear. This had the advantage of creating a defensible base area but it had the disadvantage of allowing economic blockades to be easily enforced, depriving the base area of everything from food to information (such as newspapers). Trade with outside areas was stopped. It also meant that the number of troops that could be supported by the Jinggangshan economy was limited. The winter of 1928–1929, as the economic blockade tightened, was extremely difficult. As Chen Yi wrote,

For four months [September 1928 to January 1929], the Red Army underwent unprecedented difficulties. In the thick of winter, the mountains filled with snow without a letup; food and clothing were very difficult. Because of the enemy's blockade, the Red Army was not able to go far on guerrilla missions to relieve the economy. At this time, the officers and men had only a single layer of clothing to ward off the cold, and they could only eat red rice and pumpkins. For two months they did not have a penny of spare change.[36]

It was just at this time, December 1928, that Peng Dehuai ascended the Jinggangshan with his 800 troops.

Mao's time on the Jinggangshan clearly reflects his desire to be in command and to be free of local party control. Mao was a master at maximizing his own autonomy without ever directly countermanding higher party authorities. When Mao arrived at the Jinggangshan he organized a Front Committee (*qiandi weiyuanhui*) that was responsible for military, government, and mass work. This form of organization had to be abandoned in March 1928 when Zhou Lu came to the Jinggangshan as a representative of the Hunan Provincial Party Committee, which had authority over Mao. Zhou Lu told Mao not only that the Central Committee (actually the Comintern representative, Lominadze) had revoked Mao's standing as an alternate member of the Central Committee as punishment for his failure to take Changsha, but also – erroneously – that he had been expelled from the party.[37] When

---

[36] Chen Yi, "Guanyu Zhu Mao jun de lishi jiqi zhuangkuang de baogao" (Report on the History of the Zhu–Mao Army and Its Circumstances), in Jiangxisheng dang'an guan and Zhonggong Jiangxi shengwei dangxiao dangshi jiaoyanshi, eds., *Zhongyang geming genjudi shiliao xuanbian* (Selected Historical Materials on the Central Revolutionary Base Area), 3 vols. (Nanchang: Jiangxi renmin chubanshe, 1982), vol. 2, pp. 444–463.

[37] Ying Xing, "Hongsijun lingdao jigou de bianhua yu zhuli hongjun de zuzhi xingshi," p. 17.

Mao and Zhu De finally met the following month, it was the Hunan Party Committee that decided that they should organize the Red Fourth Army. For the next four months, the Hunan Party Committee was able to keep close tabs on Mao, but in August the party committee was broken up by the GMD. With the Hunan Party Committee out of commission, the Jiangxi Party Committee stepped in and approved Mao as head of the newly created "Hunan–Jiangxi Special Committee" (*XiangGan tewei*). Mao organized a standing committee that included other party figures but not Zhu De or Chen Yi, a clear expression of tension. Mao then used joint meetings to exercise unified leadership over the Red Fourth Army and the county party committees. It was a bit arbitrary who would be invited to these meetings, and sometimes Zhu De was not invited.[38]

In the summer of 1928, when the Hunan Party Committee was ordering and then begging Mao and Zhu to return to southern Hunan, it instructed the Red Fourth Army to abolish its military commission and replace it with a Front Committee. When Mao was off in Yongxin, Zhu's troops met in Miandu, just across the border in Hunan, on July 31. In addition to agreeing to enter Hunan, they decided to re-establish the Front Committee. Because Mao was away, Chen Yi took over as secretary. When Zhu's troops returned, there was another meeting at which the Front Committee was abolished in favor of establishing an action committee with Mao as secretary.[39]

The problem was not that Mao objected to the idea of organizing a Front Committee (after all, that was the organizational structure he had originally favored), but that he objected to its being appointed by the Hunan Party Committee. Mao did not want to be under the control of a local party organization. At the time, the Party Center itself was unclear about the relationship it hoped to establish between the military, the party, and the soviets. It adopted a number of mutually contradictory resolutions, one of which was contained in a letter drafted by Li Weihan on June 4. This letter called clearly for the establishment of a Front Committee, with Mao as secretary. This letter was not received in the Jinggangshan until November 2, but when it was received, Mao readily agreed.[40]

---

[38] Ibid., p. 20.   [39] Ibid., p. 23.

[40] Ibid., p. 25. See also Li Weihan, *Huiyi yu yanjiu* (Remembrance and Study), 2 vols. (Beijing: Zhonggong dangshi chubanshe, 2013), vol. 1, p. 192.

From Mao's point of view, there were a number of advantages of having a Front Committee. First and foremost, the Front Committee was designated by the Center and its members were appointed by Shanghai. Even though the letter ambiguously stated that the party and military should be under the authority of the Hunan Party Committee when in Hunan and under the Jiangxi Party Committee when in Jiangxi, the fact that the letter was drafted in Shanghai implied that Mao was under the direct control of the Party Center, thus undercutting the authority of the local party organizations. The letter also stated that the Front Committee would exercise authority throughout the area controlled by the military. This instruction meant that the various special committees in charge of different areas could no longer exercise control over Mao and the Red Fourth Army. Although it was not yet explicitly stated, from then on Mao would report only to the Party Center in Shanghai.[41]

When Mao and Zhu departed the Jinggangshan in January 1929, they headed to Jiangxi rather than to Hunan, in part because they knew the Jiangxi Party Committee was weaker and less likely to exert control over them.

The Jinggangshan Base Area had failed. Its resources were too few to sustain an army large enough to defend the area, much less to expand it. These tensions, already evident, exploded when Peng Dehuai brought his Fifth Army to the mountain stronghold. Thus, on January 14, 1929, Mao and Zhu De led some 3,600 troops from the Red Fourth Army out of the mountain, leaving Peng Dehuai, Yuan Wencai, and Wang Zuo to defend the base against the gathering GMD armies.

Leaving the Jinggangshan was hardly safer than remaining there. As related in the previous chapter, the Red Fourth Army was under constant attack in Jiangxi, and it was on the verge of destruction when it finally reached Donggu in February 1929.

Tensions between Mao and Zhu

Mao and Zhu De stayed in Donggu for a week, resting, eating, and taking care of the wounded. While in Donggu, they learned that Peng Dehuai had not been able to hold the Jinggangshan base, so their original plan to return there had to be scrapped. With GMD troops

[41] Ibid., p. 27.

moving toward Donggu, Mao's Red Fourth Army headed northeast and then south into western Fujian, where, in the middle of March, it was able to defeat Guo Fengming and seize the county seat in Changting.[42] In Changting, the Red Fourth Army was able to rest even longer – seventeen days – before moving on. Leaving Changting, Mao and Zhu De went to Ruijin, where they were able to meet up with the remnants of Peng Dehuai's Fifth Army, which had been mauled trying to hold the Jinggangshan Base Area. Peng now led fewer than 300 soldiers.

As the Red Fourth Army crisscrossed the southern Jiangxi country-side, tensions mounted. As suggested above, the famous "Zhu–Mao" army was never the harmonious partnership depicted in the history books. Zhu was the one with the military background and his troops tended to be loyal to him. Moreover, he had brought more troops to the Jinggangshan than had Mao, giving him significant leverage. But Mao was the party representative who had been appointed by the Center. As strained as it was, party authority meant something. As a strong-willed person and head of the Front Committee, Mao was determined to exert control. If there was one thing he admired about the guerrilla move-ment in Donggu, it was that the military was under the absolute control of the party, something he hoped to duplicate. In the Jinggangshan, the tensions between Mao and Zhu could be kept under control, but leaving the Jinggangshan would bring these tensions to the fore, largely because without a base area all operations were military operations. There was not much a Front Committee, which was supposed to oversee party activities as well as military operations, could do.

The CCP's Sixth Party Congress was held in Moscow in June and July 1928. Shortly after that, the Party Center in Shanghai drafted the "February 7" letter to Mao and Zhu. This famous letter instructed the guerrilla leaders to (1) disperse their troops into small groups to mobil-ize the masses and (2) take leave of the army and come to Shanghai. This letter clearly expressed the concern of the Center that Mao and Zhu were beyond the control of the Center, and it wanted to recover

---

[42] Shi Zhongquan, "Cong 'zuozuodangshi' dao 'fajue dangshi'" (From "Looking at Party History" to "Developing Party History"), in Zhonggong Jiangxi shengwei dangshi yanjiushi et al., eds., *Donggu: Ganxinan geming genjudi shiliao xuanbian* (Selected Historical Materials on the Donggu and Southwest Jiangxi Revolutionary Base Area), 2 vols. (Beijing: Zhongyang wenxian chubanshe, 2007), vol. 1, pp. 5–6.

that control. Mao received the letter on April 3, 1929. Then in May one Liu Angong arrived from the center to take up a leading position in the Red Fourth Army. When he arrived, he gave a report on implementing the February 7 letter.[43]

Liu Angong's arrival changed party dynamics for two reasons. First, Liu had been sent not only as a messenger delivering documents but also as a "special envoy" (*teshi*) who was meant to stay on to supervise work. The instruction for Liu to remain with the Red Fourth Army was contrary to the previous directive to disperse the army into small units, but it was consistent with the Center's repeated efforts to exert more control over Mao and Zhu. The other reason why Liu's arrival changed party dynamics in Ruijin was because of the personal relationship between Zhu De and Liu. Liu was from Sichuan and had studied electrical engineering in Germany, where he had met Zhu De and had joined the Communist Third International and the Chinese Communist Party. Returning to China in 1924, he had first served as chief of staff for Yang Sen, the warlord in Sichuan where Zhu De also worked, and then in 1927 he had participated in the Nanchang Uprising. In 1928, after the failure of the Guangzhou Uprising, he had gone with Liu Bocheng to the Soviet Union for a year of training as an artillery officer. Upon his return to China, the Party Center used him as a special envoy, in this case sending him to oversee Mao and Zhu.

After Liu Angong arrived, he quickly discovered that Mao had abolished the Military Committee at the February 3 Luofuzhang Meeting (discussed in the previous chapter). The Military Committee had been replaced by the Political Department of the Red Fourth Army, and Mao became head of that department, concurrently with his position as party secretary of the Front Committee. In this way, Mao had concentrated power in his own hands and could directly oversee army movements.

Because Liu Angong had been sent from the Center, Mao quickly yielded his position as head of the Political Department to him.[44] With Liu asserting authority and no doubt talking with his old friend Zhu De, there was increasing talk among leaders of the Red Fourth Army about Mao's behavior. Mao was criticized for concentrating all power in his own hands, for abolishing the Military Committee as an

---

[43] *Mao Zedong nianpu*, vol. 1, pp. 272–273.
[44] This decision was made at a meeting held at Yudu on April 11.

"overlapping" organ, for asserting "patriarchal" authority, and for his ill-tempered verbal lashings of subordinates. In May, the Front Committee decided to restore the Military Committee, with Liu Angong taking over as head. Later that month, the Military Committee, under Liu's direction, decided that the Front Committee should only discuss the army's movements (*xingdong*) and nothing else.[45] This decision brought the tensions within the leadership to a breaking point. After Liu and Zhu De sent a report directly to the Center, without going through the Front Committee, Mao immediately pointed out this act of insubordination and sent his own letter to the Center. When the army took the town of Baisha on June 7, Mao immediately called a meeting for the next day.

Mao argued that there were three main issues. First, some people said that the party controlled too much and that too much power was concentrated in the Front Committee. Second, some people opposed the idea that party branches should manage everything, arguing that party branches were only for educating people. Finally, some people opposed the idea that individual freedoms should be restricted, and they demanded that party members should have a fair amount of freedom. Their position was that the party's authority was limited. Mao obviously disagreed with these positions, but the fact that they were raised at all showed that the firm hierarchical discipline of a Leninist party was not yet in place.

Zhu De disagreed with Mao. First, he argued that Marxism did not include the idea that the party should control everything as its highest principle. Second, he agreed with the idea that "all work belongs to the party branches," but he maintained that the Red Fourth Army did not uphold this principle because "all work is concentrated in the Front Committee." The Front Committee, he said, substituted for mass organizations when doing external work and replaced party committees at various levels when doing work within the party. Third, he argued that all party members should have iron discipline, but precisely on this point Mao Zedong did not fare well, freely expressing his views, castigating comrades without restraint, and not carrying out the

---

[45] Li Quan et al., "Junshi faxian: Zaokang huiyi kancheng Gutian huiyi qian zou qu (Discovering Military History: The Zaokang Meeting Can Be Called the Prelude to the Gutian Conference), *Jiefang junbao*, October 15, 2014, at www .81.cn/sydbt/2014-10/15/content_6179364.htm, accessed January 8, 2021.

instructions of the Center and the provincial party committees as he
should have.[46]

Mao replied that with the division between the Military Committee
and the Front Committee, his work had become impossible.
Discussions were unrealistic and, when decisions were made, they
could not be implemented because there still was disagreement.
Under such circumstances, the organizational principle of the Front
Committee directing things had come into question. "I cannot bear this
sort of untenable (*busheng busi*) responsibility and I ask that you
immediately replace me as secretary."[47]

In terms of the organizational chain of command, Mao won the day.
The Baisha meeting voted thirty-six to five to abolish the provisional
Military Committee.[48] In his June 14 letter to Lin Biao, Mao expressed
satisfaction. "Decisions based on the selfish desires of the individual" –
an apparent reference to Zhu De and Liu Angong – "will be rejected by
the masses. We need only look at the fact that at the meeting attended
by forty-one people, the Military Committee, which a minority of
comrades obstinately insisted on establishing, was abolished by
a vote of thirty-six to five. "[49] But what Mao won in organizational
terms, he lost in personal prestige. Only hours before the meeting, Lin
Biao had sent Mao a vitriolic letter, the text of which has never been
published. The timing suggests that the letter had been solicited. Lin's
letter was apparently a personal attack on Zhu De, declaring that there
were "a few leading comrades whose ambitions were vast, whose
vanity has reached an extreme." These people, Lin wrote, had used
"all sorts of feudal" methods to form "invisible cliques" and had
"egotistically launched attacks on other comrades."[50]

In his response to Lin, which is included in Mao's *Selected Works* as
"A Single Spark Can Start a Prairie Fire," Mao gave vent to his own
vitriol. He declared that the chief problem in the Red Fourth Army was
the struggle between "individualism," which he clearly identified with
Zhu De, and "party leadership," which he clearly identified with
himself. Tracing the problems in the Red Fourth Army back to its
creation, Mao declared that the party was not able to establish the
"absolute power of command" because of the "enormous power of the

[46] Xiao Ke, *Zhu Mao hongjun ceji*, p. 91.   [47] Ibid., p. 276.   [48] Ibid., p. 90.
[49] Mao Zedong, "Letter to Lin Biao," translated in Schram, *Mao's Road to Power*,
     vol. 3, pp. 177–189.
[50] Li Quan et al., "Junshi faxian."

individual." "The party," Mao wrote, "dared not attempt to allocate and transfer the guns." The issue of military equipment – guns – was clearly central to the argument between Zhu and Mao. Mao had said that in Donggu the military had to ask about every bullet; he clearly wanted the same sort of authority over Zhu De's forces. Zhu's forces were roughly double the size of those commanded by Mao, and the implicit charge was that Mao wanted to direct the better equipment to his own forces.

Addressing the issue of the Front Committee, which had led to the convening of the Baisha meeting, Mao declared that "[w]hat they really want is to have a leading organ in their hands."[51] This accusation got to the heart of the dispute, namely who was in charge. The Military Committee had been re-established with the aim of reducing the personal power of Mao more than reducing the power of the Front Committee per se.

At another meeting several days after the Baisha conference, Mao openly expressed such sentiments, saying, "The main issue in the party of the Red Fourth Army is that of individual leadership or party leadership." This was, he maintained, "the main thread of the history of the Red Army." As soon as Mao expressed this view, Xiao Ke recalls, "the arguments in the Red Fourth Army became even more heated."[52]

The Seventh Representative Meeting of the Red Fourth Army

With Mao resigning from his position, Chen Yi took over as acting secretary of the Front Committee and he began to prepare materials for the Seventh Representative Meeting of the Red Fourth Army, which was convened on June 22 at Longyan in Fujian province. Xiao Ke, then a regimental commander and later a full general, recalls the atmosphere in the Red Army at the time. It was a period, he writes, when issues were debated fully and at length. The Sixth Party Congress, the materials of which had only recently reached the Red Fourth Army, had reiterated that democratic centralism meant that, "before a decision is made, all questions in dispute can be freely discussed." "At the time," Xiao recalls, "there was no avoidance of arguments within the party." "So

---

[51] Mao Zedong, "Letter to Lin Biao," translated in Schram, *Mao's Road to Power*, vol. 3, p. 184.
[52] Xiao Ke, *Zhu Mao hongjun ceji*, p. 91.

most people, out of their concern and support for the party, let their personal views be known and they engaged in arguments."[53] At the Seventh Representative Meeting, arguments flowed freely.

The Front Committee suggested that, as head of the Political Department of the Red Fourth Army, Chen Yi chair the meeting. Chen gave a work report, and Mao and Zhu addressed the meeting. Finally, the meeting passed the "Resolution of the Seventh Representative Congress of the Red Fourth Army" (*Hongjun disijun diqici daibiao dahui jueyi'an*) and selected a new Front Committee. One of the chief issues discussed at the Seventh Representative Meeting was whether the "party controls everything" (*dangguan yiqie*). This slogan could not be found when consulting the central documents and especially the resolution of the Sixth Party Congress. In an evident effort to reach compromise, it was argued that this slogan was not contradictory to the organizational principle of the party, so it could be affirmed. But at the same time, it was declared that because it was not clear and it was subject to misunderstanding, the slogan should not be used. But the meeting did agree, however, that the army should be under the leadership of the party.

On the question of the relationship between the Military Committee, if one were to be established, and the Front Committee, the resolution recognized that the Military Committee was subordinate to the Front Committee and that Military Committee resolutions required approval by the Front Committee. The resolution further stated that some comrades demanded that the Military Committee be re-established, but under the present circumstances this would be redundant, so it should not be re-established.[54]

However, the Seventh Representative Meeting then voted on the membership of the Front Committee. Mao was re-elected to the Front Committee – but not as its secretary. This was a very personal rebuke of Mao as leader. The fact of the matter is that by the time of the meeting, there was much opposition to Mao, especially from Zhu De and his followers. Mao was disliked for his overbearing personality, his constant tongue-lashing of subordinates, and his desire to intervene in everything – every bullet and every gun. No doubt there is some truth to Lin Biao's charge that Zhu De's forces engaged in some "feudal" traditions of the warlord armies, particularly the bonds of personal

---

[53] Ibid., p. 89.   [54] Ibid., p. 96.

loyalty rather than the more abstract notions of loyalty to the party, but Mao's leadership was hardly abstract either.

At first, it seems that the two decisions – to agree with Mao to abolish the Military Committee and then to remove Mao as secretary – are contradictory, but if one assumes that the establishment of the Military Committee was intended to weaken Mao's power, then it seems apparent that Mao's "victory" in the first vote was pyrrhic. The intent all along had been to weaken or remove Mao, a goal achieved by the second vote. Zhu De and his followers were happy to have the party in charge but they were not happy to have Mao in charge of the party. The vote to oust Mao from the leadership of the Front Committee was a sharp rebuke of the strong-willed, hot-tempered leader. Chen Yi had sided with Zhu De against Mao, but he nevertheless was something of a compromise candidate as he could get along with both Zhu De and Mao.

As secretary, Chen Yi gave Mao a serious inner-party warning and Zhu a written warning, but both were instructed to continue in their positions. Criticizing both Mao and Zhu maintained a certain balance, but Mao was clearly angered at being ousted from his position. He was also apparently sick with malaria, but it is difficult to determine the degree to which his illness was political. In any event, on July 8, Mao mounted his horse and left the Red Army with his wife, He Zizhen, and a few aides to go to Jiaoyang in Shanghang county, in western Fujian, to recuperate and to deal with party affairs there.[55]

The September Letter and the Gutian Conference

At the end of the month, the Front Committee convened another meeting to discuss military strategy, but Mao declined to participate. When this meeting concluded, Chen Yi left to report on the situation to Shanghai. On his way to Shanghai, Chen stopped in Jiaoyang and had a long conversation with Mao, before proceeding through Xiamen to Hong Kong and on to Shanghai by boat.[56]

When Chen reached Shanghai, he had long talks with Zhou Enlai and Li Lisan. Xiang Zhongfa, a worker, had been named chairman of

[55] *Chen Yi zhuan* (Biography of Chen Yi) (Beijing: Dangdai Zhongguo chubanshe, 1991), p. 296.
[56] Ibid., p. 299.

the Politburo in July 1928, but he and other members of the Central Committee delegated Zhou and Li to handle the discussions. Chen prepared several reports that were discussed extensively with Zhou.[57] One of the reports, "The History of Zhu and Mao Army and Their Circumstances," has never been made public.

Army–party relations were clearly a major topic of discussion. Chen told Zhou, "Political workers and military officers frequently have disputes, just as in the old days in the National Revolutionary Army." According to Chen, there were four ways in which political workers and military officers could interact:

(1) a political worker can be equal to a military officer (just like a husband and wife), with the result that they argue every day; (2) the political worker's authority can be restricted to just political training, but in this way the military officer's authority is too great, and the political worker becomes like a concubine; (3) as in the Jiangxi Red Army's Second Regiment [this is a reference to Li Wenlin's troops], the military officer must take orders from the political worker, and in this way it becomes a father–son type of relation; or (4) the military officer and the political worker are equal, but the party secretary always dominates and all work is accountable to the party branch.

The personal relationship between Mao and Zhu certainly needed to be worked out, but the critical issue for Zhou and the Center was the relationship between the party and the military, and on this issue there could be no doubt which way Zhou would come down.

Ultimately, the Center's response, which came in a document known as the "September Letter," backed Mao. It called for Mao to be restored as secretary of the Front Committee, and it declared, "All the authority of the party should be concentrated in the leading organ of the Front Committee. This is correct, and absolutely must not be shaken. One should not mechanically use terms like 'patriarchal system' to weaken the authority of the leading organ or as a cover for ultra-democracy." At the time, the Comintern was opposing "ultra-democracy," so the September Letter opposed the sort of open discussion and debate that the Red Fourth Army had had at Baisha and at the Seventh Representative Meeting. The September Letter stated,

With regard to all issues, without question, the Front Committee should first make a decision and then give it to lower levels for discussion. It absolutely

---

[57] Chen Yi, "Guanyu Zhu Mao jun de lishi jiqi zhuangkuang de baogao."

should not first solicit the agreement of the lower levels and it should make a decision before the lower levels have expressed their opinions ... In this [way, of the lower levels first expressing their opinions], the phenomenon of ultra-democracy is extended to an extreme.[58]

The most sensitive part of the letter, the ninth and final section, has never been made public, but it is known that it discussed the relations between Mao Zedong and Zhu De. Apparently, both were criticized, and it was this relatively balanced treatment that made the letter acceptable to Zhu. It no doubt helped that Zhu and Zhou were close (Zhou had introduced Zhu into the party), and this may have eased the pain of patching relations with Mao.

Chen took the letter back with him, meeting up with Zhu De on October 22, and Zhu accepted the decision of the Center. Having discussed the issues extensively with Zhu, the Front Committee held a meeting on November 18 to build a consensus, and then Chen Yi went to Jiaoyang and asked Mao to return and again take up the position of secretary. After listening to Chen Yi, Mao said that his illness was better by one-half, and on November 28, he wrote to the Center to say that he had returned and had resumed his duties.[59]

Barely back in power, Mao convened the Ninth Representative Conference of the Red Fourth Army, better known as the Gutian Conference, on December 28–29. The issue that had set off the confrontation between Mao and Zhu was whether there were any limits on the party's power over the military. Zhu had no problem with party authority but he questioned whether it extended to "every bullet and gun." Could there not be a sphere in which the military could make its own decisions, a division of responsibilities? The Gutian Conference answered such questions in the negative. The Resolution adopted by the conference excoriated "ultra-democracy," stating that it was rooted in the "individual aversion of the petty bourgeoisie." Such thinking led to the "lack of organizational consciousness" and the "failure of the minority to submit to the majority." The Gutian Conference aimed to impose far greater discipline on the party and

---

[58] "Zhongyang gei hongjun disijun qianwei de zhishixin" (Letter of Instruction from the Center to the Front Committee of the Red Army's Fourth Army), in Zhongyang dang'an guan, ed., *Zhonggong zhongyang wenjian xuanji* (Selected Central Committee Documents of the CCP) (Beijing: Zhonggong zhongyang dangxiao chubanshe, 1989), vol. 5, p. 486.

[59] *Chen Yi zhuan*, pp. 316–317.

the army, and in doing so, it took an important step in the building of a Leninist system.[60]

More than relations between the party and the army, the Gutian Conference put into place a system in which authority was extended from the top down. This meeting was, after all, a "representative" conference. As we have just seen, the Seventh Representative Meeting had voted Mao out of his position as secretary. Indeed, before this time, the leaders of special committees (*tewei*) and military heads were decided by votes of representative conferences.[61] Even if these conferences were not democratic in any real sense, at least symbolically they indicated that authority was bestowed from the bottom up. This conference was different. It still voted, but the decision to have Mao as secretary was decided before the meeting was convened. It had, in fact, been decided by Zhou Enlai and conveyed in the September Letter – implicitly signifying that the authority of leaders derived from the top down. Indeed, after the Gutian Conference, there were no more representative meetings of the Red Army and there was no more voting.[62] Hierarchy was emphasized.

The Gutian Conference clearly exceeded the bounds of the September Letter on one important issue. The September Letter had specified that when the army was in an area where a soviet government had been established, the soviet should direct the military. The party should not manage the army directly but only through the party groups (*dangzu*) in the army. The Gutian Resolution says nothing about soviets and their role in managing the military.[63] Mao had emphasized party authority over the army, and that would remain.

Conclusion

In 1927, the CCP, with guidance from the Comintern, interpreted the bloody events of that spring – Chiang Kai-shek's violent coup and Xu Keqiang's murderous Horse Day crackdown – through the prism of Russia's history. It concluded that these setbacks, however devastating

[60] "Draft Resolution of the Ninth Congress of the Chinese Communist Party in the Fourth Red Army," translated in Schram, *Mao's Road to Power*, vol. 3, pp. 195–230.
[61] Ying Xing, "Hongsijun lingdao jigou de bianhua yu zhuli hongjun de zuzhi xingshi," p. 29.
[62] Ibid., p. 31.   [63] Ibid., p. 32.

they were for the party, did not mean that the "high tide" of revolution had passed. On the contrary, insurrections set off throughout the country would, it presumed, arouse the masses and lead the CCP to nationwide victory. Despite the use of military force in the Nanchang and Guangzhou uprisings, the party saw the path to victory not as coming from military conquest *à la* Northern Expedition, but rather coming from arousing the revolutionary fervor of the masses. But it was unlikely that insurrections, such as that in Donggu, could inspire the nation (or even one province), to rise up and sweep away "feudal" power. Donggu's success was rooted in its localness, and its localness prevented it from leading to nationwide success.

Mao was more clear-sighted about the use of violence and less interested in winning over the masses than is usually suggested. His colleagues in the leadership of the CCP criticized him repeatedly for his emphasis on military force, but Mao repeated his mantra about power growing out of the barrel of a gun and, when his efforts to take Changsha failed, he readily "went up the mountains." Mao allied with Yuan Wencai and Wang Zuo, but in the final analysis, he was an outsider and a military leader, albeit not a trained military leader. Mao's policies were radical – land was confiscated and redistributed – but such policies failed to win adherents. He was unsuccessful in recruiting peasants from the area. As he put it, "the Red Army simply could not find any peasants from the Hunan–Jiangxi border area."[64]

Zhu De brought an important infusion of military strength to the Jinggangshan that no doubt allowed the base area to survive, at least for a while. But Zhu De's troops were never really merged with Mao's, and Mao's troops were never really merged with those of Yuan Wencai and Wang Zuo. They each had their own regiment, with Mao resenting Zhu De's "feudal" control over his own troops. These tensions burst out in the open in June 1929 at the Baisha meeting and the subsequent Seventh Representative Meeting of the Red Fourth Army. The Party Center in Shanghai reaffirmed Mao's authority and Mao was able to assert his control over the military at the Gutian Conference. This accomplishment should not be underestimated. It is not easy to combine party authority and military expertise; the GMD's effort to build

---

[64] Mao Zedong, "Jinggangshan de douzheng (1928 nian shiyiyue ershiwu ri)," vol. 1, p. 63, quoted in Tang Lianying, Ye Fulin, and Ding Renxiang, *Donggu geming genjudi shilu*, p. 275.

a party army was far less successful.[65] Mao's model was light years away from what the Party Center had been thinking in the wake of Chiang's coup.

When Mao began exploring his own revolutionary path, he was still under the authority of the Hunan Party Committee. Then he accepted the idea that he would be under the authority of the Hunan Party Committee when in Hunan, but that he would be under the authority of the Jiangxi Party Committee when in Jiangxi. When Li Weihan wrote Mao in June 1929 to support the establishment of a Front Committee, Mao readily accepted Li's suggestion because Li's letter implicitly endorsed the idea that Mao and his troops would report directly to Shanghai, not to a local party committee. Therefore, by late 1929, Mao had developed an organization that reported only to the Party Center, which, fortunately for Mao, was far away in Shanghai. At the Gutian Conference, Mao had extended his party control over Zhu De and his army. Moreover, the sort of "ultra-democracy" that had burst out at the Baisha meeting and the Seventh Representative Meeting was not to reappear. Zhou Enlai had decreed that party organizations should make decisions and then discuss them in wider circles, not the other way around. Decision making should be top-down. Democratic centralism was increasingly tilted in favor of centralism. The CCP was a very different party organization than it had been before 1927 or even before 1929. It was far more hierarchical, more disciplined, and more militarized. There were still multiple centers of power, and one unit did not necessarily obey another, but the party, or at least Mao's part of the party, was on its way to becoming a real Leninist party. It still did not have a base area, and Mao's model still had not been extended throughout the party. The quest for such a base and wider party unity would lead it to violent conflict with the Donggu Base Area.

[65] William Wei, *Counterrevolution in China: The Nationalists in Jiangxi during the Soviet Period* (Ann Arbor: University of Michigan Press, 1985).

4 | Mao versus Local Forces
The Futian Rebellion

Starting in 1927, the Donggu revolutionary movement, following the Center's call for local uprisings, began to build an organization and military that had remarkable success, especially when contrasted with the general failure of such uprisings throughout the rest of the province. The Donggu movement was certainly revolutionary and it was violent, but it was also rooted in local society and its success grew out of the particularities of Donggu – its physical isolation, strong school and familial ties among its leaders, and shared characteristics of having ties to local society as well as to the broader revolutionary thinking outside Donggu. Although the Donggu movement expanded to cover some twenty-three townships, it is difficult to imagine it expanding much beyond its immediate environs. It was, after all, a local movement.

Mao's revolutionary redoubt in the Jinggangshan, in contrast, was never a local movement. Mao, with the co-operation of bandits Yuan Wencai and Wang Zuo, was able to expand his area of control, organize peasants, and carry out land reform, but he was never rooted in local society in the way Lai Jingbang and Li Wenlin were in Donggu. Mao was focused on national revolution, but he realized that tensions existed between the revolution he envisioned and the local society. Recall his statement: "The most troublesome are not the despotic gentry, but the intermediate classes."[1] Unless local society were revolutionized and reorganized in ways far beyond what local leaders had in mind, Mao could not establish a base area.

Although a clash between Mao's more centralized approach and locally organized forces was no doubt inevitable, there is nevertheless considerable irony in what eventually became a gruesome story. First

---

[1] Mao Zedong, "Report of the Jinggangshan Front Committee to the Central Committee," in Stuart R. Schram, ed., *Mao's Road to Power: Revolutionary Writings, 1912–49*, vol. 3: *From the Jinggangshan to the Establishment of the Jiangxi Soviets, July 1927–December 1930* (Armonk, NY: M.E. Sharpe, 1995), pp. 103–104.

and foremost, Li Wenlin and his local forces based in Donggu had quite literally saved Mao and his Red Fourth Army from annihilation. Moreover, Li had considered joining Mao's forces before being called back by Feng Ren and the West Jiangxi Special Committee. In addition, there was a personal relationship between Li Wenlin and Zhu De. They had worked together when Li had taught in the Nanchang Military Education Group under Zhu De. That group would eventually help break up the AB Corps in Nanchang (see below). Then, in the following year, Li would join the Nanchang Uprising and accompany the withdrawing troops as they headed south to Guangdong in hopes of establishing a base there. In short, a superficial look at these two revolutionary movements suggests that Li Wenlin might have been a strong ally of Mao in western Jiangxi. If Mao had stayed away from the area, they might well have co-operated, but when Mao returned to western Jiangxi in early 1930, tensions quickly mounted.

Return to Western Jiangxi

The sequence that set in motion the clash between Mao's outside forces and Li Wenlin's local forces might be dated from when, in September 1929, Feng Ren was transferred from secretary of the West Jiangxi Special Committee to become an inspector (*xunshiyuan*) of the West Jiangxi Special Committee, and was replaced as secretary by one Wang Baiyuan. Wang did not have the same experience and resources as Feng, so real power fell to Liu Shiqi, the chief secretary (*mishuzhang*) of the party committee. Then, in November 1929, the special committee was largely broken up by the GMD and Wang Baiyuan fled. Hence Liu Shiqi took over as party secretary.[2]

Liu Shiqi was from Hunan, and it was unusual for an outsider to take control of a local special committee, but Liu was no ordinary outsider. Following the Horse Day massacre in Hunan, the Center had sent him to Jiangxi in June 1928. There, he participated in restoring the party organization following the failure of the Nanchang Uprising and then he became a member of the Jiangxi Party Committee, a special envoy (*tepaiyuan*) to the North Jiangxi Special Committee, and then chief

---

[2]   Ying Xing, "Suqu difang ganbu, hongse wuzhuang yu zuzhi xingtai" (Local Cadres in the Soviet Area, Red Armed Forces, and the Organizational Circumstances), *Kaifang shidai*, no. 6 (2015), p. 67.

secretary of the provincial party committee. In other words, even though he was an outsider, he had held a number of important positions in the party organization, and he knew Jiangxi well. In May 1929 he was appointed chief secretary of the West Jiangxi Special Committee.

Perhaps more important, in May 1929 Liu Shiqi married He Yi, He Zizhen's younger sister, thus becoming Mao Zedong's brother-in-law. This obviously gave him a connection to the most powerful revolutionary force in the province and thus strengthened his position on the special committee.[3]

One of Liu Shiqi's primary goals was land reform, and it was this focus that would bring him into conflict with the Donggu organization.

On September 18, 1929, the Party Center – meaning primarily Li Lisan – issued a notice demanding that the soviet areas expand their armed forces and go on the attack. This approach of using the still-undeveloped military forces of the CCP to attack the cities was the chief hallmark of what would later become the so-called Li Lisan line. One Pan Xinyuan, who was an inspector, brought the Center's notice to Jiangxi and then joined a subsequent meeting of the West Jiangxi Special Committee held in Yuntian. Perhaps not surprisingly, the committee adopted a resolution to seize Ji'an, a move that would require consolidating military forces in the area. This resolution was the origin of the idea to combine the Second and Fourth Regiments, the core of Li Wenlin's local forces, to form a new Sixth Army.[4] A meeting the following January brought together representatives from the West Jiangxi Special Committee, the Hunan–Jiangxi Border Special Committee, and the military committee of Peng Dehuai's Fifth Army, which decided that local forces in Jiangxi should be reorganized as the Sixth Army. Peng Dehuai's old friend and associate, Huang Gonglüe, was named commander. Liu Shiqi was appointed party representative, and Mao's brother, Mao Zetan, was named head of the political department. Thus began an effort by outsiders to command local forces.

The decision to organize the Sixth Army, which would be confirmed at the February 7 Meeting (to be discussed below), marked the beginning of a growing rift between Mao and Li Wenlin. Li and other local leaders argued that the decision to create the Sixth Army had to be

---

[3] Ibid.   [4] Ibid., p. 69.

approved by the Party Center as well as by the provincial party committee,[5] but Mao confirmed the appointments of Huang Gonglüe, Liu Shiqi, and his brother Mao Zetan on his own. Mao tried to balance this assertion of power, at least temporarily, by appointing Li Wenlin and other local Jiangxi leaders as heads of the three brigades (*lü*) under the Sixth Army. But Mao would soon undermine Li Wenlin even further by moving him out of the regular army to be secretary of the military committee of the Southwest Jiangxi Special Committee. Li's former position as brigade commander was filled by Mao's close associate, Li Shaojiu, who could not get along with Li Wenlin would soon play a critical role in the Futian Rebellion.[6] This reorganization of military forces put outsiders from Hunan in charge of local forces. Li Wenlin protested on procedural grounds, but the issue was about control over local forces.

In addition to organizing the Sixth Army, Liu Shiqi and the West Jiangxi Special Committee began to support a more radical land redistribution policy. They advocated redistributing land on a per capita basis. This policy would undercut the interests of small landlords and rich peasants, who made up the bulk of the Donggu leadership, and would thus bring Liu Shiqi and Mao Zedong into conflict with the local leaders.

On November 17 – after the decision to form the Sixth Army but before it had actually happened – the Party Center in Shanghai reversed itself, sending an urgent telegram to the Jiangxi Party Committee telling it not to take action in response to uprisings in several areas. A newly prudent Center told the Jiangxi Party Committee that it had overestimated the situation: "Now we are moving toward a revolutionary high tide; now is not the time that we have already reached a revolutionary high tide."[7]

This message certainly affected the attitude of Jiang Hanbo, an inspector from the Jiangxi Party Committee who was then in western Jiangxi. He, too, had been at the Yuntian Meeting and had had doubts

---

[5] Gao Hua, "'Su AB tuan' shijian de lishi kaocha" (Historical Investigation into the Suppression of the AB Corps), in Gao Hua, *Lishi biji* (History Notes), 2 vols. (Hong Kong: Oxford University Press, 2014), vol. 1, p. 108.

[6] Chen Yongfa, "Zhonggong zaoqi sufan de jiantao: AB tuan an, 1930–1932" (An Examination into the CCP's Early Suppression: The Case of the AB Corps, 1930–1932), *Zhongyang yanjiuyuan, jindaishi yanjiu jikan*, no. 17, pt. 1 (June 1988), p. 207.

[7] Ibid.

about the decision to consolidate military forces. Part of his concern was procedural. He believed that the proposal to create the Sixth Army should be approved by the provincial and central authorities. He also had doubts about Liu Shiqi's proposal to adopt land redistribution on a per capita basis, as well as about the urgency to attack Ji'an. Receiving the urgent telegram from the Center reinforced his views. So, too, did going to Yanfu, an area west of the Gan river and north of Ji'an city. In Yanfu, he spoke with party leaders from that area. These leaders were very locally oriented. Also, they had all come from a relatively wealthy stratum, and they were opposed to the sort of radical land reform that Liu Shiqi was proposing. Jiang Hanbo was convinced and began to staunchly oppose the consolidation of forces.[8]

The February 7 Meeting (1930)

The February 7 Meeting was one of the major turning points in the evolution of the CCP. It would greatly expand Mao's authority and would mark an important escalation in the evolving tensions between the external forces of Mao and the local forces of Donggu that would culminate in the Futian Rebellion. At the time, there were three GMD armies, from Fujian, Guangdong, and Jiangxi, converging on Mao's position in western Fujian, so Mao and Zhu led the Red Fourth Army west across Jiangxi to the Donggu area. They stopped in the town of Beitou, a wealthy ancient town not far from Futian where the Liang clan had fostered a long line of scholars, producing six *jinshi*, or metropolitan, degree holders. More important from a revolutionary perspective, Beitou was where the West Jiangxi Special Committee had moved its headquarters after many of its leaders were seized in their previous location in the city of Ji'an. About fifty representatives from the Red Fourth Army Front Committee, the Sixth Army, the Southwest Jiangxi Special Committee, and various action committees and county party organizations attended the February 7 Meeting. Peng Dehuai's Fifth Army was stuck on the west side of the Gan river, so he asked his old friend Huang Gonglüe of the newly formed Sixth Army to represent him.[9] The authority of Mao's Front Committee to call such a meeting

---

[8] Ibid.
[9] Yu Boliu and Ling Buji, *Zhongyang suqu shi* (History of the Central Soviet) (Nanchang: Jiangxi renmin chubanshe, 2001), vol. 1, p. 201. On the details of the formation of the Southwest Jiangxi Special Committee, see Zhou Ming,

was dubious, and the decision to upgrade the Front Committee to a General Front Committee, which then took charge of all local forces, was even more suspect.

Besides confirming the creation of the Sixth Army and the decision to place all three armies (Mao's Red Fourth Army, Peng's Fifth Army, and Huang Gonglüe's Sixth Army) under Mao's General Front Committee, the February 7 Meeting made two other important decisions. First, the meeting confirmed the merger of the West Jiangxi Special Committee with the South Jiangxi Special Committee to form a new Southwest Jiangxi Special Committee. Liu Shiqi was named secretary. Second, the meeting debated and ultimately passed a new Land Law, the implementation of which would inaugurate a period of violence that would culminate in the suppression of the so-called AB Corps and lead to the Futian Rebellion.

The Land Law was the most controversial measure. In some ways, the new Land Law was an improvement over Mao's policy in the Jinggangshan. Mao's policy had been to confiscate all land, which Mao later admitted had been a failure; instead, the new Land Law confirmed private ownership. But, and this is a very important but, Mao called for equal distribution of land rather than distribution according to labor power. Back in 1927 Mao had seemed indifferent as to how land was to be distributed, but now he was very opposed to distributing land according to labor power.[10] Jiang Hanbo and Li Wenlin strongly opposed the new law. Jiang argued that distributing land according to labor would promote production. Those families with greater labor power would be able to use more land productively, while those with little labor power would be unable to use the extra land if it were distributed equally on a per capita basis as Mao wanted. Mao was quite familiar with the class implications of dividing the land

---

"Ganxinan tewei de chengli he yanbian" (The Establishment and Evolution of the Jiangxi Southwest Special Committee), *Jindaishi yanjiu*, no. 6 (1984), pp. 250–254.

[10] In an August 20, 1927, letter to the Central Committee, Mao advocated confiscating all land and letting the peasant associations distribute it "in accordance with the two criteria of 'labor power' and 'consumption' [i.e., per capita]." See Schram, *Mao's Road to Power*, vol. 3, p. 40. In a report from November 1928, Mao writes that the criterion for land distribution in the Jinggangshan base used to be that "everyone, male or female, old or young, got an equal share." But, he goes on, "we have switched to the method of the Central Committee, which takes labor power as the criterion." See ibid., p. 105.

according to labor power, having already encountered the problem in the Jinggangshan Base Area. He knew that rich peasants wanted the land to be divided according to labor power.[11] Reflecting Mao's views, Liu Shiqi argued that Jiang Hanbo "was completely taking the rural bourgeois class (rich peasant) line." The task at present, Liu said, was to win over the masses. Distributing land according to labor power would favor the rich peasants and landlords. In other words, Liu and Mao were looking for a way to mobilize the peasants against the rich peasants and landlords, the very people who made up the backbone of the leadership of the Donggu Revolutionary Base Area.[12]

Liu Shiqi was certainly right that distributing land according to labor power would favor the power of the local elites, but Jiang Hanbo and Li Wenlin were also right that distributing land according to labor power would generate greater economic growth. Mao, however, was less concerned with economic growth than he was with political power. Without pushing aside local cadres, there would be no way for Mao and his movement to take root in this area. Just as other governments had discovered, the only way to control a given area was to work through the local elite. Mao would not tolerate this situation. He wanted his power to extend right down to the grassroots. Attacking the local elite – Communists though they were – was the only way.

Closely associated with this attack on the local power structure was the need to mobilize the peasants. Peasants, as we have seen, were not always easy to mobilize. Landless laborers, vagrants and bandits were one thing, but building a power base was another. Furthermore, it was difficult to penetrate peasant society. Communist organizers could and did take up acceptable roles such as schoolteachers, but these positions were not sufficient to overturn the local power structure, as Li Lisan and Mao had discovered to their dismay in Anyuan.[13] The forces of family clans and religion were too powerful. People like Li Wenlin

---

[11] In the November 1928 report, Mao notes, "The rich peasants among the owner-peasants have put forth the demand that productive capacity should be taken as the criterion." See ibid., p. 105.

[12] "Liu Shiqi tongzhi gei Zeng Juefei tongzhi xin" (Letter from Comrade Liu Shiqi to Comrade Zeng Juefei), in Jiangxisheng dang'an guan and Zhonggong Jiangxi shengwei dangxiao dangshi jiaoyanshi, *Zhongyang geming genjudi shiliao xuanbian* (Selected Historical Materials on the Central Revolutionary Base Area), 3 vols. (Nanchang: Jiangxi renmin chubanshe, 1982), vol. 1, p. 573.

[13] Elizabeth J. Perry, *Anyuan: Mining China's Revolutionary Tradition* (Berkeley: University of California Press, 2012).

Figure 4.1 The room where the February 7 Meeting was held

could be committed Communists, but their visions of revolution were nowhere near what Mao had in mind.

Hence, Mao and Jiang Hanbo argued. Mao not only won the argument but also led the effort to expel Jiang from the Communist Party. Mao had no authority to expel Jiang from the party, so the resolution doing so stated that the action had been taken pending approval by higher levels.[14] Of course, the Jiangxi Party Committee did not exist at that time, so it is not clear whether or when any action was taken against Jiang. Nevertheless, he removed himself from politics, leaving the area and going into education.

The argument about land redistribution reflected a deeper and more serious issue – who was in control of the local party organizations. Liu Shiqi and Mao insisted that the party organizations in western and southern Jiangxi were filled with landlords and rich peasants and that such a situation constituted a "serious crisis." Party policies were "completely opportunist." "Opportunism," of course was the charge that had been leveled against Chen Duxiu at the Emergency Meeting in 1927; here Mao was introducing an ideological "line" to attack local party leaders who disagreed with him.[15] If landlords and rich peasants were not expelled from the party, Mao argued, the revolution would fail. It was necessary to quickly bolshevize the party, and it was necessary to immediately confiscate all land from landlords and rich peasants, including land of owner–cultivators, so that it could be distributed equally. The idea was to mobilize the poor peasants against the party leaders in this part of China. As Yu Boliu and Ling Buji explain, many of these leaders had come from wealthy families, but once they entered the party, they had led the peasants in revolution, sometimes even killing members of their own families.[16] This explanation may be exaggerated, as peasant protests in the area had in fact been fairly mild – generally limited to resisting rent payments and taxes. In any case, it is clear that the demand to redistribute land on a per capita basis was linked to the criticism of the local leadership for being from small landlord and rich peasant families. As Liu Shiqi explained in a letter to Jiang Hanbo, it was more important to "win over the masses" (*zhengqu minzhong*) than it was to "expand production" (*fazhan shengchan*).[17]

In order to achieve these goals, the meeting declared, it was necessary to expand the responsibilities of the Front Committee, but doing so required the establishment of a military committee. This decision may

[14] "Qianwei kaichu Jiang Hanbo dangji jueyi" (The Front Committee Expels Jiang Hanbo from the Party), in Jiangxisheng dang'an guan and Zhonggong Jiangxi shengwei dangxiao dangshi jiaoyanshi, *Zhongyang geming genjudi shiliao xuanbian*, vol. 1, pp. 576–578; and "Liu Shiqi tongzhi gei Zeng Juefei tongzhi xin."

[15] Gao Hua, "'Su AB tuan' shijian de lishi kaocha, 1930–1932," p. 110.

[16] Yu Boliu and Ling Buji, *Zhongyang suqu shi*, vol. 1, p. 204.

[17] "Liu Shiqi tongzhi gei Zeng Juefei tongzhi xin," p. 574.

seem surprising given that this was precisely the issue over which Zhu De and Mao had argued the previous summer, but both the Fifth and Sixth Armies had military committees, so Mao simply adopted their system, putting his new military committee on top.[18] The standing committee of the newly reorganized General Front Committee that would direct this military committee consisted of Mao as secretary and Zeng Shan, Liu Shiqi, Zhu De, and Pan Xinyuan, the inspector who had supported Liu Shiqi at the Yuntian Meeting that had decided on the formation of the Sixth Army.[19]

Zeng Shan is an interesting and important figure in the development of the CCP in Jiangxi. Zeng was born in Yonghe, Ji'an county, in 1899. From this background he might easily have joined one of the local guerrilla forces, perhaps one of Li Wenlin's regiments, and been one of those purged rather than one of those doing the purging. He is one of those figures that make generalizations about "locals" and "outsiders" difficult; although the distinction is real and important, there were exceptions. Zeng Shan received very little formal education, but his father was a *xiucai* under the Qing examination system, and his older brother, Zeng Yansheng, attended Shanghai University, where he joined the Communist Party. Zeng Yansheng participated in the Nanchang Uprising and then returned to the Ji'an area, where he became party secretary of the South Jiangxi Special Committee and then secretary of the Ganzhou Special Committee. He was arrested in March 1928 and executed.[20] Zeng Shan followed in his older brother's footsteps. He, too, participated in the Nanchang Uprising and then followed the defeated troops southward to Guangdong, where he participated in the Guangzhou Uprising in December 1927. In spring 1928 he returned to the Ji'an area to organize the peasants. In January 1929 he was appointed secretary of the West Jiangxi Special Committee. It was after Mao and Zhu left Donggu in February 1928 that Zeng followed the Front Committee, finally meeting up with Mao

[18] Gu Zexu, *Zhu De biezhuan: Yu Mao Zedong de enen yuanyuan* (Unauthorized Biography of Zhu De: Gratitude and Resentment with Mao Zedong), 2 vols. (Hong Kong: Tianxing chubanshe, 2020), vol. 1, p. 309.

[19] "Qianwei tonggao, diyihao" (Front Committee No. 1 Notice), in Jiangxisheng dang'an guan and Zhonggong Jiangxi shengwei dangxiao dangshi jiaoyanshi, *Zhongyang geming genjudi shiliao xuanbian*, vol. 2, pp. 172–174.

[20] Liu Mianyu, *Zeng Shan zhe yisheng* (Zeng Shan's life) (Nanchang: Jiangxi renmin chubanshe, 2015); "Zeng Yansheng," at https://baike.baidu.com/item/ %E6%9B%BE%E5%BB%B6%E7%94%9F, accessed January 11, 2021.

in March 1929. At a meeting in Chanting on March 20, he was added as a member of the Front Committee. When the Red Fourth Army began its guerrilla activities in Fujian, Zeng returned to Ji'an. In May Zeng was elected to the standing committee of the West Jiangxi Special Committee, which was then under the direction of Feng Ren. It was Feng who gave Zeng the name Shan, changing his name from Zeng Rubo, and sending him to Yanfu district to serve as party secretary.[21] From Mao's point of view, it was obviously helpful to have somebody well versed in local politics to help as he tried to develop his own power in the area. Zeng would emerge as a key figure in the purge of the AB Corps in 1930. In the 1950s he served as minister of the interior, but today he is remembered mostly as the father of Zeng Qinghong, a key aide to Jiang Zemin and later a member of the Politburo and its standing committee.

The February 7 Meeting concluded by taking one final action that marked the opening of a new phase of violence against local leaders: it executed four Communist leaders: Guo Shijun, Luo Wan, Liu Xiuqi, and Guo Xiangxian – as "four great party officials" (*sida dangguan*).[22] All four were leaders of a base area in Yanfu, about sixty miles or so from Donggu. Yanfu was densely populated but more spread out than Donggu. With rich soil, there were also local landlords. All four of these leaders came from rich peasant families, but none of them had gone to school outside the area and none of them had developed strong external ties. The result was that there was little of the internal cohesion that held Donggu leaders together or the external ties that integrated Donggu into the broader revolutionary movement. The local party organization did not have the continuity that the Donggu area had, and its leadership had clashed with higher-level party organizations.

---

[21] Liu Mianjue, "Zeng Shan zai Donggu de geming huodong" (Zeng Shan's Revolutionary Activities in Donggu), in Zhonggong Jiangxi shengwei dangshi yanjiushi, Zhonggong Ji'an shiwei dangshi gongzuo bangongshi, and Zhongguo Ji'anshi qingyuan quwei, *Donggu genjudi yu Zhongguo geming daolu de kaipi: Jinian Donggu geming genjudi chuangjian 80 zhounian xueshu taolun huiji* (The Donggu Revolutionary Base Area and the Opening of China's Revolutionary Path: Collection of Academic Discussions Commemorating the 80th Anniversary of the Founding of the Donggu Revolutionary Base) (Beijing: Zhonggong dangshi chubanshe, 2008), pp. 115–116.

[22] Dai Xiangqing and Luo Huilan, *AB tuan yu Futian shibian shimo* (A Complete History of the AB Corps and the Futian Incident) (Zhengzhou: Henan renmin chubanshe, 1994), p. 82.

Zeng Shan's time in Yanfu no doubt exacerbated this tension. Guerrilla forces in the area had been combined into the Third Independent Regiment, and that force was supposed to be integrated into the Sixth Army. When Jiang Hanbo visited Yanfu after the Yuntian Meeting, these Yanfu leaders all opposed Liu Shiqi's efforts to absorb local forces into the Sixth Army.[23]

Following the Beitou Meeting that expanded Mao's authority, a follow-up meeting was held in southern Jiangxi because leaders from the South Jiangxi Special Committee had been unable to attend the earlier meeting. This later meeting focused on ratifying the decisions made at the February 7 Meeting, particularly the merger of the West Jiangxi Special Committee and the South Jiangxi Special Committee, to form the Southwest Jiangxi Special Committee. This merger was part of Mao's consolidation of power, but it was also a reflection of the degree to which Communist leaders in southern Jiangxi, particularly in Xingguo county, were frequently landlords or rich peasants. Understandably, they had not implemented party policy on resisting rents and land redistribution. According to Jiang Hanbo, when Mao and Zhu had left Xingguo in 1929, peasants were ordered to put up slogans opposing Mao and Zhu as well as local leaders Li Wenlin and Duan Qifeng. As a result, the southern Jiangxi meeting ended with even greater violence than the February 7 Meeting: several leading cadres were expelled from the party and over ten were executed. Land redistribution began immediately after these two meetings.[24]

The Struggle against the AB Corps

It would take only two months after the February 7 Meeting for the assault on landlords and rich peasants, who had supposedly infiltrated the CCP, to be renamed a struggle against the AB Corps. There had once been an AB Corps. It had been established in 1926. At that time, the Northern Expedition had passed through Hunan and into Jiangxi,

---

[23] Ying Xing, "Suqu defang ganbu, hongse wuzhuang yu zuzhi xingtai," pp. 57–60.

[24] "Zhang Huaiwan xunshi Ganxinan baogao" (Zhang Huaiwan [Jiang Hanbo]'s Inspection Report on Western and Southern Jiangxi), in Jiangxisheng dang'an guan and Zhonggong Jiangxi shengwei dangxiao dangshi jiaoyanshi, *Zhongyang geming genjudi shiliao xuanbian*, vol. 1, p. 201.

and Chiang Kai-shek had established his headquarters in Nanchang. Even before his armies had arrived in the province, Chiang's organization man, Chen Guofu, had sent two of his people, Duan Xipeng and Zhou Lisheng, to Nanchang in September to organize the AB Corps and take control of party affairs. The "AB" of the "AB Corps" can be understood as meaning either "Anti-Bolshevik" or as two levels of a single organization, with "A" standing for the inner circle and "B" standing for the outer circle; these two meanings are not contradictory, so there is no reason to try to sort out the "real" meaning. In any event, the mission of the AB Corps was to root out the Communists in Jiangxi and to consolidate GMD control. With the Wuhan government not far away, Communist influence in Jiangxi was strong, and there was resistance to the power of the AB Corps. As tensions mounted, the Communists organized a counterattack. On April 2, 1927, the local Communist Youth League leader, Yuan Baobing, organized a group of toughs, who led a crowd to storm GMD headquarters. This action was co-ordinated with Zhu De's Military Officers and Teachers Group, which went alongside the youth group in plain clothes but with pistols hidden underneath their overcoats. The assault was successful. Although the main leaders of the AB Corps, Duan Xipeng and Zhou Lisheng, escaped, others were taken prisoner, and the AB Corps as an organized group was finished; it had existed for a total of three months.[25]

In his carefully researched article on the origins of the Futian Rebellion, Steve Averill comes away convinced that the AB Corps was revived, and that it was real and prevalent when the Communist Party campaign against the AB Corps began in 1930. However, Dai Xiangqing and Luo Huilan, who were writing their authoritative examination of the Futian Incident at the same time as Averill was writing his article, arrive at precisely the opposite conclusion. In their view, the AB Corps was never re-established after the April 2 counter-attack destroyed it. It is true that Communist documents from the period refer to the AB Corps, but Dai and Luo argue persuasively that such documents were using the term "AB Corps" as a general term to mean "conservative," rather than pointing to a specific organization.

---

[25] Dai Xiangqing and Luo Huilan, *AB tuan yu Futian shibian shimo*, pp. 35–39.

For instance, a report from the Jiangxi Provincial Party Committee states that when Nationalist military leader Zhu Peide arrived in Jiujiang to take power in the province, he seized nine members of the AB Corps and had them shot as a demonstration of strength.[26] But what this report really reveals is the hostility that existed between Jiangxi elites and Zhu Peide, who was from Yunnan. Moreover, the Jiangxi elites often co-ordinated with Chiang Kai-shek, so Zhu Peide was demonstrating his independence from Chiang as well as from the local elites. What such documents do not show, however, is that there really was an organized AB Corps, much less one that had successfully infiltrated the Chinese Communist Party.[27]

Another such document is Jiang Hanbo's April 1930 report to the Center, which discusses splits between local elites and outside military forces as well as between the Reorganizationalists (followers of Wang Jingwei) and the AB Corps. However, as Dai and Luo convincingly argue, Jiang was simply following the habit of the time by calling local elites "AB Corps," meaning pro-GMD elements. There is no evidence that an organized network actually existed.[28]

Dai and Luo note,

If the AB Corps was really a large special operations group infiltrating the CCP and sending people into the soviet areas to carry out sabotage, then surely there would be some record in GMD war histories and the various historical materials on armies, and certainly something would have been said about it by the GMD spies who surrendered or were captured.[29]

PLA general Xiao Ke, a veteran of the soviet areas and of the anti-AB movement, supports the conclusion of Dai and Luo. He writes that he later asked colleagues who had worked in the Communist intelligence system if they had known of the AB Corps. They told Xiao that they had had a pretty good understanding of the GMD in and around 1930

[26] "Zhonggong Jiangxi shengwei gei zhongyang de zonghe baogao" (A Comprehensive Report from the Jiangxi Provincial Party Committee to the Center), April 15, 1928, in Zhongyang dang'an guan and Jiangxisheng dang'an guan, *Jiangxisheng geming lishi wenjian huiji (1927–1928)* (Compilation of Historical Documents on the Jiangxi Revolution, 1927–1928) (Los Angeles: Zhongwen chubanshe fuwu zhongxin, 2013), ser. 21, vol. 15, pp. 204–205. See also Yu Boliu and Ling Buji, *Zhongyang suqu shi*, p. 1134.
[27] Dai Xiangqing and Luo Huilan, *AB tuan yu Futian shibian shimo*, pp. 57–58.
[28] Ibid., p. 61.   [29] Ibid., p. 45.

and that there had been no AB Corps. Xiao was able to confirm this conclusion with people who had worked in GMD intelligence.[30]

The February 7 Meeting had set a radical tone, and the execution of the four Communists from Yanfu had driven home that message. Shortly after the meeting concluded, the newly reorganized General Front Committee issued a notice that stated, "The Southwest Jiangxi party faces an extremely serious danger, namely that landlords and rich peasants have filled the leadership organs at all levels in our localities." This notice was the signal for Liu Shiqi, who was secretary of the group, to begin a purge. "Party policies," the notice stated,

are completely opportunist. If this is not cleared up fundamentally, not only will we not be able to carry out the great political tasks of the party but also the revolution will fail completely. The joint meeting [a reference to the February 7 Meeting] calls on the revolutionary cadres within the party to rise up and strike down opportunist political leaders, expel landlords and rich peasants from the party, and quickly bolshevize the party.[31]

Given this push against local cadres with landlord and rich peasant backgrounds and the tendency to label all local elites as "AB Corps," it is not surprising that "AB" elements were soon "discovered" in the party. The first report came in May 1930 when, not surprisingly, the Southwest Jiangxi Special Committee reported that there were AB elements in Rulin (an area straddling the Gan river in the vicinity of Yonghe) and other places.[32] On June 25, the West Route Action Committee (*Xilu xingwei*), which was under the jurisdiction of the Southwest Jiangxi Special Committee, issued a "Propaganda Outline for Opposing the Reorganizationists and the AB Corps." This outline declared that

in the various counties of western Jiangxi, the Reorganizationists are now undertaking activities to hide in the Red areas and to pretend to borrow the slogans of the Communist Party, such as dividing the land and resisting rents, in order to deceive the people and entice people into their trap. Their plot is to

---

[30] "Xiao Ke tongzhi tan zhongyang suqude chuqi sufan yundong" (Comrade Xiao Ke Discusses the Early Period of the Movement to Suppress the Counterrevolutionaries in the Central Soviet), in Zhongguo geming bowuguan yanjiushi, ed., *Dangshi yanjiu ziliao*, no. 4 (Chengdu: Sichuan renmin chubanshe, 1983), p. 403. Quoted in Dai Xiangqing and Luo Huilan, *AB tuan yu Futian shibian shimo*, p. 45.

[31] "Qianwei tonggao, Diyihao."

[32] Dai Xiangqing and Luo Huilan, *AB tuan yu Futian shibian shimo*, p. 85.

wreck the soviet government of workers and peasants as well as to wreck the division of land and to draw in the reactionary armies to arrest and kill worker and peasant revolutionary comrades. They want to fundamentally overthrow the revolution and let workers and peasants fall into the ninth level of hell so as to allow the landed bullies and landlords to own the world . . .[33]

Shortly thereafter, the Southwest Jiangxi Special Committee issued an emergency notice in which it described in great detail the organizational structure of the AB Corps – a structure that did not exist. The AB Corps, the notice declared, had a central headquarters as well as headquarters in the various provinces, prefectures, counties, districts, and branches, and small groups below that (mirroring exactly the CCP organization). The AB Corps was said to dispatch people to infiltrate Communist organizations, people who would not attract attention, whose attitudes were extremely leftist, loyal, and sincere. Such people would ferret out plans and information about the Communists and plot things such as assassinations and their own uprisings. One such person, Zhu Jiahao, was caught by the Southwest Jiangxi Special Committee. At first, Zhu would not admit that he was a member of the AB Corps, but after "strict questioning using both soft and hard methods," he admitted that both the Red Flag Lenin Youth Association and the Southwest Jiangxi Government had AB organizations. The head of these organizations was said to be one Xie Zhaoyuan, who, along with his collaborators, was arrested. It was said to be necessary to organize investigation groups at all levels to find suspicious persons. But the members of the AB Corps were "extremely devious, cunning, treacherous, and tough," so "unless the cruelest methods of torture (*zui canku kaoda*) were used, they will certainly not confess."[34]

During the summer, local party people spearheaded the movement to suppress the AB Corps. People in Yudu county were particularly

---

[33] "Fan gaizupai AB tuan xuanchuan dagang" (Propaganda Outline for Opposing the Reorganizationalists and the AB Corps), in Jiangxisheng dang'an guan and Zhonggong Jiangxi shengwei dangxiao dangshi jiaoyanshi, *Zhongyang geming genjudi shiliao xuanbian*, vol. 3, pp. 631–636.

[34] "Jinji tonggao di ershi hao: Dongyuan dangyuan qunzhong chedi suqing AB tuan" (Emergency Notice No. 20: Mobilizing the Mass of Party Members to Completely Purge the AB Corps), in Jiangxisheng dang'an guan and Zhonggong Jiangxi shengwei dangxiao dangshi jiaoyanshi, *Zhongyang geming genjudi shiliao xuanbian*, vol. 3, pp. 639–650. The reference to the "cruelest measures of torture" can be found on p. 649.

enthusiastic, and the party secretary there, one Huang Weihan, was an educated youth from Jiangxi. Between May and September Huang oversaw the arrest and execution of over 1,000 people.[35] In September the movement to oppose the AB Corps kicked into high gear. According to a notice from the Southwest Jiangxi East Route Action Committee, the AB Corps was planning an uprising to seize power on Double Ten day (October 10, the anniversary of the Revolution of 1911).[36] By October, the Southwest Jiangxi Soviet had purged one-fourth of its members.[37] Over 1,000 landlords and rich peasants were expelled from the party, and another 1,000 were killed.[38]

It should be noted that Li Wenlin, soon to be one of the chief targets of the anti-AB Corps movement, was very much a supporter of the movement when it began. Apparently not yet comprehending that it would soon be directed against local (meaning Donggu) cadres, Li accepted the paranoid belief that there really was a threat from the AB Corps. Paranoia was understandable in an area where local elites and the GMD were trying to exterminate the Communists, and Li Wenlin did not hesitate to take the lead in the effort to root out the AB Corps. Like many local cadres, he was a believer in carrying out "Red terrorism."[39]

Increasing Tensions

As the purge of suspected AB Corps members got underway in western Jiangxi, Comintern policy was evolving. This was a time when Stalinists were vigorously denouncing Bukharin's "rightist" tendencies,[40] and there was a belief that a new high tide was approaching for the Communist revolution in China. The Great Depression led many to believe that capitalism was facing collapse, while the tensions between Chiang Kai-shek, on the one hand, and warlords Feng Yuxiang and Yan Xishan, on the other, that burst out in the Central

---

[35] Yu Boliu and Ling Buji, *Zhongyang suqu shi*, p. 1139.
[36] Dai Xiangqing and Luo Huilan, *AB tuan yu Futian shibian shimo*, pp. 89–91.
[37] Ibid., pp. 91–92.   [38] Ibid., p. 83.
[39] Dai Anlin, "Futian shibian yu suqu sufan" (The Futian Incident and the Suppression of Counterrevolutionaries in the Soviet Areas), *Xiangchao*, no. 6 (2007), p. 27.
[40] Stephen F. Cohen, *Bukharin and the Bolshevik Revolution: A Political Biography 1888–1938* (Oxford: Oxford University Press, 1980), Chapter 9.

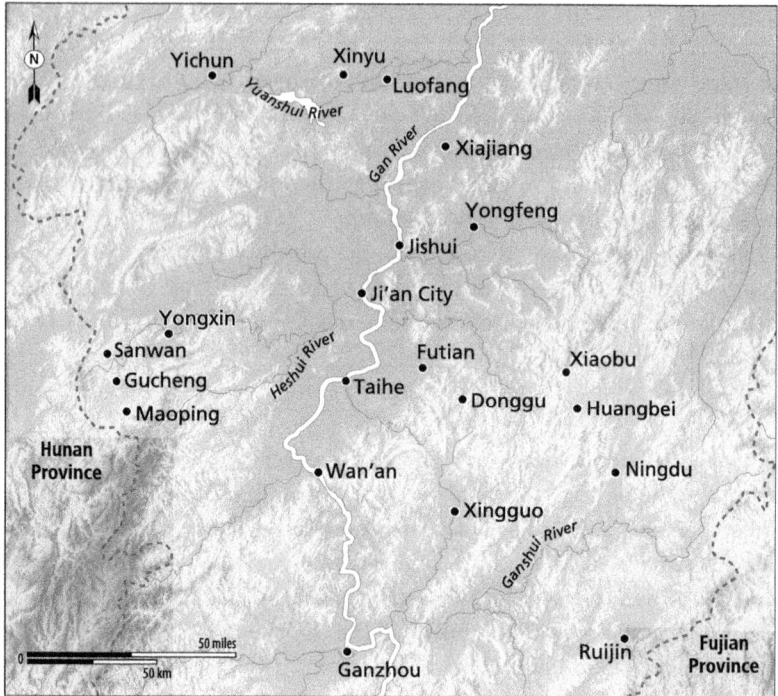

Map 4.1 Southern Jiangxi

Plains war of April 1930 suggested that the Nationalist coalition was on its deathbed.

As these crises deepened, Li Lisan began developing his thesis that the CCP should attack the major cities. In a series of articles in April and May 1930, Li argued that a new high tide of revolution was approaching and that the CCP could seize power in one or several provinces. Li focused on Wuhan as his main target, disagreeing with Mao's more modest goal of attacking Nanchang, the capital of Jiangxi. In fact, Mao, understanding that his military strength was not yet sufficient, did not want to attack Nanchang at this time, but he was willing to move in that direction in a show of compliance. In June, Li Lisan sent Mao a scorching letter, stating,

The Center has conveyed the new line to you several times in the past. We have written several times and Comrade Cai Shenxi has orally conveyed [our message]. Although our letters were all very simple and Comrade's Cai's oral message was not sufficient, all were completely in accordance with the Center's line. But up until the present you have completely not understood and have stubbornly stuck to your past line.[41]

It was at this time – May 1930 – when the Li Lisan line was being strongly asserted and when tensions between Li Lisan and Mao were developing, that Li Wenlin, Zeng Shan, and Duan Liangbi, who would later play an important role in the Futian Rebellion, went to Shanghai to participate in the All-China Congress of Representatives of the Soviet Areas. Li Lisan wanted Mao to attend the conference, but Mao declined, staying behind to write "Investigation of Xunwu" and his "Oppose Bookishism," two of his most important early writings. But Li Wenlin was in Shanghai to hear Li Lisan say,

The National Military Affairs Conference has discovered two obstacles to the development of the Red Army, one is the conservative views in the Soviet areas and the other is the strategy of narrow guerrilla-ism. Most obvious is Mao Zedong of the Fourth Army. He has his continuous guerrilla thinking. This line and the line of the Center are completely different.[42]

Li Wenlin came away from the congress as a firm believer in the Li Lisan line. Whether this was a matter of intellectual persuasion, party discipline, or personal interest, or some combination of all three, is not clear, but Li returned to Jiangxi in August believing that he understood the policies of the Party Center and that he had the full backing of Li Lisan.

Upon his return to Jiangxi, Li Wenlin chaired the Second Congress of the Southwest Jiangxi Special Committee, during which he attacked "rightism" and "conservatism." The source of intra-party struggle, Li said, was that some people supported the Trotskyites who opposed the Communist International. This struggle had brought "Red terror" to the party, with the result that many people had been executed or expelled from the party. "The central issue in this struggle," it was stated at the Congress, "was striking down those opposed to the

---

[41] "Zhongyang zhi sijun qianwei xin" (Letter from the Center to the Front Committee of the Fourth Army), in Zhonggong Jiangxi shengwei dangshi ziliao zhengji weiyuanhui and Zhonggong Jiangxi shengwei dangshi yanjiushi, eds., *Jiangxi dangshi ziliao* (Materials on Jiangxi Party History), vol. 6: *Luofang huiyi qianhou zhuanji* (Special Volume on before and after the Luofang Conference) (Nanchang: "Jiangxi dangshi ziliao" bianjishi, 1988), p. 44.
[42] Quoted in Yu Boliu and Ling Buji, *Zhongyang suqu shi*, vol. 1, p. 249.

Comintern, grasping the objectively good conditions, and adopting the correct line of expanding attacks, taking Ji'an and Ganzhou, attacking Jiujiang and Nanchang, striving for victory in Jiangxi, and meeting up [with other armies] in Wuhan." This was a pure recitation of the Li Lisan line and it was totally impractical, but there was no doubt of the depth of Li Wenlin's opposition to Liu Shiqi.[43] Li demanded that the Congress remove Liu Shiqi from his positions, so Liu was thus removed both as secretary and as political commissar of the 20th Army, and then he was expelled from the party. The party committee was reorganized, with Li Wenlin joining the standing committee. Li's attacks on Liu Shiqi were clearly meant as criticisms of Mao, and Li's demand to attack Ji'an and Ganzhou expressed his opposition to Mao's strategy of "luring the enemy in deep" (see below). Later on, Mao would accuse this congress of being completely controlled by the AB Corps.[44] All the leaders at the congress – Li Wenlin and others – would eventually be arrested and accused of being part of the AB Corps.[45]

While Li Wenlin and the others were in Shanghai, representatives from Peng Dehuai's Fifth Army were attending the All-China Congress of Representatives of the Soviet Areas (*Quanguo suweiai quyu daibiao dahui*) as well as the Red Army Representative Congress (*Hongjun daibiao huiyi*) that followed. They returned from those meetings with direct orders to attack Wuhan. But, looking at the situation, Peng and the others understood that doing so could mean the complete destruction of their army. They nevertheless moved in the direction of Wuhan, feigning that Wuhan was their destination. Believing that Peng was going to attack Wuhan, Chiang Kai-shek moved two divisions from Yueyang in northeastern Hunan toward Wuhan, leaving Yueyang open. Peng occupied Yueyang in early July and then withdrew to Pingxiang before Chiang's troops could counterattack.[46]

---

[43] "Ganxinan tewei er quanhui jueyi'an zhi er" (The Second Resolution of the Second Congress of the Southwest Jiangxi Special Committee), in Jiangxisheng dang'an guan and Zhonggong Jiangxi shengwei dangxiao dangshi jiaoyanshi, *Zhongyang geming genjudi shiliao xuanbian*, vol. 2, pp. 247–250.

[44] Chen Yongfa, "Zhonggong zaoqi sufan de jiantao," p. 209.

[45] Yu Boliu and Ling Buji, *Zhongyang suqu shi*, p. 1150; Zeng Xianxin, "Xiang Ying, Zhou Enlai jiuzheng zhongyang suqu sufan cuowu" (Xiang Ying and Zhou Enlai Corrected the Mistakes of the Central Soviet Area in the Suppression Campaign), *Bainianchao*, no. 10 (2003), p. 24.

[46] Zhao Quanjun and Zhang Zhenzhong, "Luofang huiyi qianhou zongshu" (Before and after the Luofang Meeting), *Jiangxi dangshi ziliao*, vol. 6, pp. 9–13.

At the time, the growing tensions between Chiang Kai-shek and Nationalist general Zhang Fakui burst out in confrontation. In support of Chiang, Hunan commander He Jian moved his troops south, leaving Changsha's defenses weakened.[47] Therefore, on July 27, Peng Dehuai's forces attacked and occupied Changsha. To take a provincial capital was a major accomplishment for the revolutionary forces. Even though after a few days Peng was forced to abandon Changsha, retreating again to Pingxiang and leaving vulnerable peasants and workers to be slaughtered when He Jian returned, Peng's ability to take a major city seemed to substantiate Li Lisan's line of attacking central cities. It was, it seemed, a "merciless smashing of all localisms." In other words, the idea of building up base areas now seemed "conservative."[48]

With Peng's army under attack in Pingxiang, Mao decided to withdraw from the area near Nanchang and go to Peng's aid (although he never reached Peng, causing resentment). The idea was to wipe out as many GMD troops as possible and then reoccupy Changsha. By late August, Mao was in a position to attack Changsha, even though he did not have heavy artillery. Mao and Zhu hoped to lure He Jian's troops out, but without success. After launching several attacks and taking heavy losses, Mao and Zhu made a decision on September 12 to withdraw from Changsha before Nationalist reinforcements could get there.[49]

Mao wanted to return to Jiangxi and take the city of Ji'an, but many cadres disagreed with him. They argued that they should follow the orders of Shanghai and attack Nanchang and Wuhan. These discussions became heated when Zhou Yili, a special envoy from the Center, arrived with a letter emphasizing the need to attack central cities. The issue of which way to go became a heated point of contention at a meeting in Yuanzhou on September 28.[50] But Mao knew Zhou Yili from their days working together at the Central Peasant Training Institute in Guangzhou and Mao was able to persuade Zhou of the correctness of his (Mao's) views. As a result, the Yuanzhou meeting decided to go forward with Mao's plan to attack Ji'an. On October 4,

---

[47] He Jian was originally a subordinate of military leader Zhu Peide. He was also a superior of Xu Kexiang, and it was He Jian who ordered Xu to crack down on the Communists, leading to the Horse Day massacre.

[48] Zhao Quanjun and Zhang Zhenzhong, "Luofang huiyi qianhou zongshu," pp. 13–14.

[49] Ibid., p. 18.   [50] Ibid., p. 24.

Mao's army attacked and occupied Ji'an. This was not a small accomplishment. Prior to this, the party had attacked eight times without success. Having occupied Ji'an, Mao finally turned his attention to local matters and asked about circumstances. He was told that the Southwest Jiangxi Special Committee had discovered that one-quarter of its people were members of the AB Corps. This response is consistent with a September notice put out by the Southwest Jiangxi Special Committee that claimed that the AB Corps planned to take advantage of a party meeting scheduled for October 7 to send delegates with weapons and then launch an uprising. Assassination squads would target "progressive" farmers, workers, and CCP members. Since Li Wenlin was in charge of the Southwest Jiangxi Special Committee, there is no doubt that he was convinced that the AB Corps was real; he was just as guilty of the torture of innocent people as anyone else. The fear that agents from the GMD or local landlord forces had infiltrated the CCP was real and pervasive. Despite Li's deep disagreements with Mao and Liu Shiqi, he never suspected that the campaign to purge the AB Corps would be used against himself and other local leaders. Revolutionary movements frequently have internecine struggles, but the amount of violence that this campaign directed against its own members is extraordinary (see next chapter).

The Provincial Action Committee

On October 6, the General Front Committee held a meeting with the Southwest Jiangxi Special Committee, of which Li Wenlin was a member of the standing committee, and established the Jiangxi Provincial Action Committee with Li Wenlin as chairman. This decision is difficult to understand because in August Li had engineered the ouster of Liu Shiqi as secretary of the Southwest Jiangxi Special Committee, a decision Mao deeply resented. Thus the decision to set up a Provincial Action Committee must have come from Shanghai. The difficulty with this explanation is that the Third Plenary Session of the Fifth Central Committee, held September 24–28, had criticized Li Lisan and he had left his leading position. But Mao did not know of that decision until December, so one has to assume that Li Lisan made the decision to set up the Provincial Action Committee and appoint Li Wenlin chairman before his own ouster. The General Front Committee, it appears, was simply carrying out orders that were old and outdated by the time they were executed. The establishment of the Action Committee was important because it then commanded the 20th Army, which had just been cobbled together from local guerrilla forces, and would be the main target during the Futian Rebellion. Li's appointment as chairman of the Provincial Action Committee suggests that he was not subordinate to Mao's General Front Committee, and perhaps he was even superior to Mao. Mao would strongly assert his own authority (see below), but the organization of the Provincial Action Committee seems intended to constrain Mao.

Only days later Mao would take action to countermand the impact of the new Action Committee and flout the authority of Shanghai. Shanghai had decided to set up a Central Bureau to assert supervision over Mao, and it had appointed Xiang Ying, a veteran cadre who had long been a leader in the workers' movement, as acting head until Zhou Enlain could go to Jiangxi and take leadership. Mao, in an apparent effort to pre-empt this decision, sent a letter of instruction, saying that while Xiang Ying was on his way to head the new Central Bureau, they, the General Front Committee, should go ahead and establish the bureau with Mao as acting secretary. Moreover, Mao declared that all political and military leadership would be concentrated in this Central Bureau.[51]

However one interprets the establishment of the Provincial Action Committee, Mao would continue to direct fire at the Southwest Jiangxi Special Committee. On October 14, Mao wrote to the Center, saying,

The party in southwest Jiangxi faces an extremely serious crisis. The entire party is led by leaders following the rich peasant line … Without purging the rich peasant leaders and suppressing the AB Corps and fundamentally reorganizing the party in southwest Jiangxi, we will be unable to overcome this crisis. At the moment, the General Front is planning such work.[52]

It was after seizing Ji'an that various counties set up "committees for the suppression of counterrevolutionaries," but for a time their only job was to arrest "local bullies" and impose fines on them.[53]

---

[51] Zhonggong zhongyang wenxian yanjiushi, ed., *Mao Zedong nianpu, 1893–1949* (Annual Chronicle of Mao Zedong, 1893–1949), 3 vols., revised ed. (Beijing: Zhongyang wenxian chubanshe, 2013) (hereafter cited as *Mao Zedong nianpu*), vol. 1, p. 320.

[52] Quoted in Dai Xiangqing and Luo Huilan, *AB tuan yu Futian shibian shimo*, p. 93.

[53] Yu Boliu and Ling Buji, *Zhongyang suqu shi*, p. 1145.

Seizing Ji'an would also prove important in the ongoing struggle against the so-called AB Corps because Communist cadres searching the city found what they took to be a name list of AB Corps members. One piece of evidence seized was a receipt allegedly signed by Li Wenlin's father that "proved" that he was a landlord and AB Corps member. It was later shown, however, that the signature in question was not that of Li Wenlin's father. Nevertheless, the appointment of Li as chairman of the Provincial Action Committee and the discovery of this evidence, as flimsy as it was, could only have fueled tensions between Mao and Li. Soon, there would be new sources of tension.[54]

Having taken the city of Ji'an, there were again discussions, often heated, about which direction to head in. With the Central Plains war over, Chiang Kai-shek was redirecting his troops toward western Jiangxi to prosecute what would be the first of five "extermination campaigns" intended to wipe out the Communist insurgency. Mao urged abandoning Ji'an, but many disagreed. However, Mao prevailed and began moving his troops to Luofang, about 100 kilometers north of Ji'an.

The Luofang Conference

Arriving at Luofang on October 27, Mao convened a meeting that would bring tensions between Mao and Li Wenlin to a head. Seventeen leaders, including Mao Zedong, Zhu De, Peng Dehuai, Zhou Yili, Lin Biao, Zeng Shan, and Li Wenlin, met to discuss two main issues: the strategy to be used to confront the Nationalist troops and the threat posed by the AB Corps. On the first issue, one group argued that it would be better to meet the enemy near Xiajiang, about halfway between Luofang and Ji'an – in other words, away from Donggu and the base area. Fighting in their own base area, these people argued, would cause the loss of a significant territory, would harm the people of the base area, and would create a negative influence. These concerns, as we shall see, were all too real. However, Mao argued that luring the enemy in deep would force the enemy to divide its troops and to fight on unfamiliar territory, and the Communist forces would have the support of the local people. In the end, Zhu De, Peng Dehuai, Zhou

---

[54] See www.taomingren.com/baike/8126, accessed May 12, 2021.

Yili, and others supported Mao.[55] One wonders the outcome if Zhou Yili, the envoy from Li Lisan, had carried out his instructions from Li Lisan and had supported Li Wenlin and the others who opposed the strategy of "luring the enemy in deep."

On the AB Corps threat, Mao was bent on deepening the campaign and completely reorganizing the party so that not a single landlord or rich peasant could join. Mao again carried the day, and the Luofang Conference decided, "From a political perspective, the tricks and plots of the AB Corps and their influence among the masses have to be eliminated."[56] In accordance with this decision, the Luofang Conference decided to set up a Committee for the Suppression of Counterrevolutionaries in the First Front Army (the name now given to the various armies under the control of Mao's General Front Committee). It was headed by twenty-seven-year-old Li Shaojiu, who would soon play an infamous role in the Futian Rebellion.[57]

Even after, or perhaps especially after, the Luofang Conference, there were still commanders unhappy about withdrawing from Changsha, about not attacking Wuhan, and especially about withdrawing from Ji'an. Xu Fuzu was head of the Committee for the Suppression of Counterrevolutionaries in the 22nd Army, an army that had, like the 20th Army that would be at the center of the Futian Rebellion, been recently cobbled together from local troops.[58] He later wrote that, at the time, there were people who "cursed the General Front Committee, saying that it had opposed the Center's orders by not attacking Wuhan and Nanchang and that it had even withdrawn from Changsha after seizing it [referring to Peng's brief occupation of the city]. Now it [the General Front Committee] wants to withdraw from Ji'an and return to the soviet base area. A mood of dissatisfaction is everywhere."[59] This mood bolstered Mao's determination to root out supposed AB Corps members in the military.

When the troops withdrew to Huangbei and Xiaobu in Ningdu county, where the General Front Committee had established its

---

[55] Zhao Quanjun and Zhang Zhenzhong, "Luofang huiyi qianhou zongshu," p. 36.
[56] Quoted in Dai Xiangqing and Luo Huilan, *AB tuan yu Futian shibian shimo*, p. 94.
[57] Yu Boliu and Ling Buji, *Zhongyang suqu shi*, p. 1145.   [58] Ibid., p. 1146.
[59] Quoted in Dai Xiangqing and Luo Huilan, *AB tuan yu Futian shibian shimo*, pp. 94–95.

headquarters, the General Front Committee announced that it would reorganize the army. The next day, according to Xu Fuzu's memoir,

we discovered a counterrevolutionary AB Corps organization headed by Gan Kangchen. Gan came from a landlord family in Xingguo and desired city living. Thus he was eager to attack Wuhan. When we retreated from Ji'an, Gan incited the officers and men to leave the General Front Committee's leadership, saying they would attack Nanchang themselves. They had already reached Xiajiang. This proved there were AB Corps people in the Red Army. So we established suppression committees in all our armies – in every division, every brigade, every regiment, and every company – and carried out suppression and reorganization in lightning fashion. For a time, army headquarters could not handle so many suspects, so authority was handed over to the company and platoon level.[60]

Xiao Ke recalls that when his army reached Ningdu, the anti-AB Corps work had already started.

A political propaganda person told us that we had AB Corps people in our army, and he named two. We grabbed these two. Under questioning, they would not confess. Alternating beating and questioning, they finally confessed and gave up the names of ten or so people. These people were seized, and after being beaten and questioned, they each gave up ten or so more names. By late November or early December, we had seized one or two hundred people. The political commissar, Zhang Chinan, myself, and the cadres of the various regiments did nothing else; our energies were spent on attacking the AB Corps. At that time, whether to seize someone was decided by the regimental commander; whether to kill someone was decided by the division party committee. The Front Committee and the Military Committee of the Fourth Army did not interfere. Our division killed sixty or more. After about ten days, in one evening in the first half of December, our division party committee and soldier representatives decided to kill another group of more than sixty people. Early the next morning, I went to the army political commissar's office and reported to Luo Rongcheng, saying, "Some ten days ago we executed sixty; now we are prepared to execute another sixty or more. The division party committee studied this and decided." Luo listened and said, "kill more!" Off to the side, Huang Yishan, chief secretary of the Fourth Army Military Commission, said, "kill more!" ... With the two of them saying this, I returned, and the troops took the "criminals" to the

---

[60] "Xu Fuzu huiyi Huangbei sufan" (Xu Fuzu Recalls the Suppression of Counterrevolutionaries in Huangbei), quoted in Dai Xiangqing and Luo Huilan, *AB tuan yu Futian shibian shimo*, p. 95.

execution ground. I said, "Let's not execute. Wait until the division party committee studies this and then decide." After studying it, we released thirty or so, but we still executed over twenty.

In total, the Red Fourth Army executed 1,300 or 1,400 people, about 20 percent of the 7,000 troops in the army.[61] Later Mao would say that a total of 4,400 AB Corps members were discovered and executed in the military.[62]

It is odd that a revolutionary movement purged its own forces, especially with GMD forces bearing down. It is not as if the CCP felt it had enough troops. On the contrary, it had been making every effort to recruit troops. But most peasants did not want to join the army. In part this was out of sensible family concerns – wives worried that if their husbands were killed, their livelihoods would be in jeopardy. Moreover, in general, peasants would not want to join the army if it meant leaving their counties, a fact the Red Army would run into time and again. Consequently, cadres tasked with recruiting troops resorted to tricks and coercion. In November, Zeng Shan, then in charge of the provincial soviet government, warned that cadres were exercising "commandism" (*mingling zhuyi*) and were separated from the masses (*tuoli qunzhong*), causing revulsion (*fan'gan*) among the masses. They threatened the masses with being labeled AB Corps members or they tricked the peasants by telling them they were not going to be inducted into the army. Discovering they had been duped, many ran away.[63] One can certainly understand why cadres used such methods. After all, they had quotas and doubtlessly they felt that they too could be labeled AB Corps members if they did not fulfill their assigned tasks.

Hence the suppression campaign in Huangbei can be attributed to the degree of distrust that had developed between Mao and other outsiders on the one hand and the educated youth and other disgruntled officers and men from the local area on the other. Only a month after this suppression campaign the Nationalist general Zhang Huizan would enter Donggu.

---

[61] Quoted in ibid., p. 96.

[62] Mao Zedong, "A Letter of Reply by the General Front Committee," in Schram, *Mao's Road to Power*, vol. 3, pp. 704–705.

[63] "Kuoda hongjun de zhuti banfa," in Jiangxisheng dang'an guan and Zhonggong Jiangxi shengwei dangxiao dangshi jiaoyanshi, *Zhongyang geming genjudi shiliao xuanbian*, vol. 2, pp. 528–533.

The Futian Rebellion

As the attack on the imaginary AB Corps expanded, attention inevitably focused on the Jiangxi Provincial Action Committee. A December 5 letter of instruction from the General Front Committee accused Duan Liangbi, one of the leaders of the Provincial Action Committee, of being the head of the AB Corps in the area.[64] The Provincial Action Committee, which had just been established, had its headquarters in Futian, the wealthy town in Ji'an county that had been attacked by Lai Jingbang when he first organized the Donggu Revolutionary Army. The Provincial Action Committee controlled the 20th Army, which had only recently been assembled out of local guerrilla forces. As Mao's effort to establish a provisional Central Bureau prior to Yang's arrival shows, Mao was determined to bring these forces under his control. Now, Mao moved to reinforce that determination. On December 3, Mao's General Front Committee sent a letter demanding the immediate arrest of Duan Liangbi, Li Baifang, and Xie Hanchang of the Provincial Action Committee. Duan was the secretary of the Southwest Jiangxi Special Committee, a member of the Provincial Party Standing Committee, and a leading member of the Provincial Action Committee. Li was chief secretary (*mishuzhang*) of the Special Committee and acting chief secretary of the Provincial Action Committee, and Xie was the head of the political department of the 20th Army.[65]

The December 3 letter also notified the Provincial Action Committee that the General Front Committee was in charge. As written in the letter, "Because of the needs of the struggle ... the authority of the General Front Committee must be above that of the Provincial Action Committee. All military and local affairs – all military affairs, political affairs, and party affairs – must all be under the unified direction of the General Front Committee."[66] This assertion of authority was consistent with Mao's insistence at the February 7 Emergency Meeting that the General Front Committee was in charge of all military forces in the area, and it followed from the efforts described in Chapter 3 to make Mao's Front Committee subordinate only to the Party Center in Shanghai. Mao's Hunan–Jiangxi Border Area Special Committee and its successor Front Committee had originally been subordinate to the

---

[64] Dai Xiangqing and Luo Huilan, *AB tuan yu Futian shibian shimo*, p. 99.
[65] Ibid., pp. 98–99   [66] Ibid., p. 99.

provincial party authority, but Mao had never accepted such authority. Now, in Jiangxi, he was asserting his authority not only to override the Provincial Action Committee but also to detain and torture its leaders. On the basis of more forced confessions, the General Front Committee sent a follow-up letter naming more names and instructing the Provincial Action Committee that in order to find clues, it "must not, as it did when breaking cases in the Special Committee, kill the chief culprits too quickly."[67]

As these letters were being sent out, Mao had Li Wenlin arrested and jailed. Li was without doubt the most prestigious local leader, the one who might have rallied local forces against Mao. The letter to arrest Duan Liangbi and the others was carried by Li Shaojiu, Mao's assistant and head of the Suppression Office (*sufan weiyuanhui*) in the General Front Department.

Li Shaojiu was born in Hunan's Jiahe county. His father was the head of the local hooligans. Li was kicked out of middle school for his disruptive behavior. He was an inveterate gambler and opium addict. He went to Guangdong and became party representative in Lin Boqu's army. During the Northern Expedition, he was a platoon commander. After Wang Jingwei and Chiang Kai-shek each broke with the Communists and then joined forces again, Li remained in the Nationalist Army. On the eve of the Nanchang Uprising, he was sent to Nanchang. When his company was wiped out on the morning of August 1, Li was taken prisoner. He was able to seek out Xiao Ke, who was also from Jiahe, and his old commander Lin Boqu, and thus he participated in the Nanchang Uprising on the Communist side. He followed the army south, and after its defeat in Guangdong, he went to Anyuan in Jiangxi to participate in revolutionary activities. He joined the CCP in 1928.[68] Arrested by the GMD, he declared that he was a loyal adherent of the Three Principles of the People. Li remained with the GMD army for over half a year, but he then made contact with the Jiangxi party organization. Dai Xiangqing and Luo Huilan, experts on the Futian Rebellion, describe Li as a person with "horrible thought

---

[67] Ibid., p. 99.
[68] "Suqu zhongyangju guanyu chufa Li Shaojiu tongzhi guoqu cuowu de jueyi" (Resolution of the Central Bureau of the Soviet Area on Punishing Comrade Li Shaojiu for his Past Mistake), January 25, 1932. See https://baike.baidu.com /item/%E5%AF%8C%E7%94%B0%E4%BA%8B%E5%8F%98, accessed May 2, 2021.

and character, a person of extremely evil ways," but someone who was "able to talk and do things, who was good at currying favor and deceiving the General Front into trusting him."[69]

Li Shaojiu arrived in Futian on the afternoon of December 7, with a platoon from the 12th Army, and they immediately began arresting and torturing people. According to Zeng Shan's later testimony, on December 7, he (Zeng) personally interrogated Duan Liangbi and others, who confessed under torture that a number of leaders were members of the AB Corps. Torture was creative and painful; victims were normally strung up and whipped. If that were not enough, more creative and painful methods were adopted. One county reported using over 120 different methods of torture. Between December 7 and December 12, when the Futian Rebellion broke out, over 100 AB members were "discovered" in the Provincial Action Committee, the soviet government, and the political protection guards (*zhengzhi bao-weidui*), among whom over forty were executed.[70]

On December 9, Li Shaojiu went to Donggu and seized Xie Hanchang of the Provincial Action Committee. Under torture, Xie confessed that one Liu Di, a political representative in one of the regiments of the 20th Army (the army under the Provincial Action Committee) was a member of the AB Corps. Li Shaojiu then began to interrogate Liu Di. Li Shaojiu told him that many people had named him as an AB Corps member. Liu Di responded, "Do I look like an AB Corps member?" Li responded, "Exactly! I don't believe it either. But now there are people who say you are." Liu Di asked, "Don't you believe that the members of the AB Corps have a plot to give up many Communists?"[71]

After talking a while, Liu Di used his native Changsha dialect and said to Li Shaojiu,

I am your former subordinate. My political level is very low, as you know. Now, I am fortunate that you have come. I only have to receive political education and admit my mistakes. I believe that Comrade Mao Zedong is not a member of the AB Corps, you, too, are not a member of the AB Corps, the military commander [Liu Tiechao] is not an AB Corps member. I have followed the three of you loyally. What else am I?

---

[69] Dai Xiangqing and Luo Huilan, *AB tuan yu Futian shibian shimo*, pp. 97–98.
[70] Ibid., pp. 105–106.
[71] Jing Yuchuan, "Futian shibian shi de Liu Di gei zhongyang de xin" (The Letter Liu Di Gave to the Center at the Time of the Futian Incident), *Yanhuang chunqiu*, no. 11 (2014), pp. 84–88.

In his later letter to the Party Center, Liu Di continued,

In this way, he [Liu Shaojiu] completely believed me and knocked off that false AB Corps hat, slapped me on the shoulder, grasped my hand, and said, "I never believed that you would take that road. It is certainly them plotting to harm you. You have now sincerely admitted mistakes, and I have absolutely no doubts about you. If you act under the correct instructions of the party and do things with determination, then that is right."

After talking, Li Shaojiu ordered a soldier to escort Liu Di back to battalion headquarters.

On the morning of December 12, fearing that Li Shaojiu would go back to Futian and kill the remaining leaders of the Provincial Action Committee, Liu Di and Xie Hanchang led their troops to Futian. They surrounded the Wang Family Temple, where the captured leaders were being held, and they disarmed the platoon from the 12th Army. They released Duan Liangbi, Li Baifang, and seventy other people who had been detained.[72] This was the Futian Rebellion.

Figure 4.2 The Wang Family Temple

[72] Dai Xiangqing and Luo Huilan, *AB tuan yu Futian shibian shimo*, p. 108.

Resolution of the Futian Rebellion

On the morning of December 13 soldiers of the 20th Army met at the Wang Family Temple in Futian and their leaders described what had happened. As the atmosphere became heated, the soldiers cried out, "Strike down Mao Zedong, support Zhu De, Peng Dehuai, and Huang Gonglüe."[73] Those in the 20th Army were obviously aware of the tensions between Mao and the others but they were not aware that those tensions had been sufficiently resolved by the Gutian Conference and that the leaders of the Red Army would not rise in rebellion against Mao; on the contrary, they quickly declared their loyalty to Mao.

The meeting concluded by deputing Duan Liangbi and Liu Di to write a report on the incident that Duan took to Shanghai. Duan's report has never been published, but Liu Di's letter was copied and finally published in *Yanhuang chunqiu* (Annals of the Chinese People). In it, Liu Di writes that he had heard that the Center had criticized Mao for his peasant mentality and desire to create bases, and that Mao had criticized the Center and openly published his criticism in *Red Flag.*[74]

Unfortunately for Duan Liangbi and the others, the situation had changed radically in Shanghai. The Comintern, tired of Li Lisan's unrealistic policies, had sent Pavel Mif to China to reorganize the CCP, and he did so with a vengeance. Arriving in Shanghai in December 1930, Mif convened the Fourth Plenum of the Sixth Central Committee on January 7. He organized support for his student Wang Ming and, despite strong objections by some long-time party members, Wang Ming was named party secretary. The "Li Lisan line" was criticized harshly, making the Futian rebels' support of it untenable. Therefore, when Duan Liangbi arrived with his report, he was startled to discover that the Center was happy to learn that Mao had resisted Li Lisan's policies![75] Duan exited party headquarters and disappeared into the streets of Shanghai, never to be seen again.

Before Duan Liangbi arrived in Shanghai, however, the party had sent Xiang Ying, a veteran labor leader, to Ningdu to establish a Central Bureau (which Mao had already "established," without

---

[73] Jing Yuchuan, "Futian shibian pingfan de qianqian houhou" (Before and after the Resolution of the Futian Incident), *Bainianchao*, no. 1 (2000), p. 40.

[74] Jing Yuchuan, "Futian shibian shi Liu Di gei zhongyang de xin," pp. 84–88; and Jing Yuchuan, "Futian shibian pingfan de qianqian houhou," pp. 39–44.

[75] Jing Yuchuan, "Futian shibian pingfan de qianqian houhou," pp. 39–44, 112.

authorization). As noted previously, the Party Center in Shanghai had been trying for some time to exert control over Mao. Setting up a Central Bureau would finally do that. Meeting with Mao, Zhu, and other leaders on January 10, Xiang Ying announced that Mao's General Front Committee would be abolished, replaced by the Central Bureau. Zhou Enlai was named secretary, but Xiang Ying would serve as acting secretary until Zhou arrived (Zhou would not arrive until the following December). Nine people, including Mao and Zhu De, were named to the standing committee.[76] Reviewing the events of the Futian Incident, Xiang sharply criticized the leadership of the General Front Committee (i.e., Mao) for going too far. He released Li Wenlin and assigned him, whether ironically or not, to carry out the work of suppressing the AB Corps, which Xiang still believed existed. Hoping to reconcile conflicting factions, Xiang invited the leadership of the 20th Army to return to Ningdu for a meeting. Zeng Bingchun, one of the founders of the Donggu Revolutionary Base Area and commander of the 20th Army, was sent to convince the army to return to Ningdu.[77]

Mao had his own version of events. In an impassioned letter of December 20, Mao unreservedly attacked the AB Corps for "initiat-[ing] an uprising in the rear while the front was preparing to fight a decisive war, thus sabotaging the decisive class war." Their activities had been discovered; "If there had not been severe repression," Mao wrote, "the Red Army might have already ceased to exist."[78]

Despite having read Duan Liangbi's report, Xiang Ying's report, and Mao's letter, the Party Center still seemed uncertain what to do. In a message to Ningdu, the Center agreed with Mao, saying that if Mao had moved to attack Nanchang as Li Lisan had demanded, the AB Corps and others could have "created havoc" in the rear areas. They would have been able to "enlarge their ranks, deliberately spread rumors, and slander to shake the revolutionary line and confuse the masses." But the letter went on to state that the Center did not have complete information about the incident and it had not yet received

---

[76] *Mao Zedong nianpu*, vol. 1, p. 330.
[77] Stephen C. Averill, "The Origins of the Futian Incident," in Tony Saich and Hans van de Ven, eds., *New Perspectives on the Chinese Communist Revolution* (Armonk, NY: M.E. Sharpe, 1995), pp. 79–115.
[78] Mao Zedong, "A Letter of Reply by the General Front Committee," in Schram, *Mao's Road to Power*, vol. 3, pp. 704–705.

a formal report from the Front Committee (apparently it wanted something more than the letter Mao had sent),[79] so the Party Center stated that it was delegating a group to go to the soviet area to reorganize the just-established Central Bureau. The group would have "complete authority" to investigate and resolve this issue.[80]

The Party Center designated three people – Ren Bishi, Wang Jiaxiang, and Gu Zuolin – to go to Ningdu to straighten things out. But while they were en route, Pavel Mif intervened. Having read the various reports, Mif came down strongly on Mao's side. On March 18 he issued a decision on the Futian Rebellion that declared the AB Corps was "without a doubt a primary fighting organization of the class enemy" and that it was set on "destroying our party's troops and army."[81] Casting aside the uncertainty it had just displayed, the Politburo issued its own, even harsher, judgment, declaring that the Futian Rebellion had been a "counterrevolutionary uprising led by the AB Corps."[82] All of a sudden, the plenipotentiary powers originally granted to the investigation group were revoked. A decision had been made. The "three-person group" (*sanrentuan*), as the committee became known, arrived in Ningdu on April 17. The first thing the members of the group did was to remove Xiang Ying as acting secretary and restore the authority of Mao and the General Front Committee.

The leaders of the 20th Army were unaware of these developments. Responding to the invitation issued by Xiang Ying, they arrived in Ningdu the day after Ren Bishi and his colleagues had arrived. They

[79] This statement is a bit confusing. Mao had written a report on December 20, and Xiang Ying had written a separate, and conflicting, report in January. See Zhonggong zhongyang wenxian yanjiushi, ed., *Ren Bishi zhuan* (Biography of Ren Bishi), 2 vols. (Beijing: Zhongyang wenxian chubanshe, 2014), vol. 1, p. 246.

[80] "Zhongyang gei diyi fangmianjun zongqianwei, Jiangxi shengwei, ge tewei, ge difang dangbu de xin" (Letter from the Center to the General Front Committee of the First Front Army, the Jiangxi Provincial Party Committee, Various Special Committees, and All Local Party Organizations), in Zhongyang dang'an guan, ed., *Zhonggong zhongyang wenjian xuanji* (Selection of Documents from the CCP Center) (Beijing: Zhonggong zhongyang dangxiao chubanshe, 1999), vol. 7, pp. 139–142.

[81] Li Weimin, "Cong gongchan guoji dang'an kan fan 'AB tuan' douzheng" (Viewing the Struggle against the "AB Corps" from the Files of the Communist International), *Yanhuang chunqiu*, no. 7 (2009), p. 66.

[82] "Zhongyang zhengzhiju guanyu Futian shibian de jueyi" (Central Politburo's Resolution on the Futian Incident), in Zhongyang dang'an guan, *Zhonggong zhongyang wenjian*, vol. 7, p. 203.

were immediately detained. A sentencing meeting was convened, and Liu Di was executed that same day. In the days that followed, the other leaders were similarly executed. On April 19 the three-person group sent a message back to Shanghai: "The Futian Incident has been resolved."[83]

But it was not quite resolved. More tragedy was to follow. The fighters and officers of the 20th Army were still in the field fighting. They received an order to go to Ningdu and arrived in July. Attending a meeting at the Xie Family Temple (*Xie jia sitang*), they were quickly surrounded by the troops of Peng Dehuai and Lin Biao. Handing over their rifles, they were soon bound and led off to the execution ground. Every officer, from the deputy platoon level up – some 700–800 officers – were then slaughtered. Two people managed to survive, one who was recognized and let go and another who had been on sentry duty. The designation "20th Army" was then abolished and has never been restored.[84]

The End of Donggu

On December 19, 1930, Zhang Huizan, the GMD general leading the Eighteenth Division, entered Donggu. His forces stayed in Donggu for three days, killing and burning. They then went in pursuit of the main Communist forces that were some 100 miles away in Ningdu county. Thinking that other GMD forces were nearby, Zhang's forces moved quickly – too quickly. They found themselves in a trap and all 9,000 men were forced to surrender.[85] Zhang was captured alive and taken back to Donggu where he was tried publicly. Not surprisingly, the crowd shouted "Kill! Kill!" and Zhang was promptly executed and decapitated. His head was nailed to a plank and floated down the Gan river for his comrades to recover.

Only three months later, in April 1931, the Second Extermination Campaign attacked Donggu, where the CCP had made its headquarters. Again, the Red Fourth Army was able to ambush the GMD troops, inflicting heavy losses.[86]

---

[83] Jing Yuchuan, "Futian shibian pingfan de qianqian houhou," pp. 39–44.
[84] Ibid.
[85] William Wei, *Counterrevolution: The Nationalists in Jiangxi during the Soviet Period* (Ann Arbor, MI: University of Michigan Press, 1985), pp. 36–38.
[86] Ibid., pp. 42–45.

These two major victories have been made into the stuff of legend, suggesting that Mao's strategy of luring the enemy in deep was correct. But Li Wenlin was also right – encouraging the enemy to come into the base area did indeed inflict enormous damage on the population. Donggu was originally a town of 15,000–20,000, but after these two battles, the population was reduced sharply, perhaps to only 3,000. Even by 1949, the population of Donggu was only about 4,500.[87] Because the town was burnt down in these battles, the oldest building in Donggu now dates from 1932.

The horrors inflicted on Donggu were caused not only by the GMD. Indeed, the damage done to Donggu was largely a product of the campaign against the nonexistent AB Corps, a campaign that cost thousands of lives. When Zhou Enlai arrived in Ruijin, where the Central Bureau had moved, he quickly concluded that the campaign against the AB Corps had been "excessive" (*kuodahua*), and this judgment remains in official historiography today. However, as later research by Dai Xiangqing and Luo Huilan shows, the existence of the AB Corps was not "exaggerated" – it simply did not exist. From May 1930, when the campaign to suppress the AB Corps first began, to the present, not a single case has been substantiated.[88]

Of all the Communist cadres who witnessed the *sufan* campaign, Zhu De certainly understood its history better than most. Li Wenlin had worked under Zhu in the Nanchang Military Education Group, and that group had helped break up – and end – the AB Corps in Nanchang. So why didn't Zhu stop the campaign? Peng Dehuai seems to have asked him more or less the same question. Zhu replied that he was just a plaything in the hands of Mao; he had no authority. Mao had no regard for him, and there was nothing he (Zhu) could do. The always blunt Peng slapped the table and said, "You are a coward. Why didn't you struggle?"[89] Perhaps the answer is that Zhu in fact had struggled – at the Seventh Representative Meeting of the Red Fourth Army in June 1929 – only to be repudiated by Zhou Enlai and the Gutian Conference.

---

[87] Interviews with Donggu Revolutionary Base Area museum staff.

[88] Luo Huilan, "Dangnei su AB tuan 'kuodahua' zhi shuo xinkao" (New Investigation of the Idea that the Suppression of the AB Corps in the Party was "Expanded"), *Nanchang daxue xuebao*, vol. 41, no. 3 (May 2010), pp. 86–91.

[89] Yu Boliu and Ling Buji, *Zhongyang suqu shi*, p. 1165.

Conclusion

In retrospect, the Futian Rebellion seems inevitable. The Donggu Revolutionary Base Area had been formed in response to Qu Qiubai's call for cadres to launch insurrections, and it was rooted in the social conditions of Jiangxi's hill country. That hill country provided both the bandit gangs with whom the educated youth could ally and the mountains in which the growing military force could hide. The Donggu Revolutionary Base Area was under the authority of the West Jiangxi Special Committee, but it was first and foremost a local movement. It recruited its fighters from Donggu and nearby areas, and it responded to the needs of local society, attacking the wealthy of Futian and other communities and resisting the militias sent to suppress it. When Li Wenlin replaced Lai Jingbang, ties between the party organization and the Donggu Revolutionary Base Area were perhaps closer, but Li Wenlin responded to local opportunities and needs, not to abstract commands coming from the provincial party committee and the Party Center in Shanghai.

At the same time, Mao was forming a very different sort of revolutionary group, one that was rooted in Mao's revolutionary vision, not in any particular locality. He was an outsider in the Jinggangshan, and even more so in southwest Jiangxi. He was driven out of the Jinggangshan because the ecology could not support a revolutionary group the size of Mao's and because his base area could be targeted by hostile forces. When Peng Dehuai retreated to the Jinggangshan in December 1928, Mao and Zhu De had no choice but to leave. Building a party army is a difficult matter: militaries tend to focus on military matters and not on organizing the masses, something that Mao had complained about.[90] But Mao wanted to control "every bullet and every gun," something that drew him into tension with Zhu De. With Zhou Enlai's September Letter, Zhu yielded to Mao. Following the Gutian Conference, Zhu felt that there was nothing he could do in the face of the strong-willed Mao.

By the time Mao and Zhu arrived in Beitou, the new site of the West Jiangxi Special Committee, conflicts between local forces and Mao's external forces were heating up. A notice from Li Lisan was all the

---

[90] Mao complained in 1928, "we have relied on the army rather than leading an independent struggle of the masses. This has been a very great error." See Schram, *Mao's Road to Power*, vol. 3, p. 70.

encouragement that Liu Shiqi needed to start amalgamating the local armies under his control – this was the origin of the formation of the Sixth Army, which incorporated Li Wenlin's Second and Fourth Independent Regiments. How to redistribute land, whether by labor power or by the number of persons in a household, might seem to be a minor thing, but Mao knew that control of the land was the foundation of elite control, and distributing land on a per capita basis would undermine elite control. As Mao said, he was determined to reorganize the party so that not a single small landlord or rich peasant would remain in the party. It was this determination that set him firmly against the leaders of the Donggu Revolutionary Base Area.

The "discovery" of AB Corps "members" only three months after the February 7 Meeting provided a tool for attacking the local elite. Although the AB Corps did not exist, the paranoia that sustained the campaign against it was real. As noted above, Li Wenlin, though eventually a target of the campaign, had no doubt that the AB Corps existed.

On December 3, Mao again asserted the General Front Committee's authority over that of the Provincial Action Committee, whether there was any legitimate basis for doing so or not. The arrest of Li Wenlin removed the one leader who had sufficient local support to perhaps resist Mao. It was Li's arrest that opened the way for the arrest and torture of the leaders of the Provincial Action Committee, which controlled the 20th Army. This was the only local force that had not yet been incorporated into the Sixth Army, and its independence was clearly a sticking point. The "rebellion" by those leaders, touched off by Liu Di's escape from interrogation, was a matter of fear, not rebellion. Suffering from torture, their act of rebellion was an act of desperation.

The tragic demise of the 20th Army and the continuation of the campaign against the AB Corps destroyed the Donggu Revolutionary Base Area. Former bandit leader Duan Qifeng escaped and resumed his life in the mountains before being hunted down and executed in 1932. Li Wenlin, as will be discussed in the next chapter, would be executed in 1933. Mao had complained about the resilience of the "intermediate classes," noting that "the most troublesome [people] are not the despotic gentry, but the intermediate classes."[91] In Donggu, the campaign

---

[91] Ibid., p. 104.

against the AB Corps was aimed precisely at these intermediate classes. Only by destroying the intermediate classes could Mao consolidate the foundation of his political power. At the February 7 Meeting Liu Shiqi said that he was not interested in promoting production; rather, he was interested in gaining the support of the masses. What he meant by this was that he was interested in turning the poor peasants against the "intermediate classes." This strategy was not particularly successful – peasants continued to resist joining the military, but the effort nevertheless allowed Mao's external forces to extend their reach down into the grass roots, destroy the social organization of local society, and forge Leninist rule.

5 | *The Logic of* Sufan

The campaign against the AB Corps claimed perhaps 5,000–6,000 lives by the time the Futian Rebellion was over. Although the reasons it developed are complex, it was essentially a hostile takeover. Mao's troops, coming down from the Jinggangshan and having instilled a new level of discipline at the Gutian Conference, reorganized local forces as the Sixth Army, and sought to bring the local Communist organizations under control by eliminating every landlord and rich peasant – basically the entirety of the local leadership, because those who spread communism in inland China in the wake of Chiang Kai-shek's "purification" campaign were primarily educated youth who came from those classes. What is surprising is the degree to which local Jiangxi cadres accepted the stories about the AB Corps and the dangers it supposedly posed to the revolution. As noted above, Li Wenlin was a willing participant in the witch hunt for traitors. He certainly was not the only one. This speaks to the degree of paranoia in a revolutionary group surrounded by hostile forces. The fact that CCP documents continued to use the term "AB Corps" long after that organization ceased to exist (recall that it had been suppressed in Nanchang in April 1927) no doubt made it easier to believe that it had been revived and had infiltrated the CCP.[1]

Paranoia was not the only factor at work, and *sufan* – the suppression of counterrevolutionaries – was not limited to Donggu or to Mao's suppression of local Communists in the name of eliminating the AB Corps. *Sufan* is a broader term that refers to supposed enemies of the revolution of any party or group affiliation, and it would break out throughout the Communist-controlled areas. As the center of the revolution moved eastward to Ruijin, where the "capital" of the Central Soviet was established, intra-party violence would follow.

---

[1] See Stathis N. Kalyvas, *The Logic of Violence in Civil War* (New York: Cambridge University Press, 2006) on indiscriminate violence see pp. 146–172.

Violence paused for a while after Xiang Ying arrived in Ningdu in January 1931 and declared that "education" should be the main way to resolve intra-party disagreements. However, the violence would resume after the "three-person group" – Ren Bishi, Wang Jiaxiang, and Gu Zuolin – arrived in April, restoring Mao to his position and overseeing the July execution of the 700–800 officers of the 20th Army. Indeed, these executions did not mark the end of violence but rather heralded the onset of a new wave of bloodshed.

If the logic of *sufan* is comprehensible in the case of Donggu and the Futian Rebellion, it is more difficult to understand its continuation and expansion as the movement moved from the Donggu area to the Central Soviet capital, Ruijin. Although the campaign in Donggu targeted primarily the so-called AB Corps, it always included others – the Reorganizationalists, the Social Democratic Party, and members of the Third Party. The Reorganizationalists were members of the left wing of the GMD, headed by Wang Jingwei, who demanded the party be reorganized to reduce or eliminate Chiang Kai-shek's role. Because the Wang Jingwei government was based in Wuhan, the Reorganizationalists continued to have considerable strength in Jiangxi. The Social Democratic Party was a small political party, but it became the chief target of suppression efforts in Fujian, where, according to Xiao Ke, it too was nonexistent.[2] The Third Party (*Disandang*) was organized by Tan Pingshan, who had been expelled from the CCP, and Deng Yanda, who worked to build a party that tried to carve out a middle ground between the Communists and the Nationalists. Deng had left the GMD and was later executed by it. What these various elements had in common was that they were opposed to the violence of both the CCP and the GMD, and thus they appealed to the moderates in society. The CCP clearly believed that the moderates were as much of a threat to the revolution as the GMD, so, in addition to the supposed AB Corps members, party operatives sought them out and executed them. In short, enemies of the revolution were everywhere, and so the urge to continue the *sufan* movement was ever-present.

[2] "Xiao Ke tongzhi tan zhongyang suqude chuqi sufan yundong" (Comrade Xiao Ke Discusses the Early Period of the Suppress the Counterrevolutionaries Movement in the Central Soviet), in Zhongguo geming bowuguan yanjiushi, ed., *Dangshi yanjiu ziliao*, no. 4 (Chengdu: Sichuan renmin chubanshe, 1983), p. 405.

Another reason why violence was resumed is because the Fourth Plenum of the Sixth Party Congress in January 1931 installed a new party leadership that had been trained in the Soviet Union and that imported the "ruthless struggles and merciless blows" that were taking place during Stalin's purges. We have already noted that it was Pavel Mif who decreed the execution of the leaders of the Futian Rebellion and that it was the new party leadership that condemned the AB Corps as a "counterrevolutionary" group. One has to be careful because CCP historiography has always blamed the "returned-student" faction for the violence that broke out in the Central Soviet, but, as we have seen, the *sufan* movement started shortly after the February 7 Meeting and reflected Mao's determination to root out landlords and rich peasants in the party. That effort, as we have shown, was related to the push to consolidate control in the hands of Mao, Liu Shiqi, and other outsiders, and it had nothing to do with the Fourth Plenum or those returning from the Soviet Union.

Nevertheless, it was Pavel Mif who decided that the Futian Rebellion was a "counterrevolutionary" movement engineered by the AB Corps, so it is not surprising that he was not going to let up on the *sufan* campaign even after the Futian Rebellion was "resolved." Indeed, before the execution of the officers of the 20th Army, the Party Center in June had issued instructions to the localities declaring, "the party's work of suppressing counterrevolutionaries in the soviet areas is now more important than at any other time." The instructions went on to stress that the fight against the AB Corps and other counterrevolutionary organizations was not only a physical struggle but also an ideological struggle. It was of the utmost importance, the instructions stated, to carry out the struggle against "counterrevolutionary ideology," "especially the deceptive propaganda of reformism" in the soviet areas.[3] *Sufan* would be one vehicle by which moderation in any form would be opposed and rooted out. In October, Ren Bishi and others sent a wire to the Center declaring that Xiang Ying's handling of the Futian case had been "completely wrong."[4] Under this steady

---

[3] "Zhongyang gei suqu geji dang buji hongjun de shunling" (The Center's Instructions to Party Organizations and the Red Army in the Soviet Areas), in Zhongyang dang'an guan, ed., *Zhonggong zhongyang wenjian xuanji* (Selected Central Committee Documents of the CCP) (Beijing: Zhonggong zhongyang dangxiao chubanshe, 1989), vol. 7, pp. 323–332.

[4] "Suqu zhongyangju Shiyue zhen dian (1931 nian, shi yue shiyi ri)" (Soviet Central Bureau, Soviet Area, October Wire (October 11, 1931)), in *Zhongyang geming genjudi lishi ziliao, dang de xitong* (Historical Materials on the Central

drumbeat of radical exhortation it is not surprising that local party organizations began searching for counterrevolutionaries. And they found them, whether they were real or not.

As Zhou Enlai was making his way to Ruijin, the new capital of the soviet area, he stopped in western Fujian, where the suppression of the so-called Social Democratic Party was taking place in much the same way as the purge of the AB Corps was happening in Jiangxi. Aware of the wanton violence, Zhou wrote a report to the Party Center in which he noted that many of the masses feared the Communist Party and would not go near them.[5]

When, in late December, Zhou Enlai arrived in Ruijin, the first matter he looked into was the campaign to suppress counterrevolutionaries. On the basis of his report, the Politburo discussed and approved a resolution on the handling of the suppression campaign. Although the resolution stated that the Front Committee (that is, Mao) had been "absolutely correct" (a judgment it had to make because the Communist International had already said this) in its suppression of the Futian Rebellion, it went on to state that in the way that the Front Committee had looked at the problem of the AB Corps and in the way it had handled things, it had "made many serious mistakes," and thus it "had sown the seeds for a mistaken basis for suppression work."[6] One can guess from this report that Zhou's views were closer to those of Xiang Ying than to those of Mao.

Revolutionary Base Area, The Party System) (Zhongyang wenxian chubanshe and Jiangxi renmin chubanshe, 2011), vol. 3, p. 1792; and "Suqu zhongyang lingdaoren: Mao Zedong zeng aipi yintui" (The Leaders of the Central Bureau in the Soviet Area: Mao Zedong Was Criticized and Retreated), at http://history .sina.com.cn/bk/ds/2013-10-16/165071171.shtml, accessed May 5, 2021.
[5] Dai Xiangqing, "Lun Wan'an baodong" (On the Wan'an Uprising), in Zhonggong Jiangxi shengwei dangshi ziliao zhengji weiyuanhui and Zhonggong Jiangxi shengwei dangshi yanjiushi, eds., *Jiangxi dangshi ziliao*, vol. 5: *Wan'an baodong zhuanji* (Special Volume on the Wan'an Uprising) (Nanchang: "Jiangxi dangshi ziliao" bianjishi, 1988), p. 205.
[6] "Suqu Zhongyangju guanyu sufan gongzuo jueyi an" (Resolution of the Central Bureau of the Soviet Area on the Work of Suppressing Counterrevolutionaries), at https://baike.baidu.com/item/%E8%8B%8F%E5%8C%BA%E4%B8%AD %E5%A4%AE%E5%B1%80%E5%85%B3%E4%BA%8E%E8%8B%8F% E5%8C%BA%E8%82%83%E5%8F%8D%E5%B7%A5%E4%BD%9C%E 5%86%B3%E8%AE%AE%E6%A1%88/9911331, accessed January 11, 2021.

That mistaken basis – seeing counterrevolutionaries everywhere – had led to major mistakes in suppressing counterrevolutionaries. As noted in the previous chapter, after the army had captured Ji'an in October and found lists of alleged AB Corps members, Mao's Front Committee set up a Committee for the Suppression of Counterrevolutionaries in the army (headed by Li Shaojiu). But then other organizations – the Communist Youth League organization, the military, labor unions, and "mass organizations," including hospitals – all set up their own committees. These organizations all operated on their own. The Central Bureau's report complains that most such committees did not have collective leadership, meaning that they were under the control of individuals rather than under the supervision of the local party leadership. Party organizations and governments could carry out suppression as they wished, arresting people as they wanted, questioning, and torturing them. The suppression campaign, the report said, "took killing people as a child's game." Such excesses terrified peasants and drove people to join with those opposed to the party.[7]

A later report is very explicit about the excesses of the campaign. Torture was ubiquitous. Victims were whipped, and if that did not work, there were many other more severe methods. Most could not stand the pain and confessed that they were members of counterrevolutionary organizations even though they were not. And they were forced to cough up the names of coconspirators, so the cycle would continue.[8]

This violence had very negative implications for the party. In many places, normal party work came to a halt as everything revolved around the suppression of counterrevolutionaries. If anyone was inclined not to pursue this work vigorously, he was likely to be suspected of sabotaging the party's work and of being a member of the AB Corps himself. Thus there was a real incentive to arrest and torture innocent people. The panic spread by the movement made it difficult to recruit people

[7] Ibid.

[8] "Jiangxi suqu Zhonggong shengwei gongzuo zongjie baogao (xu er)" (Summary Report from the CCP Provincial Party Committee's Work in the Soviet Area (Part Two)), in Jiangxisheng dang'an guan and Zhonggong Jiangxi shengwei dangxiao dangshi jiaoyanshi, *Zhongyang geming genjudi shiliao xuanbian* (Selected Historical Materials on the Central Revolutionary Base Area), 3 vols. (Nanchang: Jiangxi renmin chubanshe, 1982), vol. 1, pp. 476–489.

into the military. People especially feared being transferred from one unit to another because it was easy for people in the new unit to suspect the newcomer of being a counterrevolutionary. In October 1930, when the struggle against the AB Corps was just five months old, there were still more than 35,000 party members in the area. By November 1935, there were only 15,000.[9]

Morale in the party plummeted. One Politburo report states that party members came to believe that the AB Corps and other counter-revolutionary groups were larger and better organized than the Communist Party. Worse, they came to believe that the counterrevolutionary groups were welcomed by the masses. In short, they feared that the AB Corps could not be wiped out.[10]

One concrete measure Zhou Enlai took to bring the suppression campaign under control was to sanction Li Shaojiu, Mao's henchman and the person responsible for setting off the Futian Rebellion. A party decision accused him of making "serious mistakes" and "even violating the decisions of his superiors and acting arbitrarily, bringing about the extreme error of making suppression work the center [of all work]." Accordingly, he was sentenced to six months of party supervision and demoted to political commissar of the Tenth Division of the Fourth Army of the Red First Front Army. In other words, he was still being protected by Mao even after being sanctioned. When the Red Army left Jiangxi on what turned out to be the Long March, Li was left behind to carry on the struggle. He died in 1935 in unclear circumstances.[11]

Another measure Zhou took was to centralize the Political Security Bureau (*Zhengzhi baowei ju*).[12] The Political Security Bureau was conceived as an internal security force that would be in charge of investigations; decisions on executions would be referred up to the

---

[9] Ding Renxiang, "Shilun Donggu geming genjudi dang de jianshe" (Discussing the Construction of the Party in the Donggu Base Area), *Zhongguo Jinggangshan ganbu xueyuan xuebao*, vol. 6, no. 3 (May 2013), pp. 59–64.
[10] "Suqu Zhongyangju guanyu sufan gongzuo jueyi an."
[11] Dai Xiangqing and Luo Huilan, *AB tuan yu futian shibian shimo*, pp. 210–211.
[12] On January 27, 1932, the Central People's Government promulgated the *Zhonghua suweiai gongheguo guojia zhengzhi baoweiju zuzhi gangyao* (Organization Principles of the State Political Security Bureau of the Chinese Soviet Republic). See Song Lei, "Guojia zhengzhi baoweiju xianwei renzhide lishi tanyi" (Exploring the History of the State Political Protection Bureau That Few Know), at http://dangshi.people.com.cn/n/2015/1202/c85037-27881688 .html, accessed January 11, 2021.

provincial level. The objective was not to stop the hunt for counter-revolutionaries – Zhou never doubted that there were counterrevolu-tionaries – but to bring the investigations under control in order to stop the wanton violence and to prevent the negative effects Zhou had seen, particularly the disruption of party organs and the alienation of the population, from occurring. As always, Zhou wanted to impose order and make party organs function efficiently. In an effort to do this, he put his long-term associate, Deng Fa, in charge.

At the time, Zhou Enlai was in a very powerful position. The Third Plenary Session of the Sixth Central Committee in September 1930 had harshly criticized Li Lisan, ordering him to go to Moscow for "study." The Comintern had been so frustrated with Li Lisan and his colleagues that it had cut off funding for the Chinese Communist Party. The Fourth Plenum, held on January 7, 1931, was really a continuation of the Third Plenum but with much firmer direction from the Comintern. Pavel Mif had arrived in China in December and had taken charge of reorganizing the leadership of the party. His student, Wang Ming, was put in charge, though formally Xiang Zhongfa, a worker, remained chairman, a position he held from July 1928 until June 1931 when he was arrested by the GMD.[13] Lu Futan, another worker, joined the Politburo. In September, Wang Ming's close friends, Qin Bangxian, better known as Bo Gu, and Zhang Wentian, joined the Politburo along with Chen Yun and others. But Zhou was the most experienced person and he was in charge of the Organization Department and military affairs. As head of the Central Bureau, he was also in charge of the soviet areas. Xiang Ying had been acting chair, but his authority was superseded by the three-person group after they arrived in April. When Zhou finally arrived in Ruijin in December 1931, his authority should have been final. But his "moderate" policies regarding the "AB Corps" were soon challenged.

Zhou Enlai was not the only source of concern for Mao. One might think that Mao's position was very strong – the Red Army had defeated the First and Second Extermination Campaigns, albeit with enormous civilian casualties, and had survived the Third Extermination Campaign. However, Shanghai still remained wary of Mao. It will be

---

[13] This position is confirmed by the authoritative *Zhongguo gongchandang lijie zhongyang weiyuan dacidian, 1921–2003* (Central Committee Members of the Chinese Communist Party through All Sessions, 1921–2003), p. 1181.

recalled that the reason the Party Center in Shanghai decided to set up the Central Bureau in the first place was that it wanted tighter control over Mao and his military forces. This was a concern that went back to at least February 1929 when the party ordered Mao and Zhu to leave their troops and go to Shanghai, which Mao artfully but firmly refused to do (see Chapter Three).

Therefore, in 1931, Mao had good reason to be concerned about his position and authority. Xiang Ying had arrived in December 1930, then the three-person group had arrived in April, and finally Zhou Enlai had arrived in December. Those concerns would only increase when Bo Gu and Zhang Wentian arrived in 1933.

Mao arrived in Ruijin, the new capital of the Soviet area, in September 1931 to prepare for the First All-China Representative Conference. In October he wrote to the Center saying that the Central Bureau had been overly focused on the military and that Xiang Ying was "insufficient to lead." Therefore, he, Mao Zedong, would serve as acting secretary. Mao also asked to expand the Central Bureau, adding several of his followers, such as Lin Biao, Zeng Shan, and Chen Yi.[14] Shanghai was not happy with Mao's proposal. It replied that the Central Bureau was the representative of the Center in the soviet areas and it should "absolutely" not follow the military. Moreover, the Central Bureau should not be expanded, nor should it take the place of local party organs.[15]

In late October, Mao notified the Center that a provisional government had been set up in the soviet area and he was chairman. Being named chairman of the soviet – a government organ – was obviously a demotion. It did, however, confer the title "chairman" on Mao, and he used that title for the much of his life (though as chairman of the party, not the government).

The First All-China Representative Conference, which convened November 1–5 in Ruijin, soon broke into arguments over the base area, military matters, and land policy. Mao's booklet on "Oppose Bookishism," written in 1930, was criticized as "narrow empiricism" and Mao's land policies were criticized for representing the "rich peasant line" (although they were precisely the opposite). The Red

---

[14] Zhonggong zhongyang wenxian yanjiushi, ed., *Mao Zedong nianpu, 1893–1949* (Annual Chronicle of Mao Zedong, 1893–1949), 3 vols., revised ed. (Beijing: Zhongyang wenxian chubanshe, 2013), vol. 1, p. 355.

[15] Ibid., p. 356.

Army was criticized for having not given up "guerilla-ism." Such criticism must have been made by Ren Bishi and Wang Jiaxiang as leaders of the Central Bureau who likely were frustrated with Mao's continued independence. As the compilers of *Mao's Chronicles* (*Mao Zedong nianpu*) put it, the conference "started to squeeze Mao Zedong out of the leadership of the Red Army in the soviet area."[16] No wonder Mao was not happy with Zhou Enlai's criticism of the way that the campaign against the AB Corps was being carried out.

On April 22 the Provisional Central Government Executive Committee (*Linshi zhongyang zhengfu zhixing weiyuanhui*) – that is, Mao – issued a directive called "Correcting the Mistake of Relaxing the Suppression of Counterrevolutionaries." The directive stated, "Governments at various levels have misunderstood the Center's directive to set up judicial procedures as meaning not to handle counterrevolutionary work … [It seems] that the meaning of completely suppressing counterrevolutionaries has been forgotten."[17] Not long thereafter, the Jiangxi party committee sent a report to the Center stating that Jiangxi was witnessing a "passive" attitude in the work of suppressing counterrevolutionaries. The report blamed this passivity on the belief that the AB Corps had already been suppressed and the belief that the counterrevolutionaries could not come back to life.[18]

In order to inject new energy into the campaign to suppress counterrevolutionaries, the Jiangxi Party Committee, with the approval of the State Security Bureau, held a mass meeting on May 30, 1932, to commemorate the May Thirtieth Movement (of 1925). The main exhibit at the mass meeting was the execution of Li Wenlin and Zeng Bingchun, leaders of the Donggu Revolutionary Base Area. Their condemnation and execution were intended to reinvigorate the campaign to suppress counterrevolutionaries.

The journal of the Politburo in the soviet area, *Struggle* (*Douzheng*), worked hard to pump up the atmosphere. One 1933 article declared that judicial niceties were not as important as getting the masses involved. If the masses really hate a counterrevolutionary leader, the article stated, then there should be an open judgment and the masses should decide on his punishment. It was not necessary to mechanically

[16] Ibid., p. 358.
[17] Quoted in Dai Xiangqing and Luo Huilan, *AB tuan yu futian shibian shimo*, p. 216.
[18] Quoted in ibid., p. 216.

go through legal procedures.[19] Another article declared, "Soviet law was created to struggle against counterrevolutionaries."[20] In this way, the *sufan* campaign was revived. It was soon merged with a new movement, the Land Investigation Movement.

Mao's position in the soviet area, always precarious after those involved in the Central Bureau began arriving in Jiangxi, was even more so after the Ningdu Conference in October 1931 when he was relieved of all military responsibility. Others associated with him, including his younger brother Mao Zetan and Deng Xiaoping, were assigned lower-level positions as well. In 1934 the Central Bureau even recommended that Mao go to Moscow for medical treatment. Interestingly enough, Mao's later rival, Wang Ming, then the CCP representative to the Comintern, argued against the idea. Wang's objection allowed Mao to stay on in the Soviet area, to go on the Long March, and to rise to power, ultimately at Wang Ming's expense.[21]

The Land Investigation Movement

In April 1931 Gu Shunzhang, in charge of the CCP's intelligence work, escorted Zhang Guotao to the Eyuwan Base Area (see below). On his return trip, Gu lingered in Wuhan. Needing money, he used his skills as a magician to put on a public show. Unfortunately for him, he was recognized by one of his former subordinates, who reported him to the GMD. Quickly arrested, Gu turned traitor and began to reveal details about CCP organization and safe houses. Gu's betrayal was quickly exposed by an underground Communist working in GMD intelligence, but many CCP leaders were nevertheless seized. Wuhan leader Yun Daiying, then in a GMD prison but still using a pseudonym, was recognized. Xiang Zhongfa, the general secretary of the Communist Party, was soon arrested and, like Gu, he betrayed the CCP. Cai Hesen, Mao's old friend who had played a role in converting Mao to communism, was arrested in June. Shanghai had become too dangerous to work in, and party leaders began to scatter.[22]

---

[19] Ibid., pp. 222–223. [20] Ibid., p. 223.
[21] Huang Daoxuan, *Zhangli yu xianjie*, p. 22.
[22] See "Gu Shunzhang," at https://baike.baidu.com/item/顾顺章. See also Chang Kuo-t'ao (Zhang Guotao), *The Rise of the Chinese Communist Party: The*

Wang Ming returned to Moscow as the CCP representative to the Comintern. Before leaving, Wang appointed Bo Gu, then only twenty-four years old, as the "responsible person" to take charge of party affairs. Bo finally arrived in Ruijin in January 1933, and in June 1933, just as the GMD was preparing to launch its fifth and final "extermination campaign," Bo Gu began a "land investigation" movement (*chatian yundong*). This movement was ostensibly to correct mistakes made in the previous distribution of land; in particular, the movement declared that some landlords and rich peasants had been able to retain land by "disguising themselves as middle peasants." Therefore the movement was supposed to check the class standing of each household. No doubt land redistribution had been less than fair, as cadres took advantage of their positions to retain land for themselves or their relatives, but the movement was not primarily about fairness. Rather, it was mainly about extending political control, building solidarity in the face of the impending GMD assault, and raising funds.[23] In this way the movement resembled the February 7 Meeting that Mao had used to purge the Jiangxi party of local leaders and to extend his control.

Now a new leadership would use the Land Investigation Movement to deepen its hold on power. One target was Mao Zedong, who was ironically put in charge of the movement. As head of the campaign, he was supposed to correct his own previous policy.[24] Just as the February 7 Meeting had adopted new restrictions on rich peasants, the Land Investigation Movement put forth a new, harsher line, stressing "class struggle," that would heighten ideological tension in the area and lead to accusations of trying to protect landlords and rich peasants – and to the criticism of Mao for following a "rich peasant line." Another goal of the movement was extortion. The soviet was under intense financial pressures and needed money, so reviewing the class status of every household was intended to squeeze money from those peasants who had money. This burden fell primarily on middle peasants because by this time no

Autobiography of Chang Kuo-t'ao, vol. 1: *1921–1927*, vol. 2: *1928–1938* (Lawrence, KS: University of Kansas Press, 1971–1972).

23 Zhang Lihong and Xiao Wenyan, "Chatian yundong yu zhongyang suqu minzhong dongyuan" (The Land Investigation Movement and Mobilizing the Masses in the Central Soviet), *Jianghan daxue xuebao*, no. 27 (October 2008), pp. 107–112.

24 Tony Saich, *From Rebel to Ruler: One Hundred Years of the Chinese Communist Party* (Cambridge, MA: Harvard University Press, 2021), p. 88.

landlords or rich peasants were left.[25] Finally, the movement was intended to mobilize peasants – to recruit them into the Red Army – just as the February 7 Meeting's attack on local landlords and rich peasants in the local party organization was intended to mobilize people to fight for the cause. Bo Gu, and the others who had returned from the Soviet Union, were eager to apply the "ruthless blows and merciless struggles" that they had learned in Moscow. To carry out the movement, teams were composed of people from the Land Department, the Industry and Agriculture Inspection Department, and the Political Protection Department, and special inspectors were set up to oversee the movement. People from the Financial Department were to collect fines from landlords and rich peasants. People from the Military Department were sent out to organize or reorganize local forces and mobilize people to join the military. The movement also eliminated large numbers of those deemed to be class enemies.[26] Such teams would convene a mass meeting and ask the masses if so-and-so was a landlord or a rich peasant, or whether someone else was a member of the AB Corps. If the masses did not denounce the target, the team would suggest that the masses had colluded with the landlords and rich peasants. Fearing the consequences of such accusations, peasants would condemn their neighbors. But such meetings did not build solidarity; on the contrary, they alienated the masses from the party.[27] So the Land Investigation Movement extorted money by intensifying the *sufan* movement.

When the soviet government was first set up, its finances were in good shape. Red Army units could go out and find wealthy people – always identifying them as "local bullies" (*tuhao*) – and rob them in the age-old manner of local bandits. But as the GMD tightened its embargo on the area, it became impossible for the CCP to launch raids outside their area of control. Therefore, in order to address financial issues, the soviet government issued public bonds and pressured the masses to make grain contributions. According to Huang Daoxuan, the burden on peasants reached an average of 15.7 percent of their income, and sometimes as high as 30 percent.[28] Considering that taxes prior to the conflict in the area had been about 4–6 percent, the burden can be imagined. But even as government finances were strengthened, there was a sense that local

---

[25] Huang Daoxuan, *Zhangli yu xianjie*, p. 295.
[26] Zhang Hongqing and Xiao Wenyan, "Chatian yundong," p. 2.
[27] Huang Daoxuan, *Zhangli yu xianjie*, p. 296.   [28] Ibid., p. 317.

cadres were a special class. Local cadres forced peasants to work their land, and the phenomenon of eating and drinking at public expense became surprisingly common.[29]

The result of these movements was that peasants fled the area if they could and they tried to avoid serving in the Red Army. As fighting took a toll on numbers, the authorities pressed the population for recruits. But even as authorities pressed for new recruits, desertion rates grew. In the year from August 1933 to July 1934, the army was suddenly expanded by 120,000 men. This expansion was achieved through "coercion, ordering, deception, enticement, and bribing the masses (*shoumai qunzhong*)." Since the recruits were not voluntary, desertion rates were high. In one county of Ruijin, 2,500 soldiers ran away. Despite going after them and applying force, arrest and even execution, still 800–900 were able to flee. According to the General Political Department of the Red Army, in one recruitment effort, they only got three or four out of every ten who were registered; the others all fled.[30]

Part of the reason recruitment was so difficult was that peasants were perennially attached to their home areas. They were willing, even eager, to join forces that protected their villages and towns, but they were unwilling to join the main force and leave their homes. According to Xiao Ke's reminiscences, "Desertion was related to where the Red Army went. For instance, if the Red Army went to Changting to fight, the soldiers from Yongding would run away."[31]

As conditions in the soviet area became increasingly difficult, there was a vicious circle: the greater the number of soldiers lost in the fighting, the more the army had to press local areas for replacements. The more peasants left the land to fight, the fewer were left to farm. With fewer left to farm, and with land ownership so tenuous, there was less food. The less food there was, the more the army used coercion to collect grain. The more it used coercion to press peasants to fight or to contribute grain, the more the army alienated the population. The more the population was alienated, the greater the party resorted to "suppressing the counterrevolutionaries." By the time the Red Army was finally forced to leave the soviet area in Jiangxi, tens of thousands had been executed. Others had fled. The population in the fifteen counties central to the soviet area fell by some 20 percent.[32]

---

[29] Ibid., pp. 320–321. [30] Ibid., p. 332. [31] Quoted in ibid., p. 330.
[32] Xiao Ke, *Xiao Ke huiyilu* (Xiao Ke's Memoir) (Beijing: Jiefangjun chubanshe, 1997).

Mao bickered constantly with the Politburo over proper tactics to fight the surrounding GMD troops, but in the final analysis it was the brutality of the Communist Party that alienated the population and made it impossible to sustain the fighting. Such brutality extended from the suppression of the non-existent AB Corps in Donggu, to the suppression of so-called counterrevolutionaries in the Land Investigation Movement, to the use of coercion to recruit soldiers.

The Eyuwan Revolutionary Base Area

As we have seen, the Donggu Revolutionary Base Area developed in two phases, the first emerging from educated youth building a very local movement based on personal networks, kinship relations, and physical isolation, and the second based on Mao's revolutionary movement moving into the area and purging local revolutionaries on the pretext that they were members of the nonexistent AB Corps. The violence was extended into the Central Soviet area as the center of revolutionary activities moved to Ruijin and as Bo Gu and other leaders from Shanghai moved to Jiangxi, displacing Mao. Local cadres and peasants, particularly middle peasants, were the victims as outsiders tried to exert control and extract resources.

The Eyuwan base area differed from Donggu and the Central Soviet not only in that it was wealthier and that its leaders were better educated but also in that it was more decentralized and thus there was more rivalry among leaders. The story of Eyuwan has been told before, most recently by William Rowe, who has set it the context of its 700-year history of local violence, so it need not be told again here.[33] But there are important similarities to the Donggu Base Area, in particular the emergence of a leadership of an educated local elite followed by the violent imposition of external control.

The Eyuwan Base Area developed around two major areas. The first was centered around Qiliping, about sixty miles northeast of Wuhan and including the two counties of Huang'an (now Hong'an) and Macheng. The other was centered around Jinjiazhai, about eighty miles due north of Wuhan, and it included Lu'an,[34] in northwest

---

[33] William T. Rowe, *Crimson Rain: Seven Centuries of Violence in a Chinese County* (Stanford, CA: Stanford University Press, 2007).
[34] Although standard pronunciation would be *liu'an*, locals pronounce it *lu'an*.

Anhui, and Shangcheng, across the border in Hubei. In between the two areas was a no-man's-land.[35]

The key figure in the creation of the Eyuwan Base Area, particularly around Huang'an, was Dong Biwu. Born in Huang'an in 1886, Dong received a traditional education and achieved the *xiucai* degree in 1903, just two years before the examination system was abolished. In 1911, he participated in the revolution that ended the Qing dynasty and he joined Sun Yat-sen's Revolutionary Alliance. In 1914 he went to Japan, where he studied law for a year before returning to China and participating in various political movements. In 1919, he was active in the May Fourth Movement.

In 1920, Dong Biwu and two others, Chen Tanqiu and Zhang Guo'en, established the Wuhan Middle School as a private institution, and they used that school to recruit students. Overall, some two-thirds of party members in Wuhan were students.[36] Dong Biwu and others from the Wuhan Middle School attracted students primarily from their native county, Huang'an, in southern Hubei, enrolling some thirty students.[37] Others came from nearby Macheng and other areas that would become hotbeds of Communist organizing.[38] As Dong Biwu, other teachers, and their students returned to their natal villages for vacation, they would spread their radical ideas. So, as in Donggu, the early activists were primarily educated youth from relatively well-off families. As one veteran of the Eyuwan Base Area put it, "Those who were first to carry out revolution were not the peasants and not the workers, but rather the revolutionary intellectuals. It was they who propagandized the logic of revolution and who organized the peasants to carry out revolution."[39] Indeed, the activists who formed the Eyuwan Base Area were generally even better educated and wealthier than those who developed Donggu. Dong Biwu was certainly much better educated than Lai Jingbang. In 1920, Dong and Chen Tanqiu would establish the Wuhan Communist Small Group, and in the following year they would represent Wuhan at the First Party Congress in Shanghai.

[35] Odoric Y.C. Wou, *Mobilizing the Masses: Building Revolution in Henan* (Stanford, CA: Stanford University Press, 1994), especially Chapters 3 and 4.
[36] Huang Wenzhi, *Eyuwan suqu daolu: Yige minzhong dongyuan de shijian yanjiu (1920–1932)*, revised edn (Saarbrücken: Jinlang xueshu chubanshe, 2017), p. 82.
[37] Ibid., p. 48.   [38] Ibid., p. 49.   [39] Quoted in ibid., p. 42, fn. 2.

When one looks at the leaders of the major uprisings in the Eyuwan area, it turns out that nearly all of them were local intellectuals. Of the nine cadres on the party committee that organized the Macheng Uprising in 1927, seven were educated youth from the area. Of the six cadres who led the Shangnan Uprising in 1929, two were from Macheng, not far away, and the other four were from Shangcheng. There was only one peasant. Of the five cadres who led the Liuhuo Uprising in 1929, four were local intellectuals, and one was a worker from Anhui's Fengtai who had worked for a long time in Liuhuo. Lu'an county in western Anhui had forty-four party members, forty-two of whom were intellectuals. Huoqiu county originally had six party members, all of whom were intellectuals.[40] When the Northwest Hubei Special Committee was established in 1928, there were 150 cadres – 80 percent of whom were intellectuals.[41]

The earliest uprisings in the area were near the Yangtze river, in Macheng and Guangshan. These were relatively well-off places, particularly when compared to the poor places in the mountains north of them. What distinguished these places was the number of revolutionary intellectuals. Coming from elite families, they were able to influence the peasants around them, much as Zeng Tianyu had organized peasants in Wan'an (see Chapter 1). At this time, the party played little role as an organization; people followed individuals, so social standing and personal characteristics were critical.[42]

In the wake of Chiang's April 12 coup, one of Chiang's generals, Xia Douyin, from Macheng county in the area that would become Eyuwan, began marching on Wuhan, slaughtering as he went. Soon, following Wang Jingwei's split with the Communists, Xia's violence was joined by others carrying out the Wuhan government's new policy of party purification. Those cadres who had not already returned to their villages and towns before the crackdown did so immediately thereafter, joining those who had already begun organizing peasants into peasant associations.[43] At the same time, as the crackdown on Communists deepened, landlords began returning to their towns and organizing forces to root out the Communists. In some areas, Communist leaders left the party and turned themselves in. For instance, in Huang'an, all

[40] Ibid., p. 82.
[41] Chen Jie, "Eyuwan suqu ganbu qunti yanjiu" (Study of the Cadre Group in the Eyuwan Soviet District) (Zhengzhou University, MA paper, 2015), pp. 27–28.
[42] Huang Wenzhi, *Eyuwan suqu daolu*, p. 104.   [43] Ibid., p. 136.

the members of the county party committee, save two, turned themselves in. The party leadership in eight of the ten districts under Huang'an turned tail. One of the Communist survivors, Zheng Weisan, recalls that by the time of the Autumn Harvest Uprising, only one out of ten party members was still active.[44]

However, the party members in Huang'an and Macheng (often called by the single name Huangma because there was a single party organization and Huang'an had originally been part of Macheng county) were still active, if not active enough for higher levels. When the Party Center was trying to launch uprisings throughout the country, it criticized cadres in Huangma for having "not expunged the continuing poison of opportunism."[45] As the local party organization was facing this pressure from higher levels, it was also facing pressure from the landlords who had returned and organized Red Spear Societies, civil corps (*mintuan*), and "expunge-Communist groups" (*changongtuan*). According to Wang Shusheng, a Macheng county native and later a famous PLA general, landlords based in Henan's Guangshan county organized 10,000 or more Red Spear members to come south, steal cattle, destroy crops, and slaughter people. Facing this threat, only the Communist Party was well enough organized to offer protection, particularly for those who had participated in previous movements against local landlords. With the radical intellectuals leading, peasants took up arms; as clashes began, and in the face of retaliation, they became increasingly violent, eventually killing over 1,000 Red Spear adherents.[46] As they killing progressed, the peasants felt their own strength. On November 14, the uprising took the county seat, something that rarely occurred in Jiangxi. The peasants held the county seat for twenty-one days, which was long enough to demonstrate the force of an aroused peasantry and to stimulate the surrounding areas, such as Huanggang, Luotian, and Shangcheng, to undertake their own uprisings.[47] Nevertheless, official troops eventually surrounded the rebels and retook the county seat. Most of the peasants disappeared into the countryside and even some of the cadres left the party. Other cadres were able to gather enough peasants to organize guerrilla activity south of Mulan Mountain. Their activities became so extreme – killing and burning homes – that the Party Center would not recognize them, saying they were like bandits.[48]

[44] Ibid., p. 138.   [45] Ibid., p. 137.   [46] Ibid., pp. 139–140.   [47] Ibid., p. 142.
[48] Ibid., p. 143.

The Eyuwan Base Area developed steadily during its first several years, despite the setback following Wang Jingwei's decision to split with the Communist Party and, more impressively, despite two "extermination" campaigns launched by the GMD (more would be launched later). By February of 1931, the area encompassed twelve counties and perhaps a million people. There were approximately 10,000 Communist Party members in the area, and there were party branches in other counties not controlled by the party.[49] Certainly in terms of scope, the Eyuwan Base Area was even more successful than that in Donggu.

Like Donggu, however, it was very much a local movement. Its leaders were almost entirely educated youth from the area, and, as in Donggu, "class struggle" was limited. Leaders distinguished between landlords who were sympathetic to the movement and "evil gentry" who were not. So "localism" was a problem from the perspective of the Party Center in Shanghai. Much as Shanghai had tried to exert control over Mao, succeeding only when circumstances forced it to move to the Soviet area, it was determined to control the movement in Eyuwan. This task seemed urgent both because the base area was not responding to instructions from Shanghai and because, after the Fourth Plenum in January 1931, the line had changed. Li Lisan was disgraced and Wang Ming was in charge.

Zhang Guotao and the Unfolding of *Sufan*

Following the Fourth Plenum, the Party Center had requested that the Eyuwan Base Area investigate Zeng Zhongshu and Kuang Jixun, the party leaders who had been sent to the base following the Third Plenum, at which Li Lisan had been criticized. The new leadership wanted to make sure that Zeng and Kuang were not "compromising" with the Li Lisan line after it had been definitively rejected. Not hearing anything for a month, the Party Center decided to dissolve the Eyuwan Special Committee, which was under the dual control of the Yangtze Bureau and the Hubei Provincial Committee, and to set up a branch of the Central Bureau to exercise more direct control.

---

[49] Tan Kesheng and Ouyang Liang, eds., *Eyuwan geming genjudi douzhengshi jianbian* (Short History of the Struggle in the Eyuwan Revolutionary Base Area) (Beijing: Jiefangjun chubanshe, 1987), pp. 179–180.

Zhou Enlai, who was in charge of the base areas and military operations, originally appointed Ke Qingshi and Li Xishi to go to the base
area and head the new branch. They had both worked in the base area
and Ke had participated in the establishment of the Anhui Party
Committee. But Ke had supported the call by party members to hold
an emergency meeting to protest the arbitrary manner in which the
Comintern had forced the CCP to accept a new leadership at the Fourth
Plenum, so he was in political trouble. Therefore Zhou decided to
instead send Shen Zemin, Fang Ying, and Shu Chuanxian. Shen, who
was the younger brother of the famous writer Mao Dun, had recently
returned from Moscow and was considered one of the so-called 28
Bolsheviks. Fang and Shu were both from Wang Ming's native area
(Jinzhai, Anhui, not far from Lu'an); Fang was also Wang Ming's
classmate in Moscow, and Shu had close relations with Xu Jishen,
one of the leaders of the Eyuwan Base Area. Zhou Enlai was obviously
trying to balance those who would firmly implement the Fourth
Plenum line with those who would be acceptable to the leaders of
Eyuwan.[50]

However, Zhou worried that Shen Zemin did not have sufficient
prestige in the party, so he changed his order and decided to retain the
Eyuwan Special Committee, putting Shen in charge, but subordinating
that committee to the new branch of the Central Bureau. To take
charge of the new branch, Zhou turned to Zhang Guotao and Chen
Changhao. Zhang Guotao was one of the founders of the party and had
years of experience in the labor movement. Chen was considered one of
the 28 Bolsheviks. So Chen and Shen Zemin could keep an eye on
Zhang Guotao, and Shu Chuanxian would provide an entrée into
local society. Arranging personnel appointments was clearly an art!

In early June, the Red Fourth Army, unfortunately with the same
designation as Mao's army in Jiangxi, had been driven north out of its
original base area to southern Henan. Facing food shortages and seeing
that the GMD was amassing troops for its Third Extermination
Campaign against the soviet area in Jiangxi, political commissar
Zeng Zhongsheng suggested that the main force of the army move
south toward Qichun and Huangmei along the Yangtze river. Part of

---

[50] Chen Yung-fa, "Zhengzhi kongzhi he Chunzhong dongyuan: Eyuwan sufan"
(Political Control and Mass Mobilization: Suppressing Counterrevolutionaries
in Eyuwan), *Dalu zazhi*, pt. 1, vol. 86, no. 1 (January 1993), p. 30.

the plan was to attack landed bullies and evil gentry to replenish its depleted coffers. When Zhang Guotao heard of this plan, he opposed it, saying that it appeared to be a revival of Li Lisan's adventurism. It would arouse enemy opposition and make it more difficult to develop the Red Army. Instead, he proposed consolidating the base area around Shangcheng and then moving east to threaten Nanjing.[51]

The Red Fourth Army had already started south and had successfully taken several towns. Zhang Guotao called a meeting of the military commission and ordered the Red Fourth Army to first take Yingshan and then move east. The army successfully took Yingshan, but then the leadership decided that their original plan of moving south was better than Zhang's plan of heading east. Before it could go far, however, it received an order to head back north. Even as it started to move north, it convened a meeting at which it decided to reject the order. But receiving repeated orders to return north, Zeng Zhongsheng relented and started to move north. When he reached Mabu in western Anhui, Chen Changhao was there to replace Zeng as political commissar. Without replacing Zeng as political commissar, Zhang Guotao would have lost control of the Fourth Army.[52] The campaign to suppress counterrevolutionaries followed from this logic; that is to say, the need to control the local military forces.

Indeed, when Zhang Guotao first got to Eyuwan, he had already begun to emphasize the importance of suppressing counterrevolution-aries. At the First Enlarged Meeting of the Eyuwan Central Bureau Branch in late June, Zhang Guotao described *sufan* as "one of our most basic and most urgent tasks at present." In July, at the Second Representative Congress of Eyuwan, he pushed for the passage of a resolution on suppressing counterrevolutionaries. Thereafter, party organizations at various levels held meetings to make arrangements for carrying out the suppression of counterrevolutionaries. Zhang also undertook the reorganization of the Political Protection Bureau, which had responsibility for carrying out the suppression, to bring it directly under the control of the Central Bureau branch and to appoint a new head. The function of the Political Protection Bureau, as in Jiangxi, was to weed out Reorganizationalists, Third Party members, and members of the AB Corps. To this end, all people who had come over from the GMD – no matter whether they had mutinied,

[51] Ibid.   [52] Ibid., pp. 28–29.

voluntarily come over, or been captured – would be investigated, as would all with landlord or rich peasant backgrounds or intellectual backgrounds.[53]

Given Zhang's determination to root out suspected counterrevolutionaries and to take control over a movement of locals, it is not surprising that he, as an outsider, used this incident of "insubordination" to launch a *sufan* movement. Xu Jishen was a perfect target. He was from Lu'an in the heart of the Eyuwan Base Area. He had graduated from Lu'an Normal School and then was a member of the first class at the Whampoa Military Academy. During the Northern Expedition he was a regiment commander. In 1929 he went to Shanghai, where he was part of a training group for high-level cadres organized by Zhou Enlai. He returned to Hubei in 1930 and was one of the leaders of the burgeoning Communist movement. When the Eyuwan Special Committee was established in March 1930, Xu was named commander of the Twelfth Division of the Red First Army, which later was reorganized into the Red Fourth Army. Xu thus had deep roots in the Eyuwan area. He also had broad social connections, which would make him vulnerable.[54]

On November 6, 1931, Zhang Guotao oversaw the questioning and trial of Xu Jishen. There were some thirty judges and 1,000 onlookers – whose anger would make any refutation of the charges impossible. Charged with the suspicion that he intended to defect to the GMD, Xu was condemned to death by the crowd. Following Xu's conviction, the Eyuwan Branch ordered every county to investigate anyone who came from a landlord or rich peasant background, anyone who was an intellectual, and anyone who had come over from the GMD, whether by revolt or by capture. As in Jiangxi, the investigations were to be carried out by the political protection bureaus. Something of the atmosphere can be gleaned from the fact that Fang Ying, party secretary of the Northwest Anhui Special Committee, was removed from office because he had not been energetic enough in pursuing counterrevolutionaries.[55]

---

[53] Tan Kesheng and Ouyang Zhi Liang, *Eyuwan geming genjudi douzhengshi jianbian*, pp. 209–211.

[54] Chen Yung-fa, "Zhengzhi kongzhi he qunzhong dongyuan: Eyuwan sufan" (Political Control and Mass Mobilization: Suppressing Counterrevolutionaries in Eyuwan), *Dalu zazhi*, pt. 2, vol. 86, no. 2 (February 1993), p. 7 1.

[55] Chen Yung-fa, "Zhengzhi kongzhi he Chunzhong dongyuan: Eyuwan sufan," pt. 1, p. 25.

The results of the purge in the Red Fourth Army were devastating: seventeen cadres at the army level, thirty-five at the division level, forty-four at the regiment level, two-thirds of brigade-level cadres, and one-third of the cadres at the company level – some 2,500 in all, about 10 percent of the whole army – were killed.[56] At the same time, the Political Protection Bureau was brought directly under Zhang's control and expanded, and new subordinate branches were set up. These security forces spread the *sufan* movement throughout area. The Red 25th Army in Eyuwan originally had 12,000 men. After forty-three days of *sufan*, there were only 6,000 men left.[57] Overall, perhaps as many as 10,000 people were purged or killed.[58] As Rowe puts it, the *sufan* campaign marked the "near-final extermination of the Party's base of indigenous supporters in the Dabie Shan region.[59] Zhang gave credit to Mao: "We have been inspired by the lessons of Futian to root out [our enemies] here."[60]

In Huang'an's Xianju district, the local political protection bureau was arresting so many cadres that the local party secretary, in a movement resembling the Futian Rebellion, led some 50,000 peasants to surround the political protection bureau and tied up the offending cadres. This popular rebellion against the suppression campaign evoked a harsh reprisal as Zhang Guotao ordered that it be put down, which it was, at the cost of over sixty lives.[61] But it also caused Zhang to take measures to bring the movement under control. Although the suppression campaign never came to a halt, the madness that had swept the area from November 1931 until February 1932 was ended. However, the cost had been enormous. Party organizations nearly collapsed as cadres were arrested and executed. Virtually all cadres with intellectual backgrounds were killed, with the result that the cadre

---

[56] Min Zhi, "Zhang Guotao zai Eyuwan geming genjudi de cuowu 'sufan'" (Zhang Guotao's erroneous "suppression of counterrevolutionaries" in the Eyuwan revolutionary base area), *Jianghuai wenshi*, no. 3 (1994), pp. 94–107.

[57] "Xiao Ke huiyilu AB tuan sufan leiji tusha 10 wan hongjun suqu zongrenkou xiajiang 20%" (Xiao Ke's Memoir: The AB Corps Suppression Campaign Killed 100,000 in the Red Army, the Total Population Decreased 20 percent), at https://bbs.wenxuecity.com/bbs/memory/450374.html, accessed August 11, 2020.

[58] Gregor Benton, *Mountain Fires: The Red Army's Three-Year War in South China, 1934–1938* (Berkeley, CA: University of California Press, 1992), p. 313.

[59] Rowe, *Crimson Rain*, p. 315.   [60] Ibid., p. 311.

[61] Chen Yung-fa, "Zhengzhi kongzhi he Chunzhong dongyuan: Eyuwan sufan," pt. 1, p. 26; Tan Kesheng and Ouyang Zhi Liang, *Eyuwan geming genjudi douzhengshi jianbian*, p. 215.

force became far less qualified. But the "localism" of the Eyuwan Base Area, like that in Jiangxi, was eliminated.

Conclusion

The excesses so evident in the *sufan* movement are frequently ascribed to the "Wang Ming line." There is some truth to this. When Pavel Mif went to Shanghai, he sent Li Lisan to Moscow. Li had bet his political fortune on taking large cities, particularly Wuhan, but the CCP did not have the organizational strength or military force to have even a remote chance of this strategy working. With Wang Ming in charge, the CCP did adopt a strategy of sowing widespread violence. Whereas Xiang Ying, sent by the Li Lisan leadership, had seen Mao using violence indiscriminately, the "three-person group" that reached Ningdu in April carried out the Comintern's decision that the Futian Rebellion was "counterrevolutionary."

Obviously *sufan* had preceded both Wang Ming's new leadership and Bo Gu's arrival in Ruijin. For Mao, the fight against the so-called AB Corps was part of the broader *sufan* movement. This was, fundamentally, a struggle between outsiders and locals. But it was also about who was in charge. Mao was not going to yield to local leaders such as Li Wenlin. But it was also a means to mobilize lower peasants against local leaders, although there is no evidence that this strategy was very successful. Mao hoped to use this mobilization to bolster his leadership and to recruit peasants into his army. But once the mechanisms of *sufan* – particularly the political protection bureaus – were established, there was a dynamic of accusing others or being accused oneself. Such a logic was self-perpetuating. All this was fully in place before the three-person group arrived in Ningdu.

Given this logic, one can see why Zhou Enlai tried to centralize control over the *sufan* movement. But Bo Gu and the others coming out from Shanghai faced the same problem that Mao had encountered when he returned to the Donggu area. Just like Mao, Bo Gu wanted to assert his leadership, this time over Mao, and to mobilize peasants to fight landlords and the GMD. Part of the problem was simply financial – landlords were few and far between – so Bo Gu had to mobilize the peasants against rich and middle peasants, or anyone with money. The Land Investigation Movement was a product of this logic. Ultimately the efforts to mobilize the peasants to fight the GMD led to a downward spiral in which peasants were increasingly coerced to join a war they did not want to join. Desertions and coercion ensued.

Zhang Guotao faced a similar situation in Eyuwan. The Eyuwan base area had been developed by local intellectuals in much the same way as Donggu had been. Zhang Guotao was an outsider who needed to gain control over the leadership of a local movement, and "suppressing counterrevolutionaries" – *sufan* – could eliminate local opposition. A similar logic played out in other base areas as well.[62]

The *sufan* movement was incredibly costly to the CCP, whether in Donggu, the Central Soviet, or elsewhere. Altogether the *sufan* movement resulted in the execution of some 100,000 Communist Party members accused of being members of the AB Corps, Reorganizationalists, Third Party members, or Social Democrats.[63] There were many reasons for the Communist losses in Jiangxi and Hubei, but the *sufan* movement was one of them.

---

[62] Xia Yi carried out a virulent *sufan* movement in the Hunan–West Hubei Base Area. See, for instance, He Lipo, "Xia Yi yu Xiangexi suqu 'sufan'" (Xia Yi and the "Campaign to Suppress Counterrevolutionaries in the Hunan–West Hubei Soviet Area"), *Wenshi jinghua*, vol. 189, no. 2 (2006), pp. 22–29.

[63] "Xiao Ke huiyilu AB tuan sufan leiji tusha 10 wan hongjun suqu zongrenkou xiajiang 20%" (Xiao Ke's Memoir: The AB Corps Suppression Campaign Killed 100,000 in the Red Army, the Total Population Decreased 20 Percent), at https://bbs.wenxuecity.com/bbs/memory/450374.html, accessed August 11, 2020.

Conclusion

The CCP's first phase of development came to an abrupt halt when Chiang Kai-shek broke the United Front between the GMD and the CCP suddenly and violently in April 1927, followed three months later by Wang Jingwei's similar break with the CCP. The CCP was confronted with an existential crisis; party membership fell by 80 percent. The "party purification" campaign, unleashed first by Chiang Kai-shek and then by Wang Jingwei, applied relentless pressure on the CCP. The organization of the CCP was seriously weakened, both through arrests and by people leaving the party. Chen Duxiu, the only leader the CCP had known up until then, was ousted and accused of "rightist opportunism," a charge that opened up ideological challenges as the party searched for a new leader, a new structure, and a new "line." Mikhail Borodin, having told Chen Duxiu that he was no longer party secretary, took his policy of compromise back to Moscow with him, as Beso Lominadze, a Stalin confidant, brought a new militancy to the reeling party. Lominadze's close associate, Qu Qiubai, was named to replace Chen Duxiu, but the twenty-eight-year old Qu did not have the prestige, authority, or resources to rebuild the party. Thinking in terms of the Russian revolution, he called for insurrections throughout the country.

Hastily organized military insurrections in Nanchang and Guangzhou failed quickly and at great cost. The Autumn Harvest Uprisings, called for by the party at the August 7 Emergency Meeting, eschewed organized military force in favor of action by the "masses." Chinese society in the 1920s, particularly in south China, where the revolution grew, was dominated by clans, and the only ones with the resources to send their sons (and, occasionally, daughters) to school were larger, wealthier clans. One has to be careful about generalizing. Huang Kecheng grew up extremely poor, but he was intelligent and enjoyed school, so he was supported by his clan. Lai Jingbang appears to have come from modest circumstances but his family had enough money to support his

164

education. Zeng Tianyu came from a very wealthy family. It seems that the majority of such rural educated youth came from small landlord and rich peasant families. Such educated youth were critical to this phase of the revolution. These educated youth, who dominated the party organizations from the peasant associations in Hunan that were so lauded by Mao, to the organization of the peasants – and bandits – in Donggu, to the development of party organizations in Eyuwan, came from "middle-class" families but faced uncertain prospects. They were radicalized by their experiences at schools outside the villages where they grew up. Sometimes, as for Lai Jingbang, these schools were in the county seat, and sometimes, as for Li Wenlin, they encompassed schools in Nanchang and the Whampoa Military Academy in Guangzhou.

Social scientists often talk about the state imposing "legibility" on society by standardizing weights and measurements, undertaking cadastral surveys, imposing standardized education, and so forth.[1] In the case of these educated youth, it seems they reversed the process, making an outside ideology – "Marxism" – legible to their rural societies. For a society that thought in terms of clan relations, the educated youth introduced a vocabulary of class and class conflict. For a society made uncertain by encroaching markets, the spread of religion, changing landlord–tenant relations, and local militarists, they linked local problems with "imperialism" and the need for "revolution." What these educated youth meant by revolution is highly uncertain. As we have seen, the Communist Movement in and around Donggu focused primarily on rent reduction and lower interest rates. Their focus on the Wang clan in Futian mixed sub-ethnic tension (Hakka versus early settlers) with landlord–tenant relations and personal grudges. Even when the leadership of the Donggu movement was taken over by Li Wenlin and expanded well beyond the limits of Donggu itself, it is difficult to imagine that these revolutionaries thought much beyond their local arena; this was not a national revolution in the making.

In contrast, Mao did think in terms of a national revolution. Unlike Qu Qiubai, he turned very readily to military force. The base area he created in the Jinggangshan was clearly not a bottom-up movement. This was not an instance of leaders rallying locals around local grievances. On the contrary, it is quite clear that in adopting radical land

---

[1] James Scott, *Seeing Like a State: How Certain Schemes to Improve the Human Condition Have Failed* (New Haven, CT: Yale University Press, 1998).

policies (confiscation), Mao lost the support of the peasants. He did learn from that experience and would adopt more moderate land policies later on (leading to the charge that he was following a "rich peasant line"), but the failure of his land policies in the Jinggangshan reflects the degree to which his movement was an outsider movement imposed on locals. This does not mean that Mao did not organize peasants. But it was clearly an organization imposed from the top down.

Building a party army is not an easy task. Party cadres tend to be ignorant of military affairs, and military people tend to view party cadres as people meddling in matters they do not understand. Moreover, it is very difficult to organize soldiers from different areas and backgrounds into a single force. Zhu De's soldiers, veterans of the Nanchang Uprising, tended to look down on Mao's ragtag army, drawn as it was from different groups. Mao wanted to control "every bullet and every gun" but Zhu De hoped that Mao would leave military matters to him. These tensions exploded in June 1929 as leaders voted to oust the high-handed Mao from his position as secretary of the Front Committee. It was only with the intervention of Zhou Enlai that Zhu De subordinated himself to Mao. Mao's model, much influenced by his understanding of the Donggu experience, was imposed at the Gutian Conference. Zhu De, as he told Peng Dehuai, felt there was nothing he could do to influence Mao.

The different approaches of the Donggu revolutionaries and Mao were bound to come into conflict. The Donggu revolutionaries were very much a product of local society, but there was nothing local in Mao's model of revolution. Mao worried about the "intermediate" groups in society, believing it would take a long time to break up the clan system. The Donggu revolutionaries were precisely the sorts of people Mao was worried about. The leaders of the Donggu Revolutionary Base Area were modestly wealthy people – from the intermediate stratum – and their revolution was based on their understanding of local society.

The clash between these two forces, one local and the other external, developed over time – from the February 7 Conference in 1930 to the Luofang Conference in October that year. Mao's determination to reorganize the party of south Jiangxi so that not a single landlord or rich peasant could join the party was intermingled with the witch hunt to root out members of the nonexistent AB Corps. The violence that ensued, not only in Donggu, Futian, and other places, went much further in destroying the "intermediate groups" than Mao had dared hope.

If, in retrospect, the clash seems inevitable, we must still ask whether the Donggu Base Area in some respects prepared the way for Mao to take over and penetrate local society. Perhaps with his growing military power, Mao could have set up a base area somewhere else that did not have an established revolutionary movement, much as he did at the Jinggangshan (though the Jinggangshan did have bandits who agreed to welcome Mao to their area). But the Jinggangshan was a small, sparsely populated area. To move into a larger, more densely populated area with strong clans would be difficult. The Donggu revolutionary movement provided an entrée into local society, but in providing that entrée, Donggu unwittingly prepared the way for its own demise. The young revolutionaries of Donggu brought new ideological concepts to the area, challenging the old clan structure by establishing a peasant association. The growth of a military force meant that the new movement was unchallengeable, at least locally. Propaganda was important, and the way in which the peasant associations organized people to do things, including singing revolutionary songs based on indigenous tunes, built support, or at least acceptance, of a new order. The introduction of Marxist vocabulary and revolutionary organization built a similitude to Mao's movement that allowed outsiders to enter local society. Even Li Wenlin did not grasp the gulf separating the two movements. But the educated youth who had established the Donggu movement made Mao's takeover possible.

The purge of the nonexistent AB Corps made clear that Mao's external forces were taking over the Donggu Revolutionary Base Area. Xiang Ying tried to rein in the brutality, but it burst out again after the so-called three-person group arrived in Jiangxi. Although the renewed violence can be blamed in part on the Comintern, there were obviously local factors involved as well. Zhou Enlai made a strong effort to stop the wanton violence, but the violence was renewed as the Shanghai leadership moved to Ruijin, as Bo Gu moved Mao aside and took control of the party, as the party struggled for resources, as the unaccountable political protection bureaus unleashed terror, and as fear and paranoia became embedded in the party. Eventually, it was the unsustainability of a situation in which the party needed ever more soldiers, but local peasants resisted joining the Red Army (as opposed to their own self-defense forces), and in which agriculture suffered as peasants fled or were dragooned into military service. Ultimately an estimated 70 percent of the victims of the *sufan* movement were members of the CCP. Rarely do revolutionary movements direct such violence inward.[2] The GMD may have driven the CCP out of Jiangxi, but the CCP was very much to blame for its own losses in Jiangxi.

The story of Donggu raises theoretical issues about how we view the Chinese revolution. The effort by Lai Jingbang and others to create a Communist organization and military force fits the social-movement literature fairly well. There was a group of people – the educated youth – facing highly uncertain futures and influenced by the radical ideology they had come in contact with at schools away from their homes, and they took action to organize and rebel against the old order. They were defeated not by conservative forces but by a larger and more militarized group – Mao's revolutionary army – from outside the area. Such takeovers seem rare in the history of social movements.

Mao's actions, however, were constrained by the hierarchical organization of the Chinese Communist Party, still very much a branch of the Comintern. Although Mao was adept at evading the instructions of the Party Center when he was in the Jinggangshan or fighting across the Jiangxi countryside, he used the authority of the Center, as when he re-established his position after being voted out as secretary of the Front Committee, but he had to submit when directly confronted by the Center, as when he quickly yielded his position to Liu Angong in April 1929 and to Xiang Ying when Xiang arrived in Ningdu in January 1931. Li Wenlin clearly hoped that the support of Li Lisan would mean something in his confrontation with Mao, but Li Lisan was on his way out. As seriously strained as relations in the party were, Leninism still meant something. This external force clearly influenced the development of the revolution, making it neither a social movement nor, strictly speaking, a rebel organization. Much of the literature on rebellions and civil wars assumes that the primary combatants are autonomous, but the CCP was not.[3]

Ultimately, the Communist Movement in south Jiangxi failed not only because of the military pressure put on it by the GMD but

---

[2] Jeremy M. Weinstein, *Inside Rebellion: The Politics of Insurgent Violence* (New York: Cambridge University Press, 2007).

[3] Paul Staniland, *Networks of Rebellion: Explaining Insurgent Cohesion and Collapse* (Ithaca, NY: Cornell University Press, 2014); Peter Krause, *Rebel Power: Why National Movements Compete, Fight, and Win* (Ithaca, NY: Cornell University Press, 2017).

primarily because of the tension within the party and between the party and local society. The Communist movement, as it developed in 1931–1934, expressed neither the aspirations of local society, as the Donggu movement had, nor the militarized approach of Mao's group, nor the even more radical approach of Bo Gu and others from Shanghai. Rather, the Communist movement expressed the aspirations of groups struggling with one another and with local society to extract the resources necessary to fight successfully. Without the ability to move to new areas because of the GMD encirclement, the CCP could only try to extract ever greater resources from a society increasingly unwilling and unable to provide them. Defeat and retreat were the only options.

Even though the party was defeated in Jiangxi, the Jiangxi period marks an era when the party changed enormously. Although contemporary propagandists talk about Mao leading the peasants to carry out the revolution, about developing a rural strategy to surround the cities, and about carrying on protracted warfare, the reality was quite different. In 1927, the party thought that the revolution might take place quickly – that was the point of calling for insurrections. Mao's turn to rural revolution did not mean that he would organize local peasants; on the contrary, it was local activists who organized peasants in local revolution. We have no opinion surveys from those days, but from the actions of the Donggu revolutionaries, it seems that most peasants would have been happy with rent reductions and lower interest rates on loans. Nor do we have detailed information about who joined the Red Army, but it is clear that bandits, vagrants, and prisoners of war made up a large percentage. When the party divided the land and granted property to the peasants, they were usually content to plant their own crops. Peasants were certainly willing to protect their localities by joining local defense forces, but they were not eager to join the Red Army. That is why cadres used deception and coercion to force peasants into the army. Zeng Shan berated cadres for such tactics, but his words apparently had little effect – cadres were using precisely the same sorts of tactics of deception and coercion, only worse, as the revolution moved its center to Ruijin.

However, the party's time in Jiangxi forged a very different party from the one that set out to make revolution. Mao's development of a party army, ratified at Gutian, allowed him to impose his control on those building their own local revolution. In imposing his will, Mao and the party did not hesitate to use violence against party members; the control mechanisms the party built were harsh and often arbitrary, and violence was difficult to control. A new party culture, centered around authority and hierarchy, was being constructed, and it penetrated society far more deeply than Chen Duxiu or even Qu Qiubai could have imagined. The party no longer represented society; its cadres were set apart, commanding local society. The party leadership still discussed issues, but not as broadly as before; the September Letter had ended the sort of open discussions and debates that the Red Fourth Army had had at Baisha and at the Seventh Representative Meeting. Whatever the party's original intentions, it had found that revolution required a fundamental social revolution and the imposition of external control.

The development of Leninism was not complete by the time the CCP left Jiangxi. There were still multiple contenders for party leadership, an issue not worked out until late 1938 when Wang Jiaxiang brought an "oral letter" back from Moscow supporting Mao's leadership.[4] Finally in 1940–1942, the CCP launched a "rectification campaign" to unify the party organization and ideology. In the party constitution of 1945 that ideology would be called "Mao Zedong Thought." These developments were based on the organizational foundation that had been established in the crucial years between 1927 and 1934.

---

[4] Exactly what the letter conveyed remains controversial. See Guo Dehong, "KangRi zhanzheng shi yinggai jinyibu yanjiu jige wenti" (Several Issues from the History of the War of Resistance That Should Be Further Researched), at www.aisixiang.com/data/35884.html, accessed January 2, 2021.

Glossary

Anfu	安福
Anqing	安庆
Anyuan	安源
Aoshang	坳上
Baisha	白沙
baodong	暴动
Beitou	陂头
Beixia	陂下
Bo Gu	博古
busheng busi	不生不死
Cai E	蔡锷
Cai Hesen	蔡和森
Cai Shenzhao	蔡申熙
canku kaoda	残酷拷打
Changjiangju	长江局
Changongtuan	铲共团
Changsha	长沙
Changting	长汀
Chatian yundong	查田运动
Chen Changhao	陈昌浩
Chen Duxiu	陈独秀
Chen Tanqiu	陈潭秋
Chen Yi	陈毅
Chen Youkui	陈佑魁
Chiang Kai-shek	蒋介石
chiweidui	赤卫队
Dabaidi	大柏地
Dai Shuren	戴述人
dangguan yiqie	党管一切
Dangyang	当阳
dangzu	党组

dashao dasha	大烧大杀
Dayu	大余
Deng Fa	邓发
Deng Xiaoping	邓小平
Deng Yanda	邓演达
diaoyang	吊羊
Dong Biwu	董必武
Donggu	东固
Donggu baodong	东固暴动
Donggu pingmin yinhang	东固平民银行
Donglong	东龙
Douzheng	斗争
Du Yuesheng	杜月笙
Duan Liangbi	段良弼
Duan Qifeng	段起风
Duan Weilin	段蔚林
Duan Xipeng	段锡朋
duizhang	队长
Enan	鄂南
Exi	鄂西
Eyuwan	鄂豫皖
Fan Shisheng	范石生
Fan'gan	反感
Fang Ying	方英
fang'ai tongyi zhanxian	妨碍统一战线
Fang Zhimin	方志敏
fazhan shengchan	发展生产
Feng Ren	冯任
Fengbian	枫边
Fengtai	风态
Fenyi	分宜
Futian	福田
Gaizao she	改造舍
Gan Kangchen	甘康臣
Ganzhou	赣州
Gao Kenian	高克念
Gao zhuang	告状
Geming de ducai	革命的独裁
Gongan	公安

Gu Mengyu	顧孟餘
Gu Shunzhang	顾顺章
Gu Zuolin	顾作霖
Guangshan	光山
Guo Fengming	郭凤鸣
Guo Shijun	郭士俊
Guo Xiangxian	郭象贤
Guohuo	过火
Guomin gemingjun disanjun junguan jiaoyu tuan	国民革命军第三军军官教育团
Gutian	古田
He Jian	何键
He Long	贺龙
He Shuheng	何叔衡
He Yi	贺怡
He Zizhen	贺子珍
Hengshan	衡山
Hengyang	衡阳
Hong'an	红安
Hongjun daibiao dahui	红军代表大会
Hongjun disijun diqici daibiao dahui jueyi'an	红军第四军第七次代表大会决议案
hongse kongbu	红色恐怖
Hongse shuguang she	红色曙光社
Hu Shaohai	胡绍海
Huang Gongluë	黄公略
Huang Kecheng	黄克诚
Huang Ping	黄平
Huang Weihan	黄维汉
Huang Tingfang	黄庭芳
Huang Weihan	黄维汉
Huang Yishan	黄益善
Huang'an	黄安
Huangbei	黄陂
Huanggang	黄冈
Huangma	黄麻
Huangmei	黄梅
Hunan quansheng diyici daibiao dahui	湖南全省第一次代表大会

Hunan sheng zixiu daxue	湖南省自修大学
Huoqiu	霍邱
Ji'an	吉安
Jiandong Academy	间东书院
Jiang Hanbo	江汉波
Jiangling	江铃
Jiangxi	江西
Jianmie	歼灭
Jiaoyang	蛟洋
Jiefu jipin	劫富济贫
Jiahe	嘉禾
Jinggangshan	井冈山
Jinghan	京汉
Jingwei tuan	警卫团
Jinjiazhai	金价寨
jinshi	进士
Jishui	吉水
Jiujiang	九江
Ke Qingshi	柯庆施
Kuang Jixun	矿继勋
Kuang Zhenxing	邝振兴
Lai Jingbang	赖经邦
Le'an	乐安
Leiyang	耒阳
Li Baifang	李白芳
Li Dazhao	李大钊
Li Lisan	李立三
Li Pucheng	李卜成
Li Weihan	李维汉
Li Wenbin	李文彬
Li Wenlin	李文林
Li Xishi	李溪石
lian	连
Liang Mingzhe	梁明哲
Liang Yiqing	梁一清
Liling	醴陵
Linshi zhongyang zhengfu zhixing weiyuanhui	临时中央政府执行委员会
Liu Bocheng	刘伯承

Liu Di	刘敌
Liu Mu	刘木
Liu Shen	刘申
Liu Shiqi	刘士奇
Liu Shiyi	刘士毅
Liu Tiechao	刘铁超
Liu Xiuqi	刘秀气
Liuhuo	六霍
Liuyang	浏阳
lixing	厉行
Longyan	龙岩
Lu Deming	卢德铭
Lu Futan	卢福坦
Lu'an	刘安
Luling	庐陵
Luo Rongheng	罗荣恒
Luo Wan	罗万
Luo Yinong	罗亦农
Luofang	罗方
Luofufeng	罗福峰
Luofuzhang	罗福嶂
Luokeng	螺坑
Luotang	罗塘
Luotian	罗田
Lü	旅
Mabu	麻埠
Macheng	麻城
Mao Zedong	毛泽东
Mao Zetan	毛泽覃
Mari	马日
Meibei	渼陂
Meizhou	梅州
Miandu	沔渡
Mintuan	民团
mishuzhang	秘书长
Mulan	木兰
Muqian nongmin yundong jihua	目前农民运东计划
Nanchang	南昌
Nanlong	南龙

Ningdu	宁都
Ninggang	宁冈
Nongmin yundong jiangxisuo	农民运动讲习所
pai	排
Pan Xinyuan	潘心元
Peng Dehuai	彭德怀
Peng Pai	澎湃
Pingjiang	平江
Pingshi	坪石
Poyang	鄱阳
Qian Dajun	钱大钧
Qiandi weiyuanhui	前敌委员会
Qiaoshan	潮汕
Qiliping	七里坪
Qichun	蕲春
Qin Bangxian	秦邦宪
Qingnian	青年
Qu Qiubai	瞿秋白
Quanguo suweiai quyu daibiao dahui	全国苏维埃区域代表大会
Ren Bishi	任弼时
Rucheng	汝城
Ruijin	瑞金
Sandian hui	三点会
Sanheba	三河坝
sanrentuan	三人团
shalu	杀戮
Shangcheng	商城
Shanghang	上杭
Shangnan	商南
shangshan	上山
Shashi	沙市
She	畲
Shen Zemin	沈泽民
shenshi	绅士
Shezu	畲族
shoumai qunzhong	收买群众
Shu Chuanxian	舒传贤
Shuinanwei	水南圩

sida dangguan	四大党官
Song Jiaoren	宋教仁
Suichuan	遂川
sufan weiyuanhui	肃反委员会
Sun Yat-sen	孙逸仙
suqing	肃清
Taihe	泰和
Taihu	太湖
Tan Pingshan	谭平山
tangdi	堂弟
tepaiyuan	特派员
teshi	特使
Tonggu	铜鼓
Tongmenghui	同盟会
tuhao lieshen	土豪劣绅
tuoli qunzhong	脱离群众
Wan Molin	万墨林
Wan Xiyan	宛希俨
Wan'an	万安
Wang Baiyuan	王百元
Wang Chuxi	王初曦
Wang Jiaxiang	王稼祥
Wang Jingwei	汪精卫
Wang Liangzhao	王良照
Wang Qun	汪群
Wang Shouhua	汪寿华
Wang Shusheng	王树声
Wang Xiusong	王秀松
Wang Zuo	王佐
Wenhua shushe	文化书社
Wu Jiang	吴江
Wu Peifu	吴佩孚
Xiajiang	峡江
Xiang Ying	项英
Xiang Zhongfa	向忠发
XiangGan tewei	湘赣特委
Xiangnan baodong	湘南暴动
Xiangtan	湘潭
Xiangxiang	湘乡

Xianju	仙居
Xianning	咸宁
Xiao Bingzhang	萧炳章
Xiao Ke	萧克
Xiaobu	小布
xiaozu	小组
Xie Hanchang	谢汉昌
Xie Zhaoyuan	谢兆元
Xilu xingwei	西路行委
Xin Jiangxi	新江西
Xinfeng	新丰
Xin'gan	新干
xingdong	行动
xingdong weiyuanhui	行动委员会
Xingguo	兴国
Xingzi	星子
Xinyu	新余
Xinyuan	心远
Xiucai	秀才
Xiushui	修水
Xu Fuzu	徐复祖
Xu Jishen	许继慎
Xu Kexiang	许克祥
Xu Qian	徐谦
xunshiyuan	巡视员
Xunwu	寻乌
Yanfu	延福
Yang Sen	杨森
Yangxin	阳新
Yanhuang chunqiu	炎黄春秋
Yaotou	窑头
Ye Jianying	叶剑英
Ye Ting	叶挺
yichu jifa	一触即发
Yingshan	英山
Yizhang	宜章
Yongding	永定
Yongfeng	永丰
Yonghewei	永和圩

Yongxing	永兴
Youzhi	幼稚
Yu Qiu	欲球
Yuan Baobing	袁宝冰
Yuan Shikai	袁世凯
Yuan Wencai	袁文才
Yuan Yubing	袁玉冰
Yuanzhou	袁州
Yudu	于都
Yueyang	岳阳
Yuji	余几
Yun Daiying	恽代英
Yuntian	雲田
Zeng Bingchun	曾炳春
Zeng Shan	曾山
Zeng Tianyu	曾天宇
Zeng Yansheng	曾延生
Zeng Zhenwu	曾振五
Zeng Zhongshu	曾中生
Zhang Fakui	张发奎
Zhang Guo'en	张国恩
Zhang Guotao	张国焘
Zhang Huaiwan	张怀万
Zhang Shixi	张世熙
Zhang Tailei	张太雷
Zhang Wentian	张闻天
Zhang Xiaolin	张啸林
Zhangjiawan	张家湾
Zhangpu	漳浦
Zheng Weisan	郑位三
zhengqu minzhong	争取群众
zhengzhi baoweidui	政治保卫队
Zhentandui	侦探队
Zhong Ri fangdi junshi xieding	中日共同防敌军事协定
Zhongyang nongmin weiyuanhui bangongshi	中央农民委员会办事处
Zhongyang tudi weiyuanhui	中央土地委员会
Zhou Enlai	周恩来
Zhou Lu	周鲁

Zhou Tingpan	周庭潘
Zhou Yili	周以栗
Zhu De	朱德
Zhu Jiahao	朱家诰
Zhu Peide	朱培德
Zhu Shigui	朱世贵
Zou Nu	邹努
Zui canku kaoda	最残酷拷打

Bibliography

Averill, Stephen C. "The Origins of the Futian Incident." Pp. 79–115, in Tony Saich and Hans van de Ven, eds. *New Perspectives on the Chinese Communist Revolution*. Armonk, NY: M.E. Sharpe, 1995.

Averill, Stephen C. "Party, State and Local Elite in the Jiangxi Communist Movement." *Journal of Asian Studies* 46(2), 1987, pp. 279–303

Averill, Stephen C. *Revolution in the Highlands: China's Jinggangshan Base Area*. Lanham, MD: Rowman & Littlefield, 2006.

Benton, Gregor. *Mountain Fires: The Red Army's Three-Year War in South China, 1934–1938*. Berkeley, CA: University of California Press, 1992.

Bianco, Lucien. *Peasants without the Party: Grass-Roots Movements in Twentieth-Century China*. Armonk, NY: M.E. Sharpe, 2001.

Boorman, Howard L., ed. *Biographical Dictionary of Republican China*. 5 vols. New York: Columbia University Press, 1967–1979.

Chang Kuo-t'ao [Zhang Guotao]. *The Rise of the Chinese Communist Party: The Autobiography of Chang Kuo-t'ao*. Vol. 1: *1921–1927*. Vol. 2: *1928–1938*. Lawrence, KS: University of Kansas Press, 1971, 1972.

Chen Jie. "Eyuwan suqu ganbu qunti yanjiu" (Study of the Cadre Group in the Eyuwan Soviet District). MA paper. Zhengzhou University. 2015.

Chen Liming. "Zeng Tianyu." Pp. 160–185, in Zhonggong Jiangxi shengwei dangshi ziliao zhengji weiyuanhui and Zhonggong Jiangxi shengwei dangshi yanjiushi, eds. *Jiangxi dangshi ziliao*, vol. 5.

Chen Liming and He Longliang. "Zhang Shixi." Pp. 186–210, in Zhonggong Jiangxi shengwei dangshi ziliao zhengji weiyuanhui and Zhonggong Jiangxi shengwei dangshi yanjiushi, eds. *Jiangxi dangshi ziliao*, vol. 5.

Chen Yi. "Guanyu Zhu Mao jun de lishi jiqi zhuangkuang de baogao" (Report on the History of the Zhu–Mao Army and Its Circumstances). Pp. 444–463, in Jiangxisheng dang'an guan and Zhonggong Jiangxi shengwei dangxiao dangshi jiaoyanshi, eds. *Zhongyang geming genjudi shiliao xuanbian*, vol. 2.

Chen Yi zhuan (Biography of Chen Yi). Beijing: Dangdai Zhongguo chubanshe, 1991.

Chen Yongfa [Chen Yung-fa]. "Zhengzhi kongzhi he qunzhong dongyuan: Eyuwan sufan" (Political Control and Mass Mobilization: Suppressing

Counterrevolutionaries in Eyuwan). *Dalu zazhi*, pt. 1, vol. 86, no. 1 (January 1993), pp. 20–38; pt. 2, vol. 86, no. 2 (February 1993), pp. 67–78; pt. 3, vol. 86, no. 3 (March 1993), pp. 120–129.

Chen Yongfa [Chen Yung-fa]. "Zhonggong zaoqi sufan de jiantao: AB tuan an, 1930–1932" (An Examination of the CCP's Early Suppression: The Case of the AB Corps, 1930–1932). *Zhongyang yanjiuyuan, jindaishi yanjiu jikan*, pt. 1, no. 17 (June 1988), pp. 193–276.

"Chuangzao Jiangxi dangde xin shengming." Pp. 117–133, in Zhongyang dang'an guan and Jiangxisheng dang'an guan. *Jiangxisheng geming lishi wenjian huiji (1927–1928)*.

Cohen, Stephen F. *Bukharin and the Bolshevik Revolution: A Political Biography, 1888–1938*. Oxford: Oxford University Press, 1980.

Dai Anlin. "Futian shibian yu suqu sufan" (The Futian Incident and the Suppression of Counterrevolutionaries in the Soviet Areas). *Xiangchao*, no. 6 (2007), pp. 26–30.

Dai Xiangqing. "Lun Wan'an baodong" (On the Wan'an Uprising). Pp. 211–232, in Zhonggong Jiangxi shengwei dangshi ziliao zhengji weiyuanhui and Zhonggong Jiangxi shengwei dangshi yanjiushi, eds. *Jiangxi dangshi ziliao*, vol. 5.

Dai Xiangqing and Luo Huilan. *AB tuan yu Futian shibian shimo* (A Complete History of the AB Corps and the Futian Incident). Zhengzhou: Henan renmin chubanshe, 1994.

Ding Renxiang. "Dongjinggang gemingshi gaiyao" (Overview of the Revolutionary History of East Jinggang). Pp. 491–519, in Zhonggong Jiangxi shengwei dangshi yanjiushi et al., eds. *Donggu: Ganxinan geming genjudi shiliao xuanbian*, vol. 1.

Ding Renxiang. "Shilun Donggu geming genjudi dangde jianshe" (Discussing Construction of the Party in the Donggu Base Area). *Zhongguo Jinggangshan ganbu xueyuan xuebao*, vol. 6, no. 3 (May 2013), pp. 59–64.

"Donggu geming genjudi gaishu" (Introduction to the Donggu Revolutionary Base Area). Pp. 1–23, in Zhonggong Jiangxi shengwei dangshi ziliao zhengji weiyuanhui and Zhonggong Jiangxi shengwei dangshi yanjiushi, eds. *Jiangxi dangshi ziliao*, vol. 10.

"Draft Resolution of the Ninth Congress of the Chinese Communist Party in the Fourth Red Army." Pp. 195–230, in Schram, ed. *Mao's Road to Power*, vol. 3.

"Du Xiujing xiang Zhonggong Hunan shengwei de baogao" (Report by Du Xiujing to the CCP Hunan Provincial Committee). Pp. 42–46, in Jiangxisheng dang'an guan, ed. *Jinggangshan geming genjudi shiliao xuanbian*.

Duara, Presenjit. *Culture, Power, and the State: Rural North China, 1900–1942*. Stanford, CA: Stanford University Press, 1988.

Esherick, Joseph. *Accidental Holyland: The Origins of China's Shaan–Gan–Ning Border Region*. Berkeley, CA: University of California Press. Forthcoming.

"Fan gaizupai AB tuan xuanchuan dagang" (Propaganda Outline for Opposing the Reorganizationalists and the AB Corps). Pp. 631–636, in Jiangxisheng dang'an guan and Zhonggong Jiangxi shengwei dangxiao dangshi jiaoyanshi, eds. *Zhongyang geming genjudi shiliao xuanbian*, vol. 3.

Fitzgerald, John. "Cadre Nation: Territorial Government and the Lessons of Imperial Statecraft in Xi Jinping's China." *China Journal*, no. 85 (January 2021), pp. 26–48.

"Ganxinan tewei er quanhui jueyi an zhi er" (The Second Resolution of the Second Congress of the Southwest Jiangxi Special Committee). Pp. 247–250, in Jiangxisheng dang'an guan and Zhonggong Jiangxi shengwei dangxiao dangshi jiaoyanshi, eds. *Zhongyang geming genjudi shiliao xuanbian*, vol. 2.

Gao Hua. *Lishi biji* (History Notes). 2 vols. Hong Kong: Oxford University Press, 2014.

Gao Hua. "'Su AB tuan' shijian de lishi kaocha" (Historical Investigation of the Suppression of the AB Corps). Pp. 103–123, in Gao Hua. *Lishi biji*, vol. 1.

Gong Chu. *Wo he Hongjun* (The Red Army and I). Hong Kong: Nanfeng chubanshe, 1954.

"Gu Shunzhang." At https://baike.baidu.com/item/顾顺章.

Gu Zexu. *Zhu De biezhuan: Yu Mao Zedong de enen yuanyuan* (Unauthorized Biography of Zhu De: Gratitude and Resentment with Mao Zedong). 2 vols. Hong Kong: Tianxing chubanshe, 2020.

Guo Dehong. "KangRi zhanzheng shi yinggai jinyibu yanjiu jige wenti" (Several Issues from the History of the War of Resistance that Should Be Further Researched). At www.aisixiang.com/data/35884.html, accessed January 2, 2021.

Guo Dehong. *Zhongguo jinxiandai nongmin tudi wenti yanjiu* (The Land Problem of Peasants in Modern and Contemporary China). Qingdao: Qingdao chubanshe, 1993.

He Lipo. "Xia Yi yu Xiangexi suqu 'sufan'" (Xia Yi and the "Campaign to Suppress Counterrevolutionaries" in the Hunan–West Hubei Soviet Area). *Wenshi jinghua*, vol. 189, no. 2 (2006), pp. 21–29.

He Youliang. "Geming yuanqi: Nongcun gemingzhong de zaoqi lingdao qunti" (The Origins of Revolution: The Leading Group at the Beginning of the Rural Revolution). *Jiangxi shehui kexue*, no. 3 (2007), pp. 89–96.

Hu Chiao-mu [Qiaomu]. *Thirty Years of the Communist Party of China: An Outline History*. Westport, CT: Hyperion Press, 1973 [1951].

Huang Daoxuan. *Zhangli yu xianjie: Zhongyang suqu de geming (1933–1934)* (Tensions and Limits: The Revolution in the Central Soviet (1933–1934)). Beijing: Shehui kexue wenxian chubanshe, 2011.

Huang Huiyun, Shi Jinsong, and Liu Jun. *Donggu geming genjudi jianshi* (A Short History of the Donggu Revolutionary Base Area). Chengdu: Bashu shushe, 2011.

Huang Kecheng. *Huang Kecheng zishu* (Autobiography of Huang Kecheng). Beijing: Renmin chubanshe, 1994.

Huang Kun. *Cong baodong dao xiangcun geju, 1927–1929: Zhongguo gongchandang geming genjudi zenyang jianli qilaide* (From Insurrections to Rural Bases, 1927–1929: How the CCP Revolutionary Bases Were Established). Shanghai: Shanghai shehui kexueyuan chubanshe, 2006.

Hsiao, Tso-liang. *Power Relations within the Chinese Communist Movement, 1930–1934.* Seattle, WA: University of Washington Press, 1961.

Huang Wenzhi. *Eyuwan suqu daolu: Yige minzhong dongyuan de shijian yanjiu (1920–1932)* (The Road to the Eyuwan Soviet Base: A Study of Mass Mobilization and Practice (1920–1932)). Revised. ed. Saarbrücken: Jinlang xueshu chubanshe, 2017.

Jiang Boying. "Cong Mao Zedong de lunshu kan Donggu geming genjudi de lishi gongxian" (Looking at the Historical Contributions of the Donggu Revolutionary Base from Mao Zedong's Remarks). *Dangde wenxian*, no. 5 (2007), pp. 53–58.

"Jiangxi gongzuo qingkuang: zonghexing baogao" (The Present Circumstances in the Work in Jiangxi: A Comprehensive Report). Pp. 254–264, in Zhongyang dang'an guan and Jiangxisheng dang'an guan. *Jiangxisheng geming lishi wenjian huiji (1927–1928).*

"Jiangxi quansheng qiubao shandong dagang" (Outline of Inciting Autumn Harvest Uprisings throughout Jiangxi). Pp. 25–34, in Zhongyang dang'an guan and Jiangxisheng dang'an guan. *Jiangxisheng geming lishi wenjian huiji (1927–1928).*

"Jiangxi shengwei zhi Ganxibian tewei de xin" (A Letter from the Jiangxi Provincial Committee to the West Ganxi Special Committee). P. 39, in Jiangxisheng dang'an guan, ed. *Jinggangshan geming genjudi shiliao xuanbian.*

"Jiangxi suqu Zhonggong shengwei gongzuo zongjie baogao (xu er) (Summary Report on the CCP Provincial Party Committee's Work in the Soviet Area (Part Two)). Pp. 476–489, in Jiangxisheng dang'an guan and Zhonggong Jiangxi shengwei dangxiao dangshi jiaoyanshi, eds. *Zhongyang geming genjudi shiliao xuanbian*, vol. 1.

Jiangxisheng dang'an guan, ed. *Jinggangshan geming genjudi shiliao xuanbian* (Selected Historical Materials on the Jinggangshan Revolutionary Base Area). Nanchang: Jiangxi renmin chubanshe, 1985.

Jiangxisheng dang'an guan and Zhonggong Jiangxi shengwei dangxiao dangshi jiaoyanshi, eds. *Zhongyang geming genjudi shiliao xuanbian* (Selected Historical Materials on the Central Revolutionary Base Area). 3 vols. Nanchang: Jiangxi renmin chubanshe, 1982.

Jing Yuchuan. "Futian shibian pingfan de qianqian houhou" (Before and After the Resolution of the Futian Incident). *Bainianchao*, no. 1 (2000), pp. 39–44.

Jing Yuchuan. "Futian shibian shi de Liu Di gei zhongyang de xin" (The Letter Liu Di Gave to the Center during the Time of the Futian Incident). *Yanhuang chunqiu*, no. 11 (2014), pp. 84–88.

"Jinji tonggao di ershi hao: Dongyuan dangyuan qunzhong chedi suqing AB tuan" (Emergency Notice Number 20: Mobilizing the Mass of Party Members to Completely Purge the AB Corps). Pp. 639–650, in Jiangxisheng dang'an guan and Zhonggong Jiangxi shengwei dangxiao dangshi jiaoyanshi, eds. *Zhongyang geming genjudi shiliao xuanbian*, vol. 3.

Jowitt, Ken. "The Leninist Phenomenon." Pp. 1–49, in Kenneth Jowitt. *The New World Disorder: The Leninist Extinction.* Berkeley: University of California Press, 1992.

Kalyvas, Stathis N. *The Logic of Violence in Civil War.* New York: Cambridge University Press, 2006.

Krause, Peter. *Rebel Power: Why National Movements Compete, Fight, and Win.* Ithaca, NY: Cornell University Press, 2017.

"Kuoda hongjun de zhuti banfa." In Jiangxisheng dang'an guan and Zhonggong Jiangxi shengwei dangxiao dangshi jiaoyanshi, eds. *Zhongyang geming genjudi shiliao xuanbian*, vol. 2, pp. 528–533

Li Quan et al. "Junshi faxian: Zaokang huiyi kancheng Gutian huiyi qian zou qu" (Discovering Military History: The Zaokang Meeting Can Be Called the Prelude to the Gutian Meeting). *Jiefang junbao*, October 15, 2014. Available at www.81.cn/sydbt/2014-10/15/content_6179364.htm, accessed January 11, 2021.

Li Weihan. *Huiyi yu yanjiu* (Remembrance and Study). 2 vols. Beijing: Zhonggong dangshi chubanshe, 2013.

Li Weimin. "Cong gongchan guoji dang'an kan fan 'AB tuan' douzheng" (Viewing the Struggle against the "AB Corps" from the Files of the Communist International). *Yanhuang chunqiu*, no. 7 (July 2009), pp. 65–70.

Liu Dai. "Donggu songxin dao Jinggang" (Donggu Sends Letters to Jinggang). P. 137, in Zhonggong Jiangxi shengwei dangshi ziliao zhengji weiyuanhui and Zhonggong Jiangxi shengwei dangshi yanjiushi, eds. *Jiangxi dangshi ziliao*. vol. 10.

Liu Jingfang. "'Li Wenlin shi' genjudi yu Zhongguo tese geming daolu de kaipi" (The "Li Wenlin"-Style Base Area and the Opening of a Revolutionary Path with Chinese Characteristics). Pp. 30–42, in Zhonggong Jiangxi shengwei dangshi yanjiushi, Zhonggong Ji'an shiwei dangshi gongzuo bangongshi, and Zhongguo Ji'anshi qingyuan quwei. *Donggu genjudi yu Zhongguo geming daolu de kaipi*.

Liu Mianjue. "Zeng Shan zai Donggu de geming huodong" (Zeng Shan's Revolutionary Activities in Donggu). Pp. 112–127, in Zhonggong Jiangxi shengwei dangshi yanjiushi, Zhonggong Ji'an shiwei dangshi gongzuo bangongshi, and Zhongguo Ji'anshi qingyuan quwei. *Donggu genjudi yu Zhongguo geming daolu de kaipi*.

Liu Mianyu. *Zeng Shan zhe yisheng* (Zeng Shan's Life). Nanchang: Jiangxi renmin chubanshe, 2015.

"Liu Shiqi tongzhi gei Zeng Juefei tongzhi xin" (A Letter from Comrade Liu Shiqi to Comrade Zeng Juefei). Pp. 571–576, in Jiangxisheng dang'an guan and Zhonggong Jiangxi shengwei dangxiao dangshi jiaoyanshi, eds. *Zhongyang geming genjudi shiliao xuanbian*, vol. 1.

Luo Huilan. "Dangnei su AB tuan 'kuodahua' zhi shuo xinkao" (New Investigation into the Idea that the Suppression of the AB Corps in the Party was "Exaggerated"). *Nanchang daxue xuebao*, vol. 41, no. 3 (May 2010), pp. 86–91.

"Luo Ming guanyu Minxi qingkuang gei Fujian shengwei de xin" (A Letter from Luo Ming to the Fujian Party Committee on Conditions in Western Fujian). Pp. 13–29, in Zhongyang dang'an guan and Fujiansheng dang'an guan. *Fujian geming lishi wenjian huiji*, vol. 15: *Minxi tewei wenjian (1928–1936 nian)*.

McAdam, Doug, Sidney Tarrow, and Charles Tilly. *Dynamics of Contention*. Cambridge: Cambridge University Press, 2001.

Mao Zedong. "Jinggangshan de douzheng (1928 nian shiyiyue ershiwu ri)" (The Struggle in the Jinggang Mountains (November 25, 1928)). Pp. 57–84, in Zhonggong zhongyang wenxian yanjiushi, ed. *Mao Zedong xuanji*, vol. 1.

Mao Zedong. "Letter from the Fourth Red Army Front Committee to the Central Committee." Pp. 147–152, in Schram, ed. *Mao's Road to Power*, vol. 3.

Mao Zedong. "A Letter of Reply by the General Front Committee." Pp. 704–713, in Schram, ed. *Mao's Road to Power*, vol. 3.

Mao Zedong. "Letter to Lin Biao." Pp. 177–189, in Schram, ed. *Mao's Road to Power*, vol. 3.

Mao Zedong. "Plan for the Current Peasant Movement." Pp. 411–413, in Schram, ed. *Mao's Road to Power*, vol. 2.

Mao Zedong. "Report of the Jinggangshan Front Committee to the Central Committee." Pp. 80–121, in Schram, ed. *Mao's Road to Power*, vol. 3.

Mao Zedong. "Report on the Peasant Movement in Hunan." Pp. 429–464, in Schram, ed. *Mao's Road to Power*, vol. 2.

Mao Zedong. "The Significance of Dividing the Troops to Win Over the Popular Masses, and Our Line." Pp. 273–279, in Schram. *Mao's Road to Power*, vol. 3.

Mao Zedong nianpu. See Zhonggong zhongyang wenxian yanjiushi, ed. *Mao Zedong nianpu, 1893–1949.*

Maruf, Harun and Dan Joseph. *Inside Al-Shabaab: The Secret History of Al-Qaeda's Most Powerful Ally.* Bloomington, IN: Indiana University Press, 2018.

Meisner, Maurice. *Mao's China and After: A History of the People's Republic.* 3rd ed. New York: The Free Press, 1999.

Olenik, J. Kenneth. "Deng Yanda and the Third Party." Pp. 111–134, in Roger B. Jeans, ed. *Roads Not Taken: The Struggle of Opposition Parties in Twentieth-Century China.* Ann Arbor, MI: University of Michigan Press, 1992.

Pang Xianzhi and Jin Chongji, eds. *Mao Zedong zhuan* (Biography of Mao Zedong). 2nd ed. 6 vols. Beijing: Zhongyang wenxian chubanshe, 2011.

Perry, Elizabeth J. *Anyuan: Mining China's Revolutionary Tradition.* Berkeley, CA: University of California Press, 2012.

Polachek. James M. "The Moral Economy of the Kiangsi Soviet (1928–1934)." *Journal of Asian Studies*, vol. 42, no. 4 (August 1983), pp. 805–829.

"Poyang dangtuan gongzuo baogao" (Report on the Work of the Party and Youth League in Poyang). Pp. 95–103, in Zhongyang dang'an guan and Jiangxisheng dang'an guan. *Jiangxisheng geming lishi wenjian (1927–1928).*

"Qianwei kaichu Jiang Hanbo dangji jueyi" (The Front Committee Expels Jiang Hanbo from the Party). Pp. 576–578, in Jiangxisheng dang'an guan and Zhonggong Jiangxi shengwei dangxiao dangshi jiaoyanshi, eds. *Zhongyang geming genjudi shiliao xuanbian*, vol. 1.

"Qianwei tonggao, diyihao" (Front Committee No. 1 Notice). Pp. 172–174, in Jiangxisheng dang'an guan and Zhonggong Jiangxi shengwei dangxiao dangshi jiaoyanshi, eds. *Zhongyang geming genjudi shiliao xuanbian*, vol. 2.

Ren Bishi zhuan. See Zhonggong zhongyang wenxian yanjiushi, ed. *Ren Bishi zhuan.*

Ren Wei. "Geming baoli de yuanqi yu tezhi: Yi 'hongse kongbu' wei zhongxin de tantao" (The Origin of Revolutionary Violence: A Case Study of "Red Terror"). *Taiwan shida lishi xuebao*, no. 51 (June 2014), pp. 51–85.

Rowe, William T. *Crimson Rain: Seven Centuries of Violence in a Chinese County.* Stanford, CA: Stanford University Press, 2007.

Rue, John E. *Mao Zedong in Opposition, 1927–1935.* Stanford, CA: Stanford University Press, 1966.

Saich, Tony. *From Rebel to Ruler: One Hundred Years of the Chinese Communist Party.* Cambridge, MA: Harvard University Press, 2021.

Saich, Tony. *The Rise to Power of the Chinese Communist Party: Documents and Analysis.* Armonk, NY: M.E. Sharpe, 1996.

Schram, Stuart R. ed. *Mao's Road to Power: Revolutionary Writings, 1912–49.* Vol. 2: *National Revolution and Social Revolution, December 1920–June 1927.* Armonk, NY: M.E. Sharpe, 1994.

Schram, Stuart R. ed. *Mao's Road to Power: Revolutionary Writings, 1912–49.* Vol. 3: *From the Jinggangshan to the Establishment of the Jiangxi Soviets, July 1927–December 1930.* Armonk, NY: M.E. Sharpe, 1995.

Schwartz, Benjamin I. *Chinese Communism and the Rise of Mao.* Cambridge, MA: Harvard University Press, 1979.

Scott, James. *Seeing Like a State: How Certain Schemes to Improve the Human Condition Have Failed.* New Haven, CT: Yale University Press, 1998.

Sheel, Kamal. *Peasant Society and Marxist Intellectuals in China: Fang Zhimin and the Origin of a Revolutionary Movement in the Xinjiang Region.* Princeton, NJ: Princeton University Press, 1989.

Shi Zhongquan. "Cong 'zuozuodangshi' dao 'fajue dangshi'" (From "Looking at Party History" to "Developing Party History"). Pp. 1–15, in Zhonggong Jiangxi shengwei dangshi yanjiushi, et al., eds. *Donggu: Ganxinan geming genjudi shiliao xuanbian.*

Song Lei. "Guojia zhengzhi baoweiju xianwei renzhide lishi tanyi" (Exploring the History of the State Political Protection Bureau That Few Know). December 2, 2015. Available at http://dangshi.people.com.cn/n/2015/1202/c85037-27881688.html, accessed January 11, 2021.

Staniland, Paul. *Networks of Rebellion: Explaining Insurgent Cohesion and Collapse.* Ithaca, NY: Cornell University Press, 2014.

"Suqu zhongyangju guanyu chufa Li Shaojiu tongzhi guoqu cuowu de jueyi" (Resolution of the Central Bureau of the Soviet Area on Punishing Comrade Li Shaojiu for His Past Mistake). January 25, 1932. At https://baike.baidu.com/item/%E5%AF%8C%E7%94%B0%E4%BA%8B%E5%8F%98, accessed May 2, 2021.

"Suqu zhongyangju guanyu suqu sufan gongzuo jueyi an" (Resolution of the Central Bureau of the Soviet Area on the Work of Suppressing Counterrevolutionaries). At https://baike.baidu.com/item/%E8%8B%8F%E5%8C%BA%E4%B8%AD%E5%A4%AE%E5%B1%80%E5%85%B3%E4%BA%8E%E8%8B%8F%E5%8C%BA%E8%82%83%E5

%8F%8D%E5%B7%A5%E4%BD%9C%E5%86%B3%E8%AE%AE
%E6%A1%88/9911331, accessed January 11, 2021.

Tan Kesheng and Ouyang Zhiliang, eds. *Eyuwan geming genjudi douzheng shi jianbian* (Short History of the Struggle in the Eyuwan Revolutionary Base Area). Beijing: Jiefangjun chubanshe, 1987.

Tang Jingtao. "Zhongyang suqu de diyikuai jishi: Li Wenlin ji Li Wenlin-shi genjudi" (The Number One Cornerstone of the Central Soviet Area: Li Wenlin and the Li Wenlin-Style Base Area). *Dangshi zongheng*, no. 6 (1992), pp. 39–41.

Tang Lianying, Ye Fulin, and Ding Renxiang. *Donggu geming genjudi shilun* (Historical Discussion of the Donggu Revolutionary Base Area). Shanghai: Huadong shifan daxue chubanshe, 2019.

Tang Xiaobing. "Dageming qianhou zhongxiao zhishi fenzi de ningju yu zhengzhihua" (The Cohesion and Politicization of Middle and Lower Intellectuals before and after the Great Revolution). N.p.

Tarrow, Sidney G. *Power in Movement: Social Movements and Contentious Politics*. Revised and updated 3rd ed. Cambridge: Cambridge University Press, 2011.

Tawney, R.H. *Land and Labor in China*. London: George Allen & Unwin Ltd., 1932.

Tilly, Charles. *The Vendée*. Cambridge, MA: Harvard University Press, 1964.

"Tonggao: Jun zi, di erhao" (Notice: Military, No. 2). Pp. 528–533, in Jiangxisheng dang'an guan and Zhonggong Jiangxi shengwei dangxiao dangshi jiaoyanshi, eds. *Zhongyang geming genjudi shiliao xuanbian*, vol. 2.

Van de Ven, Hans J. *From Friend to Comrade: The Founding of the Chinese Communist Party, 1920–1927*. Berkeley, CA: University of California Press, 1991.

Wang Caiyou. "Tudi geming de difang yinying: Yi Donggu genjudi fentian yundong wei zhongxin" (The Local Response to Land Reform: Taking the Division of Land in the Donggu Base Area as the Focus). *Kaifang shidai*, no. 8 (August 2011), pp. 5–35.

"Wang Ching-wei." Pp. 369–376, in Boorman, ed. *Biographical Dictionary of Republican China*, vol. 3.

"Wang Shouhua." At https://baike.so.com/doc/5816499-6029312.html, accessed July 17, 2019.

Wang Tiexian and Liu Fuqin, eds. *Qu Qiubai zhuan* (Biography of Qu Qiubai). Beijing: Renmin chubanshe, 2011.

Wei, William. *Counterevolution: The Nationalists in Jiangxi during the Soviet Period*. Ann Arbor, MI: University of Michigan Press, 1985.

Weinstein, Jeremy M. *Inside Rebellion: The Politics of Insurgent Violence*. Cambridge: Cambridge University Press, 2007.

Wou, Odoric Y.K. *Mobilizing the Masses: Building Revolution in Henan.* Stanford, CA: Stanford University Press, 1994.

"Wu Zhenpeng: Jiangxi dang zuzhi de fazhan yu xianzhuang" (Wu Zhenpeng: The Development and Present Circumstances of the Jiangxi Party Organization). Pp. 158–160, in Zhongyang dang'an guan and Jiangxisheng dang'an guan. *Jiangxisheng geming lishi wenjian huiji (1927–1928).*

Xiao Ke. *Xiao Ke huiyilu* (Xiao Ke's Memoir). Beijing: Jiefangjun chubanshe, 1997.

"Xiao Ke huiyilu AB tuan sufan leiji tusha 10 wan hongjun suqu zongrenkou xiajiang 20%" (Xiao Ke's Memoir: The AB Corps Suppression Campaign Killed 100,000 in the Red Army, the Total Population Decreased by 20 Percent). At https://bbs.wenxuecity.com/bbs/memory/450374.html, accessed August 11, 2020.

"Xiao Ke tongzhi tan zhongyang suqude chuqi sufan yundong" (Comrade Xiao Ke Discusses the Early Period of the Movement to Suppress the Counterrevolutionaries in the Central Soviet). Pp. 401–412, in Zhongguo geming bowuguan yanjiushi, ed. *Dangshi yanjiu ziliao*, no. 4. Chengdu: Sichuan renmin chubanshe, 1983.

Xiao Ke. *Zhu Mao hongjun ceji* (Sidelights of the Zhu–Mao Red Army). Beijing: Zhonggong zhongyang dangxiao chubanshe, 1993.

Yang Kuisong. *"Zhongjian de didai" de geming: Guoji dabeijingxia kan Zhongguo chenggong zhidao* (Revolution in the "Intermediate Zone": Looking at the Success of the CCP in a Global Context). Taiyuan: Shanxi renmin chubanshe, 2010.

Ye Fulin. "Donggu Aoshang huiyi yu dangde baqi huiyi guanxi kaobian" (Investigation into the Relationship between the Aoshang Meeting in Donggu and the August 7 Meeting). *Jinggangshan daxue xuebao*, vol. 32, no. 3 (May 2011), pp. 9–13.

Ye Fulin. "Donggu geming genjudi zhuanti yanjiu" (Specialized Research on the Donggu Revolutionary Base Area). Ph.D. dissertation, East China Normal University, 2010.

Ying Xing. "Hongsijun lingdao jigou de bianhua yu zhuli hongjun de zuzhi xingshi" (The Evolution of the Leadership Organ of the Red Fourth Army and the Organizational Forms of the Main Force of the Red Army). *Suqu yanjiu*, no. 3 (2016), pp. 14–42.

Ying Xing. "Suqu difang ganbu, hongse wuzhuang yu zuzhi xingtai" (Local Cadres, Red Armed Forces, and the Organizational Situation in the Soviet Areas). *Kaifang shidai*, no. 6 (June 2016), pp. 53–81.

Ying Xing and Li Xia. "Zhonggong zaoqi difang lingxiu, zuzhi xingtai yu xiangcun shehui: Yi Zeng Tianyu jiqi lingdao de Jiangxi Wan'an baodong wei zhongxin" (Local Leaders, Organizational Circumstances, and Rural

Society in the Early Communist Period: Taking Zeng Tianyu's Leadership of Jiangxi's Wan'an Uprising as the Focus). *Shehui*, vol. 34, no. 5 (2014), pp. 1–40.

You Haihua. "Jitai pendi de shengtai huanjing yu Donggu geming de xingqi" (The Ecological Environment of the Ji–Tai Basin and the Rise of the Donggu Revolution). Pp. 523–546, in Zhonggong Jiangxi shengwei dangshi yanjiushi, Zhonggong Ji'an shiwei dangshi gongzuo bangongshi, and Zhongguo Ji'anshi qingyuan quwei. *Donggu genjudi yu Zhongguo geming daolu de kaipi*.

Yu Boliu and Ling Buji. *Zhongyang suqu shi* (History of the Central Soviet). 2 vols. Nanchang: Jiangxi renmin chubanshe, 2017.

Zeng Xianxin. "Xiang Ying, Zhou Enlai jiuzheng zhongyang suqu sufan cuowu" (Xiang Ying and Zhou Enlai Correct the Mistakes of the Central Soviet Area in the Suppression Campaign). *Bainianchao*, no. 10 (2003), pp. 21–27.

"Zeng Yansheng." At https://baike.baidu.com/item/%E6%9B%BE%E5% BB%B6%E7%94%9F, accessed January 11, 2021.

Zhang Hongqing. *Nongmin xingge yu Zhonggong de xiangcun dongyuan moshi: Zhongyang suqu wei zhongxin de kaocha* (Peasant Characteristics and the CCP's Style of Mobilizing in the Countryside: An Investigation Centered on the Central Soviet Area). Beijing: Zhongguo shehui kexue chubanshe, 2012.

Zhang Hongqing and Xiao Wenyan. "Chatian yundong yu zhongyang suqu minzhong dongyuan" (The Land Investigation Movement and the Mobilization of the Masses in the Central Soviet). *Jianghan daxue xuebao*, vol. 27, no. 5 (October 2008), pp. 107–112.

"Zhang Huaiwan xunshi Ganxinan baogao" (Zhang Huaiwan [Jiang Hanbo]'s Inspection Report on Western and Southern Jiangxi). Pp. 180–212, in Jiangxisheng dang'an guan and Zhonggong Jiangxi shengwei dangxiao dangshi jiaoyanshi, eds. *Zhongyang geming genjudi shiliao xuanbian*, vol. 1.

Zhang Junyi. *Du Yuesheng zhuan* (Biography of Du Yuesheng). 4 vols. Taipei: Zhuanji wenxue zazhishe, 1968.

Zhang Lihong and Xiao Wenyan. "Chatian yundong yu zhongyang suqu minzhong dongyuan" (The Land Investigation Movement and Mobilizing the Masses in the Central Soviet). *Jianghan daxue xuebao*, no. 27 (October 2008), pp. 107–112.

Zhang Shouchun. "'Li Wenlinshi' Donggu geming genjudi" (The "Li Wenlin-Style" Donggu Revolutionary Base Area). At www.jsdsw.org.cn/ web/detail/detail.html?id=787, accessed April 19, 2021.

Zhao Quanjun and Zhang Zhenzhong. "Luofang huiyi qianhou zongshu" (Before and after the Luofang Meeting). Pp. 1–43, in Zhonggong Jiangxi shengwei dangshi ziliao zhengji weiyuanhui and Zhonggong Jiangxi shengwei dangshi yanjiushi, eds. *Jiangxi dangshi ziliao*, vol. 6.

Zhao Shenghui. *Zhongguo gongchandang zuzhishi gangyao* (An Outline Organizational History of the Chinese Communist Party). Hefei: Anhui Renmin chubanshe, 1987.

Zhong Rixing. *Xiangcun shehuizhong de geming dongyuan: Yi zhongyang suqu weili* (The Revolutionary Mobilization in Rural Society: Taking the Central Soviet Area as an Example). Beijing: Zhongguo shehui kexue chubanshe, 2015.

Zhonggong Jiangxi shengwei dangshi yanjiushi et al., eds. *Donggu: Ganxinan geming genjudi shiliao xuanbian* (Donggu: Selected Materials on the Revolutionary Base Area in Southwestern Jiangxi). 2 vols. Beijing: Zhongyang wenxian chubanshe, 2007.

Zhonggong Jiangxi shengwei dangshi yanjiushi, Zhonggong Ji'an shiwei dangshi gongzuo bangongshi, and Zhongguo Ji'anshi qingyuan quwei. *Donggu genjudi yu Zhongguo geming daolu de kaipi: Jinian Donggu geming genjudi chuangjian 80 zhounian xueshu taolun huiji* (The Donggu Revolutionary Base Area and the Opening of China's Revolutionary Path: Collection of Academic Discussions Commemorating the 80th Anniversary of the Founding of the Donggu Revolutionary Base). Beijing: Zhonggong dangshi chubanshe, 2008.

Zhonggong Jiangxi shengwei dangshi ziliao zhengji weiyuanhui and Zhonggong Jiangxi shengwei dangshi yanjiushi, eds. *Jiangxi dangshi ziliao* (Materials on Jiangxi Party History). Vol. 5: *Wan'an baodong zhuanji* (Special Volume on the Wan'an Uprising). Nanchang: "Jiangxi dangshi ziliao" bianjishi, 1988.

Zhonggong Jiangxi shengwei dangshi ziliao zhengji weiyuanhui and Zhonggong Jiangxi shengwei dangshi yanjiushi, eds. *Jiangxi dangshi ziliao* (Materials on Jiangxi Party History). Vol. 6: *Luofang huiyi qianhou zhuangji* (Special Volume on before and after the Luofang Conference). Nanchang: "Jiangxi dangshi ziliao" bianjishi, 1988.

Zhonggong Jiangxi shengwei dangshi ziliao zhengji weiyuanhui and Zhonggong Jiangxi shengwei dangshi yanjiushi, eds. *Jiangxi dangshi ziliao* (Materials on Jiangxi Party History). Vol. 10: *Donggu geming genjudi zhuanji* (Special Volume on the Donggu Revolutionary Base Area). Nanchang: "Jiangxi dangshi ziliao" bianjishi, 1989.

"Zhonggong Jiangxi shengwei gei Changjiangju de baogao" (Report from the Jiangxi Provincial Party Committee to the Yangtze Bureau). Pp. 52–55, in Zhongyang dang'an guan and Jiangxisheng dang'an guan. *Jiangxisheng geming lishi wenjian huiji (1927–1928)*.

"Zhonggong Jiangxi shengwei gei Zhonggong Ganxi tewei de yifeng xin" (A Letter from the Jiangxi Provincial Committee to the CCP West Jiangxi Special Committee). Pp. 8–14, in Jiangxisheng dang'an guan, ed. *Jinggangshan geming genjudi shiliao xuanbian.*

"Zhonggong Jiangxi shengwei gei zhongyang de zonghe baogao" (A Comprehensive Report from the Jiangxi Provincial Party Committee to the Center). April 15, 1928. Pp. 203–227, in Zhongyang dang'an guan and Jiangxisheng dang'an guan. *Jiangxisheng geming lishi wenjian huiji (1927–1928)*.

"Zhonggong Jiangxi shengwei tongbao (di shisan hao) (Jiangxi Provincial CCP Committee Notice (No. 13)). Pp. 39–41, Zhongyang dang'an guan and Jiangxisheng dang'an guan. *Jiangxisheng geming lishi wenjian huiji (1927–1928)*.

"Zhonggong Jiangxisheng di erci daibiao dahui guanyu Suweiai quyu jueyi an" (Resolution on the Soviet Areas [adopted at] the Jiangxi Provincial CCP Second Representative Congress). Pp. 322–329, in Zhongyang dang'an guan and Jiangxisheng dang'an guan. *Jiangxisheng geming lishi wenjian huiji (1927–1928)*.

"Zhonggong Jiangxisheng zhi zhongyang xin" (Letter to the Center from the Jiangxi Provincial CCP Committee). Pp. 73–78, in Zhongyang dang'an guan and Jiangxisheng dang'an guan. *Jiangxisheng geming lishi wenjian huiji (1927–1928)*.

"Zhonggong XiangGanbian tewei he hongsijun junwei xiang Zhonggong Hunan shengwei de baogao" (Report from the Hunan–Jiangxi Border Special Committee and the Military Committee of the Red Fourth Army to the Hunan Provincial CCP Committee). Pp. 47–49, in Jiangxisheng dang'an guan, ed. *Jinggangshan geming genjudi shiliao xuanbian*.

Zhonggong zhongyang dangshi yanjiushi. *Zhongguo gongchandang lishi* (The History of the Chinese Communist Party). Vol. 1. Beijing: Renmin chubanshe, 1991.

Zhonggong zhongyang shujichu. *Liuda yilai dangnei mimi wenjian* (Secret Party Documents since the Sixth Party Congress). 2 vols. Beijing: Renmin chubanshe, 1981.

Zhonggong zhongyang wenxian yanjiushi, ed. *Mao Zedong nianpu, 1893–1949* (Annual Chronicle of Mao Zedong, 1893–1949). 3 vols. Revised ed. Beijing: Zhongyang wenxian chubanshe, 2013.

Zhonggong zhongyang wenxian yanjiushi, ed. *Mao Zedong xuanji* (Selected Works of Mao Zedong). 2nd ed. 4 vols. Beijing: Renmin chubanshe, 1991.

Zhonggong zhongyang wenxian yanjiushi, ed. *Ren Bishi zhuan* (Biography of Ren Bishi). 2 vols. Beijing: Zhongyang wenxian chubanshe, 2014.

Zhonggong zhongyang wenxian yanjiushi, ed. *Zhu De zhuan* (Biography of Zhu De). 2 vols. Beijing: Zhongyang wenxian chubanshe, 2016.

Zhonggong zhongyang zuzhibu and Zhonggong zhongyang dangshi yanjiushi, eds. *Zhongguo gongchandang lijie zhongyang weiyuan da cidian, 1921–2003*

(Central Committee Members of the Chinese Communist Party through All Sessions, 1921–2003). Beijing: Zhonggong dangshi chubanshe, 2004.

Zhongyang dang'an guan, ed. *Zhonggong zhongyang wenjian xuanji* (Selected Central Committee Documents of the CCP). 18 vols. Beijing: Zhonggong zhongyang dangxiao chubanshe, 1989.

Zhongyang dang'an guan and Fujiansheng dang'an guan. *Fujian geming lishi wenjian huiji* (Collection of Historical Documents on the Fujian Revolution). Vol. 15: *Minxi tewei wenjian (1928–1936 nian)* (Documents of the West Fujian Special Committee (1928–1936)). Fuzhou: Fujian renmin chubanshe, 1987.

Zhongyang dang'an guan and Jiangxisheng dang'an guan. *Jiangxisheng geming lishi wenjian huiji (1927–1928)* (Compilation of Historical Documents on the Jiangxi Revolution, 1927–1928). Ser. 21. Vol. 15. Los Angeles: Zhongwen chubanshe fuwu zhongxin, 2013.

"Zhongyang gei diyi fangmianjun zongqianwei, Jiangxi shengwei, ge tewei, ge difang dangbu de xin" (Letter from the Center to the General Front Committee of the First Front Army, the Jiangxi Provincial Party Committee, Various Special Committees, and All Local Party Organizations). Pp. 139–142, in Zhongyang dang'an guan, ed. *Zhonggong zhongyang wenjian xuanji*, vol. 7.

"Zhongyang gei hongjun disijun qianwei de zhishixin" (Letter of Instructions from the Center to the Front Committee of the Red Army's Fourth Army). Pp. 473–490, in Zhongyang dang'an guan, ed. *Zhonggong zhongyang wenxian xuanji*, vol. 5.

"Zhongyang gei suqu geji dang buji hongjun de shunling" (The Center's Instructions to Party Organizations and the Red Army in the Soviet Areas). Pp. 309–329, in Zhongyang dang'an guan, ed. *Zhonggong zhongyang wenjian xuanbian*, vol. 7.

"Zhongyang zhengzhiju guanyu Futian shibian de jueyi" (Central Politburo's Resolution on the Futian Incident). Pp. 203–209, in Zhongyang dang'an guan, ed. *Zhonggong zhongyang wenjian xuanji*, vol. 7.

"Zhongyang zhi sijun qianwei xin" (Letter from the Center to the Front Committee of the Fourth Army). Pp. 44–47, in Zhonggong Jiangxi shengwei dangshi ziliao zhengji weiyuanhui and Zhonggong Jiangxi shengwei dangshi yanjiushi, eds. *Jiangxi dangshi ziliao*, vol. 6.

Zhou Ming. "Ganxinan tewei de chengli he yanbian" (The Establishment and Evolution of the Jiangxi Southwest Special Committee). *Jindaishi yanjiu*, no. 6 (1984), pp. 250–254.

Zhu De zhuan. See Zhonggong zhongyang wenxian yanjiushi, ed. *Zhu De zhuan.*

Zhu Qihua. *China 1927: Memoir of a Debacle*, tr. Zhu Hong. Portland, ME: MerwinAsia, 2013.

Index

AB (Anti-Bolshevik) Corps
  generally, 11–12, 13–14
  in armies, 126–127
  attacks on, 14–15, 113, 115–117
  Chiang Kai-shek and, 79, 112–113, 114
  Comintern on, 134, 142
  "discovery" of elements of, 115–116, 138
  in Donggu Revolutionary Base Area, 136, 138, 141
  doubts as to existence of, 113–115, 136
  executions of members, 126–127, 130, 163
  in Eyuwan Base Area, 160
  Front Committee and, 115, 126, 143
  historical existence of, 112–113
  in Ji'an, 124, 144
  Jiang Hanbo, report of, 114
  Jiangxi Provincial Action Committee and, 130
  Jiangxi Provincial Party Committee and, 114
  Land Law leading to, 106
  Li Wenlin opposing, 117, 120, 122, 133, 138, 140
  Loufang Conference, strategy at, 125
  Mao Zedong opposing, 120, 123, 133, 138–139, 162, 166, 167
  Nanchang Military Education Group and, 102
  Northern Expedition and, 112–113
  overestimation of strength, 145
  Politburo on, 145
  Red Fourth Army and, 126, 127
  Southwest Jiangxi Special Committee and, 115–117, 122
  sufan movement and, 162, 163
  20th Army and, 130

  Xiao Ke on, 114–115, 126–127
  Zeng Shan opposing, 111
  Zhou Enlai and, 136
  Zhu De opposing, 79
The AB Corps and a Complete History of the Futian Incident (AB tuan yu Futian shibian shimo) (Dai and Luo), 13–14
All-China Congress of Representatives of the Soviet Areas, 119, 120
Anhui Party Committee, 158
Annals of the Chinese People (Yanhuang chunqiu), 132
Aoshang (village), 56
Autumn Harvest Uprisings (1927)
  generally, 42, 55–56, 156
  Emergency Meeting and, 42, 55–56
  Mao Zedong and, 75, 81
  peasants and, 22–23
  violence and, 29
Averill, Stephen, 83, 113

Baisha Meeting (1930), 92, 93, 96, 99–100
Beiping China University, 41
Beitou (township)
  February 7 Meeting. *See* February 7 Meeting (1930)
  Mao Zedong in, 105, 137
  Red Fourth Army in, 105
  West Jiangxi Special Committee in, 105
  Zhu De in, 105, 137
Bo Gu
  Land Investigation Movement and, 150, 151
  Mao Zedong and, 8, 9, 147, 162, 167
  Party Center and, 6
  in Politburo, 146
  radicalism of, 169

198 *Index*

clan-dominated nature of society, 39, 42

Communism, tension with, 101, 168–169

destruction of, 2–3, 15–16, 139

difficulty in restoring former order following destruction of, 53

Donggu Revolutionary Base Area and, 101, 137, 166

GMD, destruction by, 2–3

Mao Zedong, penetration by, 8–9, 167

new party culture, impact of, 169–170

peasant associations and, 53

sufan movement and, 12

in Wuhan, 44

Lominadze, Beso, 20, 79, 86, 164

Long March, 149

Lu Deming, 84

Lu Futan, 146

Luofang Conference (1930)
  generally, 166
  AB Corps, strategy regarding, 125
  disagreements at, 125
  Lin Biao at, 124–125
  Li Wenlin at, 124–125
  Mao Zedong at, 124–125
  Nationalist Army, strategy regarding, 124–125
  Peng Dehuai at, 124–125
  Zeng Shan at, 124–125
  Zhu De at, 124–125

Luo Huilan, 13–14, 113, 114–115, 129–130, 136

Luo Rongheng, 126

Luo Shibing, 50–51

Luo Wan, 111

Luo Yinong, 31–32, 44–45

"luring the enemy in deep" strategy, 11, 120, 124–125, 136

Macheng (county), uprising in, 155

Mao Dun, 158

Maoping (city)
  generally, 1
  Mao Zedong in, 77

Mao's China and After (Meisner), 4

Mao's Chronicles, 148

Mao Zedong

AB Corps, opposing, 120, 123, 133, 138–139, 162, 166, 167

assertion of authority, 128–129, 169

Autumn Harvest Uprisings and, 75, 81

bandits and, 77–78

in Beitou, 105, 137

Bo Gu and, 8, 9, 147, 162, 167

capture of, 77

Central Bureau and, 123, 128, 132–133, 147, 148, 149

Changsha, failure to capture, 23, 99

Changsha Uprising and, 74–75, 76–77

Chen Duxiu and, 70

Chen Yi and, 87, 95, 97

Chen Youkui and, 82

in combat, 64

Comintern and, 134, 170

consolidation of power, 142

in Donggu, 1–3

Donggu Revolutionary Base Area, clash with, 5, 8, 138, 166–167

at Emergency Meeting, 23, 75

February 7 Meeting, consolidation of power at, 112

First All-China Representative Conference and, 147–148

Front Committee and, 86–88, 90–92, 93, 94–95, 96–97, 100, 134, 168

on Futian Rebellion, 133

General Front Committee and, 110, 138

in GMD, 71, 72–73

guerrilla warfare and, 85, 119, 147–148

Gutian Conference and, 166, 169

Hunan Provincial Party Committee and, 74, 76–77, 86–87, 100

on "individualism," 91–93

Ji'an, attack on, 121–122

Ji'an, withdrawal from, 124

Jiang Hanbo and, 108–109

Jiangxi Provincial Action Committee and, 122–124

Jiangxi Provincial Party Committee and, 87, 88, 100

in Jinggangshan Base Area, 13, 23, 44, 77–78

Lai Jingbang compared, 85, 101